Journal of Semitic Studies Supplement 9

THE BOOK OF THE ISLAMIC MARKET INSPECTOR

Nihāyat al-Rutba fī Ṭalab al-Ḥisba
(*The Utmost Authority in the Pursuit of Ḥisba*)
by ʻAbd al-Raḥmān b. Naṣr al-Shayzarī

Translated with an Introduction and Notes

by

R. P. Buckley

Published by Oxford University Press
on behalf of the University of Manchester

1999

OXFORD
UNIVERSITY PRESS

Great Clarendon Street, Oxford OX2 6DP

Oxford University Press is a department of the University of Oxford.
It furthers the University's objective of excellence in research, scholarship,
and education by publishing worldwide in

Oxford New York

Athens Auckland Bangkok Bogotá Buenos Aires Calcutta
Cape Town Chennai Dar es Salaam Delhi Florence Hong Kong Istanbul
Karachi Kuala Lumpur Madrid Melbourne Mexico City Mumbai
Nairobi Paris São Paulo Singapore Taipei Tokyo Toronto Warsaw

with associated companies in Berlin Ibadan

Oxford is a registered trade mark of Oxford University Press
in the UK and in certain other countries

Published in the United Kingdom
by Oxford University Press, Oxford

First published 1999

A catalogue for this book is available from the British Library

Library of Congress Cataloguing in Publication Data
(Data available)

ISSN 0022-4480
ISBN 0-19-922434-X

Subscription information for the *Journal of Semitic Studies* is available from

Journals Customer Services
Oxford University Press
Great Clarendon Street
Oxford OX2 6DP
UK

Journals Marketing Department
Oxford University Press
2001 Evans Road
Cary, NC 27513
USA

Printed by the Charlesworth Group, Huddersfield, UK, 01484 517077

CONTENTS

		Page
Preface		v
Ḥisba and the *Muḥtasib*		1
al-Shayzarī and the *Nihāya*		12
The Manual		25
Chapter 1	The Conditions and Recommendations of *Ḥisba* enjoined upon the *Muḥtasib*	28
Chapter 2	Supervision of the Markets and Roads	36
Chapter 3	*Qinṭār*s, *Raṭl*s, *Mithqāl*s and *Dirhām*s	40
Chapter 4	Scales, Measures, Standard of Coins, *Raṭls* and *Mithqāl*s	43
Chapter 5	Grain and Flour Merchants	46
Chapter 6	Bakers	47
Chapter 7	Oven Keepers	49
Chapter 8	Makers of *Zulābiyya*	50
Chapter 9	Slaughterers and Butchers	52
Chapter 10	Sellers of Roast Meat	54
Chapter 11	Sellers of Sheep's Heads	56
Chapter 12	Fryers of Fish	57
Chapter 13	Cooks	58
Chapter 14	Makers of *Harīsa*	60
Chapter 15	Sausage Makers	62
Chapter 16	Confectioners	63
Chapter 17	Apothecaries	65
Chapter 18	Perfumers	70
Chapter 19	Makers of Syrups	76
Chapter 20	Sellers of Clarified Butter	78
Chapter 21	Cloth Merchants	81
Chapter 22	Brokers and Bazaar Criers	84
Chapter 23	Weavers	85
Chapter 24	Tailors	87
Chapter 25	Cotton Carders	89
Chapter 26	Flax Spinners	90
Chapter 27	Silk Makers	91
Chapter 28	Dyers	92
Chapter 29	Shoemakers	93
Chapter 30	Money Changers	94
Chapter 31	Goldsmiths	97
Chapter 32	Coppersmiths and Blacksmiths	99
Chapter 33	Veterinarians	100
Chapter 34	Traders in Slaves and Animals	102
Chapter 35	Baths and their Attendants	104
Chapter 36	Phlebotomists and Cuppers	108
Chapter 37	Physicians, Eye Doctors, Bone Setters and Surgeons	114

Chapter 38	Educators of Boys	119
Chapter 39	*Ahl al-Dhimma*	121
Chapter 40	The Affairs of *Ḥisba* in General and Particular	124

Appendices

I	al-Ghazālī on *Ḥisba*	139
II	The Diploma of Investiture	191

Bibliography	203
Index	209

Preface

The present translation is of al-Shayzarī's *Nihāyat al-Rutba fī Ṭalab al-Ḥisba* (*The Utmost Authority in the Pursuit of Ḥisba*) edited by al-Sayyid al-Bāz al-'Arīnī and published in Cairo in 1946 by the Maṭba'at Lajnat al-Ta'līf. This edition was based mainly on a manuscript written by the Egyptian Abū Bakr 'Alī al-Bahnasī and dated 711 AH (AD 1310/11), which was both more complete than the other extant versions and also nearer to the date of the original author. It therefore represents the best source for the original text. Other manuscripts were used by the editor to resolve any ambiguities, discrepancies or omissions.

In translating the *Nihāya*, footnotes have been provided in order to clarify certain words and references so as to render the text more accessible to the reader. Notes have also been provided which add information regarding the nature of the *muḥtasib* and his duties. These have often been gleaned from the historical sources, in contradistinction to the *ḥisba* treatises, and are intended to supplement particular points raised by the text and to provide an historical context for some of al-Shayzarī's remarks.

Ḥisba and the *Muḥtasib*

The term *ḥisba* is used with two meanings by Muslim writers. First, it is used in a broad sense to denote the religious obligation theoretically incumbent upon all Muslims to perform the Qur'ānic injunction to "order good and forbid evil" (*al-amr bi'l-ma'rūf wa'l-nahī 'an al-munkar*). Second, it is used to indicate the supervision of an official explicitly appointed by the state, either directly or indirectly, over the markets in particular and moral and social behaviour in general, this official being called a *muḥtasib*.

The numerous works dealing with *ḥisba* tend to limit themselves to one or other of these meanings, with a certain amount of overlap, and deal with either public morality or the office and jurisdiction of the mandated *muḥtasib*.

Regarding the first type of work, the association of *ḥisba* with a moral and religious ideal achieves its fullest expression in the *Iḥyā' 'Ulūm al-Dīn* of al-Ghazālī (see Appendix I), where the term *muḥtasib* is hardly discussed as a governmental position at all, but rather refers to the pious individual who takes upon himself the religious duty of "ordering good and forbidding evil".

As to those works which concentrate on the mandated *muḥtasib*, a further distinction may be seen. Some concentrate on the concept of *ḥisba* and the duties, both religious and juridical, arising from this which are incumbent on the *muḥtasib*. A prime example of this is the chapter devoted to the *muḥtasib* in al-Māwardī's *al-Aḥkām al-Sulṭāniyya*. Others are more administrative in nature and detail the practical aspects of the *muḥtasib*'s responsibilities. The present translation is of a work of this latter type.

Whatever the case, the particularly Islamic or religious nature of *ḥisba* receives more or less stress in the treatises dealing with it. This emphasis is seen to manifest itself in a number of ways. One of the most common of these is the constant resort to Prophetic tradition and Qur'ānic injunction as the proof-texts from which the foundations of the *muḥtasib*'s activities are derived. Thus, it is alleged not so much that he is charged with such and such a duty because of its tendency to promote well-being, but more because the Qur'ān ordered it, or Muḥammad was seen to endorse it.

Regarding the primarily religious nature of the *muḥtasib*'s duties, it is not only with reference to the writings on *ḥisba* that this is seen. First and foremost, the very title *muḥtasib* is derived from the verb *iḥtasaba* which means, among other things, "to try to gain honour in God's eyes by acting righteously". Second, from the earliest times there was often an intimate relationship between the office of the *muḥtasib* and that of the Islamic judge which resulted in a certain amount of institutional diffusion between the two posts. The Islamic judge is the arbitrator of Islamic law and the one individual most concerned with its practical application. One of the shared qualities of the two posts which facilitated such a close association was the ostensibly religious foundations of their respective jurisdictions. This is also seen in the use of terms normally applied to the judicial procedure of the judge being also applied to the equivalent process of the *muḥtasib*, as it is in the technical term for the *muḥtasib*'s punishments - *ta'zīr* - a term from the vocabulary of Islamic law. Finally, during the Fatimid period the identification of the *muḥtasib* with a religious ideal received official sanction and in the classification of state functionaries his position was classed as a religious one (*waẓīfa dīniyya* or *khidma dīniyya*).

A Brief Historical Review of the *Muḥtasib*

1 The Proto-*Muḥtasib*: the *'Āmil al-Sūq*

Prior to the advent of Islam there is no mention of any official charged with responsibilities over the market place. This is despite the existence of some very large markets in Arabia. Some of these were of local importance, such as that of al-Ḥajar, the biggest and richest oasis on the peninsular; some were international, such as that of al-Ḥīra, the capital of the Lakhmids and a vital caravan city on the route between Persia and Arabia, or such as Dumat al-Jandal, an oasis town on the direct route between Medina and Damascus and one of the principle markets of Northern Arabia. Then there was the famous market of 'Ukāẓ near Mecca and that of Medina upon which the oasis totally depended for its prosperity. There must presumably have existed some mechanism of control over these markets, some authority to which claims of unfair treatment were directed and which would dispense justice. But if there was one, it is not identified in the sources. There is, however, an isolated account which refers to a certain Ḥākim b. Umayya who is stated to have been a *muḥtasib* in Mecca during the pre-Islamic period "ordering good and forbidding evil".[1] The title is certainly anachronistic, but perhaps the report can be taken to indicate that Ḥākim was a market inspector of sorts.

With the coming of Islam, it is in Mecca and Medina that the prophet Muḥammad is said to have appointed the first persons with jurisdiction over the market. In the light of the importance of these markets, and bearing in mind Muḥammad's interest in commercial affairs, it is easy to imagine that these first officials were to ensure the orderly running of business transactions and if not exactly to dispense justice then at least to report any infringement of what was considered fair.

Muḥammad is said to have engaged Sa'īd b. Sa'īd b. al-'Āṣ over the market of Medina sometime after the conquest of Mecca in AD 629.[2] Also, interestingly, he is said to have employed a woman in this post, Samrā bint Nuhayk al-Asadiyya, also in Medina.[3] She is not the only woman to have been so entrusted, for somewhat later the caliph 'Umar b. al-Khaṭṭāb (r. 644-55) is reported to have employed al-Shifā bint 'Abd Allah over the Medinan market.[4] It is not unlikely that these women had jurisdiction over the women's section of the market - a common feature of Muslim markets today and no doubt then also. However, no further women are ever identified in this role.

With regard to the time of the Rightly Guided Caliphs who succeeded Muḥammad, several traditions exist. It is alleged that 'Umar, apart from the woman already mentioned, had two men working for him over the market of Medina: al-Sā'ib b.

---

[1] Ibn Ḥazm, *Jamharat Ansāb al-'Arab* (Cairo, 1962) p. 263: "[Ḥākim b. Umayya] was a *muḥtasib* in Mecca during the Jāhiliyya, ordering good and forbidding evil".
[2] Ibn 'Abd al-Barr al-Qurṭūbī, *al- Isti'āb fī Ma'rifat al-Aṣḥāb* (Cairo, n.d.) 2:261.
[3] *al- Isti'āb* 4:183.
[4] *Jamharat Ansāb al-'Arab* pp.150, 156.

Yazīd and ʻAbd Allah b. ʻUṭba b. Masʻūd.[5] This tradition is noteworthy in that it quotes Sā'ib as stating that he was an *ʻāmil ʻalā sūq* (market officer) in Medina in the time of ʻUmar.[6] This is the first occurrence of a term which was to form the basis of the official designation of the eastern market inspector until it was replaced by the title *muḥtasib*.

Similarly noteworthy is another report concerning ʻAbd Allah b. ʻUṭba in which, while nothing is said regarding his function as a market inspector, it is stated that he was a judge in Kufa for Muṣʻab b. Zubayr.[7] Later, the third caliph ʻUthmān b. al-ʻAffān (r. 644-56) is said to have appointed al-Ḥārith b. al-Ḥakam over the market of Medina,[8] but as in the other examples no dates are given nor any indication as to the scope and duties of the office.

References to market inspectors continue during the ensuing Umayyad period (661-750), although these reports are very few. With the inclusion of the former Byzantine and Sasanian territories into the Muslim empire, however, we begin to hear of them in places outside of the Hijaz. Five market inspectors are mentioned: a certain Saʻīd b. Mīna who was employed in the market of Mecca for ʻAbd Allah b. al-Zubayr (d. 692);[9] Mahdī b. ʻAbd al-Raḥmān, who had jurisdiction in the market of Wāsiṭ under the governor of Iraq and the east for the Umayyad caliph Yazīd II (r. 720-24); ʻUmar b. Hubayra; and Iyās b. Muʻāwiya, the grandson of the above Mahdī b. ʻAbd al-Raḥmān, who also administered the market of Wāsiṭ after his grandfather.[10] Finally, in the course of relating a story to Walīd b. ʻAbd al-Malik (r. 705-15) the narrator refers to his meeting a man whom he takes to be the *ʻāmil al-sūq* in Medina. No name is mentioned.[11]

Such is the extent of the information on the *ʻāmil al-sūq* from the birth of Islam to the accession of the Abbasids. But although this would appear to be the limit of our Islamic west valuable information may be added.

---

[5] *al- Istiʻāb* 2:576.
[6] Ibn Sallām, *Kitāb al-Amwāl* (Cairo, 1976) p. 533.
[7] Ibn Saʻd, *Kitāb al-Ṭabaqāt al-Kabīr* (Leiden, 1908) 6:82.
[8] al-Balādhurī, *Ansāb al-Ashrāf* (Jerusalem, 1936) 5:47.
[9] al-Azraqī, *Akhbār Makka* (Beirut, n.d.) 1:215.
[10] al-Wakīʻ, *Akhbār al-Quḍāh* (Cairo, 1947) 1:353.
[11] Abū'l-Faraj al-Iṣfahānī, *Kitāb al-Aghānī* (Beirut, n.d.) 17:108.

When the Abbasids gained power in the east in 750 a member of the ousted Umayyad family fled to Spain where he subsequently established a new Umayyad dynasty. Many elements of the old regime were transferred to Spain, including much of the theory of Islamic law and its judicial institutions. It was at this time that the market inspector made his appearance in the new dynasty, being called *ṣāḥib al-sūq* and clearly a transposition of the eastern *'āmil al-sūq*. This being so, much can be learnt from the earliest extant treatise on market inspection, that of Yaḥyā b. 'Umar (c. 825-901) which deals with market inspection in the Islamic west.[12] This treatise may be taken to present a fair picture of the duties of the *'āmil al-sūq* as they were when the Umayyads set up their caliphate in Spain in 756. Significantly, the post appears to have had no religious connotations nor to have generally concerned itself with censure of public morals, but rather alluded primarily to affairs of relevance only to the orderly running of the market place, particularly with regard to weights, measures and scales. Thus, the original *'āmil al-sūq* may be seen to have been a largely secular official, for if his duties had included anything of a religious nature this would presumably have manifested itself when the office was transplanted to Spain. At the time of the writing of Yaḥyā b. 'Umar's treatise, the *'āmil al-sūq* had already given way in the east to the Islamicised office of the *muḥtasib*, while in the west the nature and jurisdiction of the post continued much as before.

As to what the *'āmil al-sūq* was actually concerned with, it is probable that chief among his duties was the control of weights and measures. This duty, as testified by the emphasis which the majority of treatises on *ḥisba* place on it, was given the utmost significance, and its exercise in the early days of Islam and throughout the Umayyad period must have been no less important. It is hardly surprising that someone should have been delegated to attend to something so fundamental to the market's orderly and fair working, so near to the Prophet's interests and so open to fraud and swindling.

Some later commentators allude to the duties of the *muḥtasib* being undertaken by the early caliphs. While it is a commonplace that traditions often give us an insight into the particular view and circumstances of those who propound them rather than

[12] Yaḥyā b. 'Umar, *al-Naẓar wa 'l-Aḥkām fī Jāmi' Aḥwāl al-Sūq* (Tunis, 1975).

recording historical fact, these allusions may be taken as indicating that before the appearance of the Islamic *muḥtasib* characteristic duties of *ḥisba* - those concerned with the upholding of religious and moral probity - were at least in theory performed by the caliphs themselves. It is stated, for example, that 'Umar b. al-Khaṭṭāb was the first person to perform *ḥisba*,[13] that is, the function of guardian of religious precepts and morality which distinguishes the *muḥtasib* from the *'āmil al-sūq*. Similarly, 'Alī b. Abī Ṭālib (r. 656-61) is the subject of traditions which show him to have engaged in *ḥisba*. It is said that the Prophet enjoined him to "order good and forbid evil",[14] the Qur'ānic phrase used to denote the *muḥtasib*'s general function. The same source also states that 'Alī used to go round the markets every morning "like a *muḥtasib*". He is alleged to have gone to the cloth merchants and exhorted them not to give short measure, likewise the grain merchants. Elsewhere it is related that 'Alī on his way through the Kufan markets urged the merchants to deal fairly, and examined a story-teller to see whether he was religiously fit to speak to the people.[15] Finally, it is stated in general terms that in former times the rulers carried out *ḥisba*.[16]

Once again, the implication is that the office of the old *'āmil al-sūq* had no religious connotations. Indeed, the very fact of renaming this official as *muḥtasib* was intended to indicate a change in function and in spirit, an Islamicising of the post.

Regarding the origins of the *'āmil al-sūq* and the *muḥtasib*, there is sometimes a great similarity between the classical Greek *agoranomos* and the Muslim market inspector, and it is perhaps tempting to conclude that the functions of the former were the model for those of the latter; the *agoranomos*, including checking the frauds of the merchants, was also appointed to maintain control over the temples in the market and to make sure that no crimes were committed in them. However, as we have seen, reports of an official over the market are available during the time of Muḥammad, that is, before the Muslim conquests and the Byzantine influence which followed. Similarly problematic are the further reports of market officials under

[13] al-Qalqashandī, *Ṣubḥ al-A'shā* (Cairo, 1913) 5:452. For other anecdotes regarding 'Umar as a proto-*muḥtasib* see al-Ṭabarī, *Tarīkh al-Rusul wa'l-Mulūk* (Leiden, 1879-1901) 1:2744, 2745.
[14] "A Zaidi Manual of Hisbah of the 3rd Century (H)", edited by R. B. Serjeant from his *Studies in Arabic History and Civilisation* (London, 1981) (pp.VII 1-34) pp. 11-12.
[15] *Akhbār al-Quḍāh* 2:196.
[16] Ibn al-Ukhuwwa, *Ma'ālim al-Qurba fī Aḥkām al-Ḥisba* (Cambridge, 1937) p. 21; al-Māwardī, *al-Aḥkām al-Sulṭaniyya* (Cairo, 1983) p. 223.

'Umar b. al-Khaṭṭāb so soon after the beginning of the Arab expansion. On the whole, it does not seem necessary to search for any outside influence; there is no good reason why the *'āmil al-sūq* and the *muḥtasib* should not have arisen as a response to internal requirements and needing no foreign precursor for their appearance.

2 The First *Muḥtasib*s

It was during the early years of the Abbasid caliphate that the *'āmil al-sūq* was replaced with his Islamic counterpart, the *muḥtasib*. According to our sources the first *muḥtasib*s are mentioned during the caliphate of Abū Ja'far al-Manṣūr (r. 754-75). 'Āṣim al-Aḥwal is reported to have held the office of *ḥisba* in either Kufa or al-Madā'in and to have died c. 759, that is, during the early years of Abū Ja'far's reign. It is also said that he was one of the jurisprudents (*faqīh*s) of Baghdad and was a judge in al-Madā'in.[17] Another was Yaḥyā b. Zakariyā whom Abū Ja'far appointed as *muḥtasib* of Baghdad in 774.[18]

The next *muḥtasib* to occur in the sources makes his appearance in the old centre of the Muslim empire, Medina. Nāfi' b. 'Abd al-Raḥmān the Qur'ān reciter is recorded as having been a *muḥtasib* in Medina, his birthplace, and to have died in that city in 785/6,[19] thus probably performing his duties during the caliphate of either Abū Ja'far or al-Mahdī (r. 775-85). Somewhat later, Aḥmad b. al-Ṭayyib, sometimes known as al-Sarakhsī, is reported to have taken the office of *ḥisba* in Baghdad, either prior to or during the reign of al-Mu'taḍid (r. 892-902).[20] Alongside this he is also credited with simultaneously holding the office concerned with inheritances (*mawārīth*) and the slave market.

---

[17] *Kitāb al-Ṭabaqāt al-Kabīr* 7 part 2 p. 65. See also al-Khaṭīb al-Baghdādī, *Tarīkh Baghdād* (Cairo, 1931) 12:243, 244, 245; *Akhbār al-Quḍāh* 3:304.
[18] *Tarīkh al-Rusul wa'l-Mulūk* 3:324.
[19] Ibn Khallikān, *Ibn Khallikan's Biographical Dictionary* translated by B. M. de Slane (London, 1843) 3:522; Abū'l-Fidā, *al-Mukhtaṣir fī Akhbār al-Bashr* (Beirut, 1968) 2:12.
[20] 'Umar Riḍā Kaḥḥāla, *Mu'jam al-Mu'allifīn* (Damascus, 1957) 2:157; al-Mas'ūdī, *Murūj al-Dhahab* (Paris, 1873) 8:179.

While there were notable exceptions, the *'āmil al-sūq* and his successor the early *muḥtasib* must often have been little more than humble servants of the state. It is for this reason that they only receive mention in the sources insofar as they were notable for other attainments, were women above their usual station or were involved in revolts. These meagre accounts are in contrast to the much greater attention paid to *muḥtasib*s commencing with the Fatimid period (909-1160). During this time the *muḥtasib* achieved a position in society which his predecessor did not, becoming a grand dignitary and possessing great influence.

This increased prestige and status may be seen in many aspects of the Fatimid *muḥtasib* but perhaps in none more so than in the ceremonies connected with his appointment. This period witnessed the appearance of an elaborate ceremony of investiture which seems to have been substantially the same for all the highest officials of state, amongst whose ranks we now find the *muḥtasib*. There are several reports giving some of the details of these ceremonies. In 1023, for example, the newly appointed *muḥtasib*, after being awarded a heavy cloak and a turban,

> went in great procession, preceded by twelve noble female camels.[21]

Similarly, upon the appointment of Bāqī al-Khādim al-Aswad to the two *shurṭa*s (police forces) and the *ḥisba* in 1024:

> A heavy voluminous cloak, a judge's golden turban and a sword of gold were conferred upon him ... then he was carried on a horse with a golden saddle and a golden bridle.[22]

In one of the earliest reports, Ḥamīd al-Mufliḥ upon being re-appointed as *muḥtasib* in 992 "went around escorted with drums and banners",[23] while Jābir b. Manṣūr al-Jawdarī on being appointed to the *ḥisba* and the ports in 1000 had

---

[21] al-Maqrīzī, *Itti'āẓ al-Ḥunafā'* (Cairo, 1967) 1:135.
[22] *Itti'āẓ* 1:150. The two *shurṭa*s were those of the *shurṭa al-suflā* and the *shurṭa al-'ulyā*, the police forces of Miṣr/Fusṭāṭ and al-Qāhira respectively.
[23] *Itti'āẓ* 1:276.

> a heavy long-sleeved gown conferred upon him and a handkerchief containing gold, while many robes were carried before him and he was invested with a sword.[24]

It will be noticed that in the above reports cloaks or clothes of some kind are mentioned as being "conferred upon" the newly appointed official. In other accounts it simply says "He was conferred upon" (*khuli'a 'alayhi*) with no mention of what the conferred object was.[25] Derived from this verb, however, is the noun *khil'a* or "robe of honour", it being considered from the earliest times in the Near East a considerable honour to be given the clothes once worn by one's superior. In practice, among the Muslims this was translated into the conferring of garments embroidered with the high dignitary's name rather than actually having been worn by him. It is probable then that the cloaks given to the *muḥtasib* were of such a nature, as were perhaps the "many robes" carried in front of Jābir b. Manṣūr, that is, a mark of the ruler's esteem.

As far as the turban referred to is concerned, this was the most essential item for showing rank and prestige, and it was not unusual for persons living during this period to lavish more money on their turbans than they did on the rest of their apparel put together. That one of the above *muḥtasib*s was granted a turban of golden cloth, and of the same kind as a judge's, is testimony indeed to their elevated position in society.

In addition to these ostentatious displays it was also common practice in Egypt to have the diplomas of investiture read out from the pulpit of the main mosque, either that of Aḥmad b. Ṭūlūn[26] or that of 'Amr b. al-'Āṣ[27] and sometimes both of them.[28]

Such was the *muḥtasib*'s status in society that the candidate was usually from "among the prominent people, honest people, and their people of distinction",[29]

---

[24] *Itti'āẓ* 2:31.
[25] See, for example, al-Maqrīzī, *Khiṭaṭ* (Beirut, 1967-8) 1:464, 2:297. *Itti'āẓ* 1:145.
[26] *Itti'āẓ* 1:145.
[27] *Itti'āẓ* 2:91. The mosque referred to is the "ancient mosque" (*al-jāmi' al-'atīq*) which was the alternative name for the mosque of 'Amr b. al-'Āṣ, the first to be built in Egypt.
[28] *Itti'āẓ* 2:73; *Khiṭaṭ* 1:464.
[29] *Ṣubḥ al-A'shā* 3:483.

which included judges - whose powers far exceeded those of the traditional Islamic judge, sometimes being more akin to a ruler or a governor - police chiefs, wazīrs and at least on one occasion the caliph himself, al-Ḥākim (r. 996-1021) being alleged to have undertaken the office.[30] At times, their authority was such that when a favourite of al-Ḥākim became ill, the caliph went to visit him in person, sending him five thousand dinars and twenty-five horses with saddles and bridles, and later appointing him to the *ḥisba*, a post commensurate with his place in the caliph's affections.[31]

This process of aggrandisement continued until under the Mamluks (1250-1517) the Egyptian *muḥtasib* was considered to be fifth in rank of all the judicial posts, coming immediately below the Head of the Public Treasury, or even above him if he was more learned.[32]

Indeed, both preceding and during the time of al-Shayzarī the post of *muḥtasib* probably amounted to little more than a sinecure, the honorary conferment of a post the day-to-day duties of which would not be carried out by its nominal holder. That this must often have been the case is supported by a number of considerations. First, the jurisdiction of the *muḥtasib* often covered such an extensive area that this would positively prohibit him from having any but the most minor role in the responsibilities theoretically attached to the office. Thus, in the Fatimid period we hear of a single *muḥtasib* being appointed to Miṣr, al-Qāhira and al-Jazīra simultaneously.[33] The situation in Egypt under the Fatimid regime perhaps occasionally corresponded to that existing under the Mamluks when there were only three *muḥtasib*s in the whole country at any one time: the *muḥtasib* of al-Qāhira who had authority over all of Lower Egypt apart from Alexandria, the *muḥtasib* of Alexandria, and the *muḥtasib* of Fusṭāṭ/Miṣr whose jurisdiction included all of Upper Egypt.[34]

---

[30] Badr al-Dīn al-'Aynī, *al-Sayf al-Muhannad* (Cairo, 1966) pp. 159-60, where it is stated that "[al-Ḥākim] used to work alone as a *muḥtasib*, going round the markets on one of his donkeys". See also Ibn Taghrībirdī, *al-Nujūm al-Zāhira fī Mulūk Miṣr wa'l-Qāhira* (Cairo, n.d.) 4:184.
[31] *Itti'āẓ* 2:91.
[32] *Ṣubḥ al-A'shā* 4:34 f.
[33] *Itti'āẓ* 2:91. al-Jazīra was the Jazīrat al-Rawḍa, the site of the oldest dock in Cairo where there was a large market.
[34] *Ṣubḥ al-A'shā* 4:37.

Second, in the relatively numerous reports in which *ḥisba* is just one of a number of offices incumbent upon the same individual, and particularly where it is not the most prestigious of those offices, it cannot be conceived that he would devote his attention to *ḥisba* to the exclusion of all else. It must therefore be presumed that when we hear of a *muḥtasib* who was at the same time a judge, for example, his responsibilities over the market were in obeisance to his more jurisprudential ones.

Finally, the sometimes purely nominal nature of the *muḥtasib*'s office becomes evident in those situations where the quantity of offices under the authority of a single individual positively precluded him from executing them all. The most extreme illustration of this is that of Ya'qūb b. Yūsuf b. Killis, who was the first wazīr appointed under the Fatimid regime. In 937 he was assigned to a large number of administrative and judicial posts including the tax department (*kharāj*), the department dealing with inheritances (*mawārīth*), the two *shurṭa*s (police forces) of al-Qāhira and Miṣr, the ports (*sawāḥil*) and the *ḥisba*.[35]

Thus, despite the many instructions given to the *muḥtasib* in al-Shayzarī's *Nihāya*, we should perhaps not visualise him as a familiar and everyday feature of the market place, making his rounds from shop to shop and checking on all the occupations. Instead, it is rather his assistants, scouts and informants that we see, for it is surely these with whom the people of the market more readily came into contact. This largely nominal role of al-Shayzarī's *muḥtasib* would indeed explain Goitein's remark that

> The *muḥtasib*, the official who, according to the textbooks, should be expected more than anyone else to represent the government to the populace, is all but absent from the Geniza papers during the Fatimid period.[36]

[35] Jamāl al-Dīn 'Alī b. Ẓāfir, *Akhbār al-Duwal al-Munqaṭi'a* (Cairo, 1972) p. 38.

[36] S. D. Goitein, *A Mediterranean Society* (California, 1971) 4:40. The term "Geniza papers" is applied to a very extensive deposit of discarded bills, contracts, commercial agreements, memoranda, letters and so forth which were fortuitously discovered in Egypt. They relate predominantly to the Fatimid and Ayyubid periods, and form the basis of Goitein's four-volume work.

al-Shayzarī and the *Nihāya*

The Author

There is no extant biography of the author of the *Nihāyat al-Rutba fī Ṭalab al-Ḥisba* and little is known concerning him. Even his full name is open to question. The different manuscript versions of the manual refer to his *laqab* (nickname) as either Taqī al-Dīn, Zayn al-Dīn or Jamāl al-Dīn. Similarly, there is no agreement concerning his *nisba* (name of kinship or place of association), some offering al-Nibrāwī, al-Ṭabrīzī, al-'Adawī, al-Shīrāzī or al-Shayzarī.[37] More recently, Carl Brockelmann refers to him as Jalāl al-Dīn al-Najīb al-Faḍā'il 'Abd al-Raḥmān b. Naṣr b. 'Abd Allah b. Naṣr b. 'Alī al-Shayzarī al-Ṭabrīzī al-'Adawī al-Shīrāzī,[38] thus incorporating most of the *nisba*s mentioned above. What seems clear, however, is that he was called 'Abd al-Raḥmān b. Naṣr b. 'Abd Allah, as this is the name offered by most of the manuscripts. As to his *nisba*, this was most probably al-Shayzarī, as can be seen from the beginning of the chapter on weights and measures where the author refers to Shayzar before any other town in Syria.

Concerning al-Shayzarī's date of death, Brockelmann remarks that this was in 1193,[39] the year that the Ayyubid Ṣalāḥ al-Dīn (Saladin) died. Whether this date can be accepted is debatable since he offers no source for his information. Certainly, al-Shayzarī was still alive after the death of Atabek Tughtakin in 1128, as the sultan is mentioned in Chapter 1 of the *Nihāya*. He was also a contemporary of Ṣalāḥ al-Dīn, as another of al-Shayzarī's books, *al-Nahj al-Maslūk fī Siyāsat al-Mulūk*, contains a dedication to him from the author.[40] One wonders whether the *Nihāya* was written in response to Ṣalāḥ al-Dīn's urging.

From the many references to Syrian towns in the *Nihāya*, there is no doubt that al-Shayzarī at least spent some time in that place and was familiar with its circumstances, but whether he was of Syrian origin is not known. Ḥājjī Khalīfa

[37] See Ḥājjī Khalīfa, *Kashf al-Ẓunūn 'an Asāmī al-Kutub wa'l-Funūn* (Leipzig, 1835) 3:510, 5:507.
[38] C. Brockelmann, *Geschichte der Arabischen Literatur: Supplementband* (Leiden, 1937) 1:832-33.
[39] *Supplementband* 1:832.
[40] al-Shayzarī, *al-Nahj al-Maslūk fī Siyāsat al-Mulūk* (Cairo, 1326 AH) p. 13.

remarks that he was a judge in Tabarayya (Tiberias), Syria,[41] while Wüstenfeld states that he was a physician in Aleppo.[42] Once again, no evidence is offered for these statements and they are therefore difficult to substantiate. al-Shayzarī was well versed in medical matters, as his lengthy and detailed chapters on apothecaries, phlebotomists and cuppers, physicians, eye doctors, bone setters and surgeons would indicate. His knowledge of Islamic law is also readily testified to in the *Nihāya*. There is, however, no convincing reason to presume that he was employed in either of these professions. Similarly, notwithstanding al-Shayzarī's composition of the *Nihāya*, there is no reason to presume that he was himself a *muḥtasib*.

Of the other writings attributed to al-Shayzarī, Brockelmann mentions the following:

1 *al-Nahj al-Maslūk fī Siyāsat al-Mulūk*
3 *al-Īḍāḥ fī Asrār al-Nikāḥ*
4 *Rawḍat al-Qulūb wa Nuzhat al-Muḥibb wa'l-Maḥbūb* (about love)
5 *Khulāṣat al-Kalām fī Ta'wīl al-Aḥlām* (doctrine of interpretation of the dreams of Gabdorrhachaman, the son of Nasar).

The Manual

The *Nihāyat al-Rutba fī Ṭalab al-Ḥisba* is a practical manual for the specific use of the *muḥtasib*, and in his absence probably also for the *muḥtasib*'s assistants, in the correct exercise of the duties of *ḥisba*. It is the earliest extant book of its kind to appear in the Islamic east. Prior to this, other writers had dealt with the subject of *ḥisba* and the *muḥtasib*, notably al-Māwardī (d. 1058) in his *al-Aḥkām al-Sulṭāniyya* and al-Ghazālī (d. 1111) in his *Iḥyā' 'Ulūm al-Dīn*, but these were primarily concerned with the juridical, moral and religious connotations of *ḥisba* as opposed to its practical application.

Of the book's contemporary importance there can be little doubt, and it formed the basis of the celebrated *ḥisba* manuals which were to follow. Thus, the Egyptian Ibn al-Ukhuwwa (d. 1338) appropriated much of al-Shayzarī's material in the

[41] *Kashf al-Ẓunūn* 3:510.
[42] F. Wüstenfeld, *Geschichte der Arabischen Aertze und Naturforscher* (Göttingen, 1840) p. 100.

composition of his *Ma'ālim al-Qurba fī Aḥkām al-Ḥisba*. Similarly, the Egyptian Ibn Bassām (14th century AD) founded much of his manual on al-Shayzarī, even naming it after the earlier work. These borrowings were often verbatim and even extended to the order of the chapters. The authors did, however, expand the content, adding new and more detailed information where appropriate, and including material of current interest and relevance.

The significance and practical value of al-Shayzarī's *Nihāya* is further underlined by the unusually large number of its extant manuscripts. Of the fourteen manuscripts which still exist, eight are in Egypt while the remainder are held in non-Arab countries.

From the reliance placed on the manual by subsequent Egyptian writers, and the location of the majority of the manuscript versions, we must conclude that it was primarily used in Egypt. In one or two places in the text al-Shayzarī clearly has an Egyptian audience in mind, such as his remark "the Egyptian *raṭl* - may God protect it". It seems probable, however, that the manual was written in Syria, or at least that al-Shayzarī drew on his personal knowledge of that country for much of his information. Thus, in Chapter 3 on weights and measures, al-Shayzarī mentions predominantly those of Syria (Aleppo, Damascus, Homs, Hama, Ma'arra and Shayzar). Similarly, in Chapter 4 he speaks of scales from Damascus. While elsewhere, in Chapter 6 on phlebotomists and cuppers, he recounts an anecdote regarding two phlebotomists he came across in Aleppo.

As regards western interest in the *Nihāya*, the only scholar to pay serious attention to the manual was Walter Behrnauer. In 1860 he translated it into French, largely using a single copy of the manuscript held in the Bibliothèque Impériale de Vienne which was considerably shorter than the present translation. It was published in two parts in the *Journal Asiatique* under the title "Mémoire sur les institutions de police chez les Arabes, les Persans et les Turcs" (No.16, 5 serie [1860] pp. 347-92, and the second part in No.17, 5 serie [1861] pp. 5-76). Aside from this, some passages from the *Nihāya* which were incorporated by Ibn al-Ukhuwwa were coincidentally translated by Rubin Levy in his edition of the latter's *Ma'ālim al-Qurba* (Cambridge, 1937).

Before turning to the contents of al-Shayzarī's *Nihāya*, perhaps a word is in order regarding the extent to which these correspond to the actual duties carried out by the *muḥtasib* and/or his various assistants.

The main sources outlining the responsibilities of the *muḥtasib* and his assistants are of course the *ḥisba* manuals and treatises and the diplomas of investiture. It might, however, be supposed that these are essentially descriptions of an ideal state of affairs and that in practice the *muḥtasib* was not expected to apply himself with equal vigour, if any at all, to everything that was theoretically within his purview. Aside from the works devoted to *ḥisba*, the historical sources can be resorted to for corroboration, and these occasionally do report a number of incidents in which the *muḥtasib* attends to some of the more important functions of his office. Such reports are, however, few and far between.[43] In general, the vast bulk of the duties ascribed to the *muḥtasib* as located within the works on *ḥisba* receive no substantiation in the historical sources. As noted above, early pre-Buwayhid reports concerning the *muḥtasib* rarely focus on him simply by virtue of his having held the post. He is usually mentioned due to some other characteristic, such as the office also having been held by a judge, or its holder having taken an instrumental part in a rebellion or some other unusual circumstance. This applies equally well when we consider the dearth of historical information regarding the *muḥtasib*'s day-to-day business; it is generally only mentioned insofar as it was unusual, of major importance (as with weights and measures) or as it served as an illustration of the enactment of certain government policies which received particular emphasis.

The above remarks need not lead one, however, necessarily to assume that the duties described by the *ḥisba* manuals did not come under the aegis of the *muḥtasib* or his representatives. The constant injunctions against a certain practice are perhaps evidence enough that it existed, and that the *muḥtasib* is constantly enjoined to attend to these affairs indicates that at least at times he, and/or his representatives, probably did so.

[43] Many of these have been incorporated in the notes to the translation.

Regarding the contents of al-Shayzarī's *Nihāya*, it is clear that the duties attached to the office of the *muḥtasib* may be divided into two broad categories: those concerned with the orderly and equitable running of the market, and those which have as their aim the maintenance of public morals and the correct execution of Islamic ritual and law. These two aspects of the market inspector's office receive more or less stress in all the manuals and miscellaneous chapters dealing with *ḥisba*, despite the fact that a writer may choose to highlight one aspect or another. al-Māwardī, for example, places much more emphasis on the moral and religious functions than he does on those more mundane, whereas al-Shayzarī generally shows more concern for subjects of direct relevance to commercial dealings in the market place. No doubt the *muḥtasib*s themselves emphasised one or other sphere depending on personal inclination or governmental injunction. In effect, the duties of the *muḥtasib* were subject to the different circumstances occasioned by place and time. Thus, the Zaydī *Kitāb al-Iḥtisāb* includes among the *muḥtasib*'s responsibilities the censure of any individuals intending to export weapons to anti-Zaydī Muslims;[44] while al-Shayzarī goes into some detail regarding supervision of the *dhimmī*s, the non-Muslim protected peoples, who during the Crusades were considered as a potential source of treachery, and regarding the predominantly Shi'ite Bāṭinī movements, which to some extent were victims of the Sunni revival then current in many parts of the Islamic world.[45]

Concerning commercial dealings within the market place, in the course of the *Nihāya* al-Shayzarī deals with a great number of trades and professions along with their most common deceitful practices. This is to enable the *muḥtasib* to monitor these and detect and remedy the swindles associated with them. The one feature common to many of these occupations was the use of weights, scales and measures.

We have earlier seen that the old *'āmil al-sūq* was primarily concerned with the more material affairs of the market place and that it was only with the advent of the

[44] "A Zaidi Manual" p. 27.

[45] As another example of the often strong relationship between the *muḥtasib*'s duties and the time and place, al-Māwardī remarks that under certain circumstances the *muḥtasib* is responsible for the collection of the *ṣadaqāt* (charitable gifts) (*al-Aḥkām al-Sulṭāniyya* p. 214). Now, al-Māwardī wrote his treatise under the Buwayhids (945-1055), and it is noteworthy that while he is the sole writer to mention this duty, the only other allusion to it occurs in a diploma of investiture from the Abbasid

Abbasids that he was endowed with a character and responsibilities of a more directly religious and moral nature. However, from all the available information, both in the *ḥisba* treatises and other sources, it is clear that the more mundane side of the *muḥtasib*'s activities always remained paramount. Thus, whatever variations there may have been in the responsibilities of the market inspector, his regard for correct weights, measures and scales always continued to be the primary one. The overriding importance of this area of his jurisdiction is readily attested by the great significance accorded to it by the *ḥisba* treatises. Among other things, this importance can also be seen in one of the reports concerning the first known *muḥtasib*, 'Āṣim al-Aḥwal:

> 'Āṣim al-Aḥwal was in al-Madā'in over the weights and measures, that is, as if he was a *muḥtasib*.[46]

Here, "over the weights and measures" is used almost as a synonym for *muḥtasib*.

Not surprisingly then, this subject similarly receives great attention in the *Nihāya*, and al-Shayzarī provides some valuable and fascinating information regarding the numerous weights and measures in circulation and their equivalents, as well as a number of ruses which tradesmen employ in the use of these to deceive the unwitting customer.

Just as the units of weights and measure suffered from a lack of uniformity and therefore lent themselves to fraud and swindling, so the coinage suffered from the same disadvantages. An obvious target for the *muḥtasib*'s attentions was the money changers who were a common feature in the markets, exchanging the numerous kinds and qualities of dirhams and dinars in circulation. While dealing with these, al-Shayzarī supplies examples of the various coins available in the market place.

Further occupations dealt with by al-Shayzarī include sausage makers, confectioners, fryers of fish, bazaar criers, sellers of sheep's heads, sellers of clarified butter, slaughters and butchers, and numerous others. Not only are many

---

caliph to the Buwayhid Amir Fakhr al-Dawla giving him jurisdiction in *ḥisba* and *ṣadaqāt* (*Ṣubḥ al-A'shā* 10:15).

[46] *Tarīkh Baghdād* 12:244.

trades mentioned the existence of which might otherwise be unknown, but intimate details are often provided regarding their workings. Such, for example, is the case regarding the various makers and vendors of foodstuffs, where recipes and methods of preparation are occasionally elaborated so that the *muḥtasib* can ensure that everything is being done in a satisfactory manner. In addition, al-Shayzarī refers to a number of medicinal preparations and remedies, the constituents of different perfumes, and a wealth of produce and ingredients coming from places as far afield as India, North and East Africa, China, Persia, Central Asia, Europe, and so on.

The *Nihāya* likewise emphasises the avoidance of anti-social behaviour and the maintenance of public welfare. Thus, those trades which use smoke-producing ovens should be distanced from such as the perfumers and the cloth merchants, and the roads of the market place must remain unobstructed and clean. This latter is a subject which receives attention in all the *ḥisba* treatises without exception and is sometimes mentioned in diplomas of investiture, both from the Buwayhid and later periods. Also included here is the separating of the different trades into their own particular areas, this being considered to be commercially more viable and no doubt enabled the authorities to exercise firmer control over them. An exception to this rule is deemed to be the bakers, who must be distributed throughout the town so that all the inhabitants have easy access to them regardless of how far they live from the market. The *muḥtasib* must also ensure that the bakers have a prescribed quantity of flour from the millers and that they bake a stipulated amount of bread so that there will be enough in the town.

Regarding the references to bakers and grain merchants, it is interesting to note that during the Fatimid caliphate one of the main functions of the *muḥtasib* was probably the exercise of control over these tradesmen, this being no doubt the reason why al-Shayzarī stressed this in his manual. Grain and bread were of crucial importance throughout the Islamic empire both prior and subsequent to the Fatimids. In no place is the utter dependence of the populace on this commodity more easily seen than in the great efforts of the Fatimid caliphs to ensure an uninterrupted supply, and it seems that the *muḥtasib* was one of the chief agents of control. One of his general duties was to ensure that no one hoarded foodstuffs so as to wait for a rise in prices before selling them, or perhaps to create a rise in prices by monopolising a commodity and withholding it from the market. Likewise, the *muḥtasib* is recommended to keep a check on the bakers by recording their names and the position of their shops in his register.

Elsewhere, al-Shayzarī shows concern for matters of general hygiene. Cooking pots, trays, vessels and so on must be washed according to the best methods, flies, maggots and similar vermin must be kept away from edibles, and rotten produce must be dumped on the municipal tips outside the town.

The welfare of animals, too, comes under the jurisdiction of the *muḥtasib*. They should not be left standing with loads on their backs, not bear too great a burden, they should be fed properly, not beaten too severely, and the veterinarian should observe the rules laid down for him.

One particular duty of the *muḥtasib* which al-Shayzarī curiously does not refer to, but which perhaps deserves mention here due to the attention it receives elsewhere, is jurisdiction over the ports (*sawāḥil*). Under the Fatimids there was a great expansion of bureaucracy and numerous new government posts were brought into existence, making the situation very elaborate and complex. It is under this regime that the office of *sawāḥil* makes its appearance and is added to that of *ḥisba*.[47] Although this post is quite often referred to by the sources they do not contain any details regarding its nature. Neither its scope of jurisdiction nor the duties incumbent upon its holder are anywhere elucidated. It seems probable, however, that the individual charged with its execution would, as the plural term *sawāḥil* (river harbour, anchorage) suggests, have responsibilities concerned with at least the three ports of al-Qāhira and Miṣr/Fusṭāṭ. It is also possible that his sphere of influence would extend as far as the port of Qūṣ in Upper Egypt which under the Fatimids became an important market on the trade route with the Far East. The port in al-Qāhira was constructed by the Fatimids on the site of an old fortified town known as Tendunyas to the Romans (Arabic: Umm Dunayn), and apart from being a trading port was also the anchorage of the military fleet. An older port was that of Miṣr/Fusṭāṭ which was concerned almost entirely with affairs of a commercial nature

[47] *Akhbār Miṣr* p. 14; *Khiṭaṭ* 1:277, 2:31, 135.

and called Dār al-Ṣinā'a. By far the oldest of the three ports in the capital was that of Jazīrat al-Rawḍa which was in use during Pharaonic times.

Perhaps the connection between the office of the *sawāḥil* and that of the *muḥtasib* is not so unusual when we consider that these ports were also the sites of large market areas. At any rate, the *muḥtasib* is sometimes credited with duties which would have inevitably taken him to the ports. al-Maqrīzī, quoting Ibn al-Tuwayr, one of the most important authorities for late Fatimid times, says that the *muḥtasib* must:

> Ensure that the ship owners do not carry more than a safe load.[48]

Likewise, al-Māwardī:

> And the *muḥtasib* should forbid the ship owners from carrying that which the ships cannot accommodate and which he is afraid may cause them to sink. Similarly, he should stop ships from setting sail in strong winds. If the ship owner carries men and women he must separate them with a partition. And if the ships are large enough he should install toilets for the women so that they do not have to go out [i.e. on to the deck and in the presence of the men] at the time of need.[49]

Aside from regulation of the trades and professions and the maintenance of public welfare, the *Nihāya* also urges the *muḥtasib* to attend to the censure of immoral behaviour. This includes the prohibition of sodomy and homosexuality, but inevitably revolves more generally around the regulation of public relations between males and females. For example, al-Shayzarī recommends that the bakers' youths and errand boys must be immature because they enter people's houses and meet their womenfolk, and that prospective buyers not be allowed to be alone with female slaves or to look at them unclothed. Similarly, the *muḥtasib* must forbid the cotton carders from talking with the women and from giving them a seat by the doors of their shops while they wait for the carding to be completed. The same applies to any merchant whose trade brings him into contact with the fairer sex. In general, the sexes are to be kept strictly segregated and the privacy and seclusion of women must remain undisturbed.

---

[48] *Khiṭaṭ* 1:463.

[49] *al-Aḥkām al-Sulṭāniyya* p. 222. Ibn al-Ukhuwwa also includes a short chapter on ship owners, see *Ma'ālim al-Qurba* Arabic text p. 222.

One additional and most obvious arena for immoral behaviour was the public baths (*ḥammām*), and al-Shayzarī also enjoins the *muḥtasib* to extend his control over them. These places of public utility and recreation were naturally open to all manner of evils, and the protection of general decency in them includes such things as not allowing an effeminate man to have his beard shaved and chastising anyone who reveals his nakedness and anyone who sees it.

Supplementing the above functions attached to the *muḥtasib*'s office were others which had a more or less direct bearing on the maintenance and correct observance of Islamic ritual and law and which receive considerable attention in the *Nihāya*. Thus, animals must be slaughtered in the religiously prescribed manner, gambling, the various forms of usury and certain methods of concluding a sale are to be prohibited, alcohol and the playing of musical instruments are forbidden.

The religio-legal concerns of the *muḥtasib* are also evident in his jurisdiction over the mosques. That he must ensure the correct maintenance of the mosques, order seemly behaviour in them, ensure that the statutory prayers are performed and that the Qur'ān is only recited according to the law of Islam are recurrent themes, found not least in the Fatimid diplomas of appointment. Connected with these is a function which receives special emphasis in the *Nihāya* and the other sources, that is, the *muḥtasib*'s concern for the muezzin and the correct performance of the call to prayer. In this, al-Shayzarī stresses that the muezzin should be aware of the times of the prayers, for if he should summon the people at the wrong time the prayers will be invalid.

Another major feature of the *muḥtasib*'s responsibilities which comes under the general heading of the religio-legal was the enforcement of those discriminatory measures which ensured the differentiation between Muslims and the non-Muslim *dhimmī*s. Most of the *ḥisba* treatises deal with this. It is probable, however, that as was the case with others of the *muḥtasib*'s functions, this one varied much according to place and time, and cannot have been performed throughout the *muḥtasib*'s history with the same amount of conscientiousness and zeal as the treatises would have us believe. Whatever the case may have been under previous regimes, however, there is ample evidence that at least under certain of the Fatimid caliphs such discriminatory measures were enforced. This is particularly the case during the reign of al-Ḥākim bi Amr Allah.

In all his duties, the *muḥtasib* was empowered to detect crimes and to inflict a suitable punishment. Generally speaking, the *Nihāya* and the other *ḥisba* manuals instruct him to make the severity of his punishment correspond to that of the transgression. In conformity with the usually lower status afforded to the *muḥtasib* vis-à-vis the judge, he had no jurisdiction in those crimes which were punishable with the statutory penalties (*ḥadd* pl. *ḥudūd*) prescribed by Islamic law. The type of penalty he was entitled to administer was called *ta'zīr*, which was a discretionary punishment inflicted for transgressions for which there was no prescribed *ḥadd*. In theory, however, once the judge had exercised his judicial prerogative and had reached a decision concerning a particular case, the *muḥtasib* was empowered to put that decision into effect on the judge's behalf. Doubtless coming under this heading are two miscellaneous penalties which al-Shayzarī maintains the *muḥtasib* may carry out: in cases of pederasty he takes the criminal and throws him from the highest place in town, but only after the offence has been proved in the presence of the Imam; and secondly, he may take control of the lapidation of offenders. This latter punishment is, of course, a *ḥadd*. al-Shayzarī remarks that if the adulterer is a man who has concluded and consummated a valid marriage (*muḥṣan*) then the *muḥtasib* collects the people around him outside the town and orders them to stone him. If, on the other hand, the adulterer is a woman (*muḥṣana*) then he digs a hole for her and puts her in it up to her waist before ordering the people to stone her.

Aside from all this, and intended to obviate the need for it, the *muḥtasib* was generally enjoined to intimidate those whom he suspected might commit a crime. For this reason, the instruments of punishment, the *dirra* (whip) and the *ṭurṭūr* (tall conical cap), should hang from the *muḥtasib*'s booth in the market place, so as to act as a deterrent to any potential miscreants. This intimidation extended not only to those who looked as if they were about to commit a crime, but also to those who were simply in an advantageous position to do so. Thus, as regards the apothecaries, whose swindles and deceits were impossible for the *muḥtasib* to be fully aware of and which were considered to be the most pernicious to mankind, al-Shayzarī instructs the *muḥtasib* to "intimidate them, exhort them and warn them of punishment and chastisement". Indeed, one of the justifications for the use of the *dirra* and the *ṭurṭūr* is that they are "more awe-inspiring and intimidating to the general public".

In all his duties the *muḥtasib* had necessarily to rely largely on the assistance of hired helpers, and he was forced to depend upon the word of these that some offence had been committed, particularly in those circumstances where no tell-tale evidence remained. For this reason, al-Shayzarī is very careful to stress that these helpers must be of a high moral character and trustworthy. This was an important consideration also in that they were in a position of considerable trust which naturally lent itself to bribery; an unscrupulous merchant offering a sum for silence. al-Shayzarī remarks that in order to maintain public confidence in his administration, the *muḥtasib* must dismiss them if they take a bribe or are even accused of anything similar.

al-Shayzarī distinguishes between the ordinary hired helper and a different type of assistant known as the *'arīf* ("he who knows") who had a distinct function to perform. Whereas the ordinary helper was concerned with the generality of things, the *'arīf* possessed intimate knowledge about one or other of the trades and was thus in a position to detect the various devices and ruses employed by the tradesmen to swindle their customers.

During the Fatimid era, the distinction between the ordinary helper and the *'arīf* conforms with information gathered from the historical sources. It is clear though that following from our remarks concerning the predominantly honorary status of the *muḥtasib* during this time, the assistants must if anything have been yet more important and active. As before, the Fatimid *muḥtasib* was empowered to appoint his deputies as he saw fit, and was similarly enjoined not to be satisfied with any but he who did his job proficiently and effectively. He was also authorised to pay his deputies himself, being credited with the money thus disbursed - probably from the Public Treasury.[50] This, however, was only on condition that he could furnish living

[50] *Ṣubḥ al-A'shā* 11:215. This is referred to in a diploma of investiture from the Fatimid period. It would seem to contradict the conclusion of Goitein who, writing of this general period, remarks that lower officials who came into contact with the general public "apparently didn't receive any fixed

proof of having actually hired somebody to work for him, and thus was not attempting to receive reimbursement for bogus employees.

salary from the office employing them. Instead they were remunerated with a small gratuity for each service rendered by the persons concerned" (*A Mediterranean Society* 2:358).

The Manual

In the Name of God the Compassionate the Merciful

The Shaykh, the Unique Imam, the Learned ʻAbd al-Raḥmān b. Naṣr b. ʻAbd Allah al-Shayzarī says:

I praise God for what He has bestowed and ask His help in that which He has enjoined. I bear witness that there is no god but He alone and that the Sublime, the Almighty has no partner. And I bear witness that Muḥammad is His servant and His prophet, God bless him, his family and Companions and grant them salvation.

I was asked by someone who held the office of *ḥisba*, was appointed to look after the interests of the citizens and inspect the general populace and the tradesmen, to compile a suitable brief summary of the lawful methods of *ḥisba*. This was to act as a support for his administration and a buttress for his supervision. So I responded to his request, attempting to be concise and without prolixity, and set down some of the information for him. I embellished this with some narratives and traditions, put information in it regarding the deceptions of salesmen and the swindles of tradesmen, revealed their hidden secrets and removed their well-guarded screens. I did this hoping for the Benefactor's reward on the Day of Judgement. I restricted myself to mentioning only those occupations well known due to their necessity and divided it into forty chapters. The *muḥtasib* can take them as a model and proceed according to them. I called it *The Utmost Authority in the Pursuit of Ḥisba*.

I have no success except by God. In Him I trust and to Him I turn in repentance.

CHAPTER ONE

The Conditions and Recommendations of *Ḥisba* enjoined upon the *Muḥtasib*

As *ḥisba* is the ordering of good and the forbidding of evil, and the establishment of order between the people, the *muḥtasib* has to be a *faqīh*,[1] aware of the rules of Islamic law so as to know what to order and what to forbid. For good conduct is only that of which Islamic law approves, and bad conduct is that of which it disapproves. The intellect has no access to knowledge of good and evil except by means of the Book of God and the Sunna[2] of His Prophet. An ignorant man may condone that which Islamic law disapproves of and thus inadvertently commit what

[1] A *faqīh* is someone with an understanding of *fiqh* (Islamic jurisprudence). It is interesting to note that there was at times a certain amount of institutional diffusion between the office of the *muḥtasib* and that of the Islamic *qāḍī* or judge. Even before the first appearance of the *muḥtasib* there are several indications that his precursor, an official known as the *'āmil al-sūq*, was occasionally also a judge. Sometimes his appointment over the market appears to have been stepping stone on the way to becoming a judge, as was the case with 'Abd Allah b. 'Uṭba b. Mas'ūd who administered the market for the caliph 'Umar b. al-Khaṭṭāb (r. 644-55) (*al-Isti'āb* 2:576) and who later became a judge in Kufa (*Kitāb al-Ṭabaqāt al-Kabīr* 6:82). Sometimes the market inspector was a judge first and only latterly concerned with the markets, as illustrated by Iyās b. Mu'āwiya who is said to have had jurisdiction in the market of Wāsiṭ, Iraq, probably sometime after 723 (*Akhbār al-Quḍāh* 1:353), while another source reports that the same individual was employed as a judge in 718 in either Basra or Kufa (*Tarīkh al-Rusul wa'l-Mulūk* 2:1347). When the *'āmil al-sūq* was transformed into the *muḥtasib* this, albeit nebulous, connection between the judiciary and the market inspector continued. The very first *muḥtasib* to appear in the sources, 'Āṣim al-Aḥwal (d. 759), who worked in the market of Kufa, is also alleged to have taken the judgeship of al-Madā'in, Iraq, for the caliph Abū Ja'far al-Manṣūr (r. 754-75) (*Kitāb al-Ṭabaqāt al-Kabīr* 7 part II:65; *Akhbār al-Quḍāh* 3:304; *Tarīkh Baghdād* 12:245, 247). What is particularly noteworthy in this context is the evidently close relationship between the two offices, for one report states that 'Āṣim administered the market of al-Madā'in "being similar to a judge" (*Tarīkh Baghdād* 12:243) while another states that he was in al-Madā'in with jurisdiction over the weights and measures "as if he was a *muḥtasib*" (*Tarīkh Baghdād* 12:244). During the Fatimid period a diploma of investiture written on behalf of the caliph al-Ḥākim (r. 996-1021) enjoins the judge to undertake several of the market inspector's traditional functions: to check the mosques, the Imams, the public speakers, the muezzins and so on (*Ṣubḥ al-A'shā* 10:384 ff.). Another diploma written on behalf of the caliph al-'Āḍad (r. 1160-71) concerning the jurisdiction of a judge states among other things that he must ensure that the roads to the markets are unobstructed (*Ṣubḥ al-A'shā* 10:433). Often, it is unequivocally declared that the judge is to have authority over the *ḥisba* (see, for example, *Ṣubḥ al-A'shā* 10:350; al-Kindī, *Kitāb al-Wulāt wa Kitāb al-Quḍāt* [Beirut, 1908] p. 596; *Itti'āẓ* 1:217). Ibn Khaldūn remarks that

> The position of *muḥtasib* ... is subordinate to the office of judge. In many Muslim dynasties, such as the 'Ubaydid [i.e. Fatimid] in Egypt ... the office of *muḥtasib* fell under the general jurisdiction of the judge, who could appoint anyone to the office at discretion (*Muqaddimah*, trans. F. Rosenthal [Princeton, 1958] 1:462).

[2] That is, the collected sayings and doings of the prophet Muḥammad, which are established as legally binding precedents and form one of the bases of Islamic law.

is forbidden.[3] For this reason, the search for knowledge is a religious duty for every Muslim, as the Prophet said.

* *

The first thing that the *muḥtasib* must do is to act according to what he knows, and for his words not to contradict his actions. When God criticised the Israelite scholars He said: "Do you order the people to act correctly and yet forget yourselves?"[4] Anas b. Mālik[5] related that the Prophet said: "One night I saw some men passing by me whose lips were being cut with scissors. I said: 'Gabriel, who are these men?' Gabriel replied: 'They are preachers from your community who order the people to be pious and yet forget themselves.'" And God, in talking about Shu'ayb[6] when he forbade his people from giving short weight and measure, said: "I don't want to oppose you in that which I forbid you to do. I only want to improve what I can."[7]

The *muḥtasib* should not be like those Ibn Hammām al-Salūlī[8] referred to when he said:

> When they are asked to speak they speak well,
> But fine words are contradicted by the deed.
> They say the world is bad for us,
> While they suck its milk until it is dry.

Someone else said:

> Don't forbid someone then do the same as him.

---

[3] The *ḥisba* treatises invariably begin by enumerating the requisite virtues of the *muḥtasib*. al-Māwardī, for example, states that "Among the conditions upon the *muḥtasib* is that he should be a freeman, of good character, judicious, stern, uncompromising in religion and with knowledge of obvious objectionable actions" (*al-Aḥkām al-Sulṭāniyya* p. 208. See also *Ma'ālim al-Qurba fī Aḥkām al-Ḥisba* p. 7).
[4] Qur'ān 2:44.
[5] A Companion of the Prophet and one of the most prolific relaters of traditions from him. d. 709/711.
[6] A prophet mentioned in the Qur'ān and identified by later commentators as the Old Testament Jethro, the father-in-law of Moses. Besides teaching monotheism, he mainly urges his countrymen to be honest in weights and measures.
[7] Qur'ān 11:88.
[8] Unidentified.

A great shame on you if you do.

* *

The *muḥtasib* must strive to achieve God's design and to seek His pleasure with both word and deed. He must be of good intentions, corrupted neither by hypocrisy nor insincerity. He must avoid arguing with people and boasting before his fellows in his supervision.[9] This is so that God will spread over him the mantle of approval and the banner of success, instil his dignity and honour in people's hearts and make them respond obediently to what he says. Indeed, the Prophet has said: "Whoever pleases God but gains the anger of the people, He will protect him from their malice. And whoever pleases the people but gains the anger of God, He will leave him to them. Whoever acts correctly in what is between him and God, God will act

---

[9] While a number of *muḥtasib*s do seem to have answered to these qualities, others were less than paragons of virtue. That this was the case may be seen in al-Māwardī's complaint at the end of his chapter on *ḥisba* where he claims that he has devoted so much space to the subject because *ḥisba* has declined in respectability, the rulers appointing to it "those who are contemptible" (*al-Aḥkām al-Sulṭāniyya* p. 223). Perhaps the individual uppermost in al-Māwardī's mind when he wrote this was the notorious Ibn al-Ḥajjāj (d. 1000), who is said to have been one of the greatest poets among the Shi'ites and who died while al-Māwardī was in his twentieth year. He was also the *muḥtasib* in Baghdad for the Buwayhid 'Izz al-Dawla Bakhtiyār. Judging from reports, his poetry would seem to have left much to be desired on the part of the more orthodox circles, while he himself was "noted for his licentiousness, humour and gaiety", becoming a "proverb for foolishness, philandery and ridicule". He was eventually dismissed, but only after having served in office for quite some time (*Biographical Dictionary* 1:448-50; *al-Nujūm al-Zāhira* 4:204; *Ma'ālim al-Qurba* p. 7; he is also mentioned by al-Shayzarī in Chapter 38 of the present translation). Another such was al-Danyālī. It appears that in 931 al-Ḥusayn b. al-Qāsim was appointed to the wazirate on the strength of a forged document in the name of the prophet Daniel. The forger, curiously named al-Danyālī, received his reward from the grateful wazīr by being employed as *muḥtasib* of Baghdad with a monthly emolument of one hundred dinars. Being dissatisfied with this, and being in a good position to bargain, the monthly stipend was duly increased to two hundred dinars. At which point we hear no more (Ibn Miskawayh, *Tajārib al-Umam*, [Cairo, 1914] 1:317). Among the other, perhaps unlikely candidates was Abū 'Abd Allah the Shi'ite, the Ismā'īlī propagandist who paved the way for the Fatimid regime in North Africa. He is often mentioned with the epithet "the *muḥtasib*" and is said to have occupied such a post in the yarn market of Basra prior to his sojourn in Africa (Ibn Khaldūn, *Kitāb al-'Ibar* [Cairo, 1971] 3:362, 6:31-32; *Itti'āẓ* 1:45,51). Another character was Yaḥyā b. Zakariyā who was appointed as *muḥtasib* of Baghdad in 774. It appears that he abused his position of trust and confidence by allying himself to the partisans of Muḥammad b. 'Abd Allah and his brother Ibrāhīm, the two proto-Shi'ites who led abortive revolts in the Hijaz and Basra in 762. Urging the people to rise in revolt, Yaḥyā was apprehended and executed on the caliph's order in the same year (*Tarīkh al-Rusul wa'l-Mulūk* 3:324). Yet another was al-Sarakhsī who also held the office of *ḥisba* in Baghdad. He is said to have been a pupil of the philosopher and physician al-Kindī and to have written a great number of books, including works on astrology, government, arithmetic, medicine, music and, interestingly, two treatises on *ḥisba*, *Ḥisba al-Kabīr* and *Ḥisba al-Ṣaghīr*, which although not extant are the earliest known works on the subject (*The Fihrist of Ibn Nadim*, trans. B. Dodge [Columbia, 1970] 2:278-79). He is also credited with a volume entitled *Amusement, Instruments for Singing, Singers, Court Companions, Sittings Together and Varieties of Stories and Anecdotes* (*Fihrist* 2:627). He was the court tutor of al-Mu'taḍid (r. 892-902) before the latter became caliph, finally being executed by his former pupil in 899 due to some court intrigue.

correctly in what is between him and the people. Whoever improves his inner being, God will improve his outer being; and whoever works for the Hereafter, God will protect him from this world."

It is related that Atabek Tughtakīn,[10] the Sultan of Damascus, was looking for a *muḥtasib* and a knowledgeable man was mentioned to him. So he gave orders that he be brought before him. When he saw him, he said: "I am giving you jurisdiction of *ḥisba* over the people, the ordering of good and the forbidding of evil." The man replied: "If this is the case, then get off that mattress and remove that cushion, for they are made of silk. And take that ring off, for it is made of gold. Concerning silk and gold, the Prophet said: 'These two things are unlawful for the men of my community but lawful for women.'" So the Sultan got off his mattress, ordered that his cushion be removed, took the ring off his finger and said: "I'm also making you responsible for the affairs of the *shurṭa*."[11] And the people had never seen a more venerable *muḥtasib*.

---

[10] Atabek Tughtakīn (d. 1128) was the ruler of Damascus and founder of the Burid dynasty. He was involved in the wars against the Crusaders. Regarding the mandating of the *muḥtasib*, this was generally done either by the caliph or by his deputies. Indeed, it would appear that the authorities took pains to discourage any from assuming this office, on a voluntary basis, apart from those specifically chosen to do so. The following extract indicates the government's concern at a very early stage with maintaining control over the office:

> It is related that the caliph al-Ma'mūn heard that someone was acting as *muḥtasib* and going among the people ordering them to do good and forbidding them from evil, while not being commissioned to do so by him. So he ordered that the man be brought before him. When he appeared, the caliph said: "I have heard that you consider yourself qualified to order good and forbid evil without me having charged you to do so" (al-Ghazālī, *Iḥyā' 'Ulūm al-Dīn* [Cairo, 1915] 2:278-79).

The caliph, however, rather than rebuking the man, was so impressed by his piety and obvious suitability for the post that he told him to "continue what you are doing, with our order and on the authority of our opinion". Somewhat later, Ibn Khaldūn in his summary of *ḥisba* also mentions this point. *Ḥisba*, he says, "rests with the person in charge of the affairs of Muslims. He appoints to the position men whom he considers qualified for it" (*Muqaddimah* 1:462-63). During the Buwayhid period, the Buwayhid amirs seem often to have done the commissioning in the name of the Abbasid caliphs. It is from this time, both in Baghdad and a little later in Fatimid Egypt, that the first diplomas of investiture are preserved. The earliest example is from the first Buwayhid amir Mu'ayyid al-Dawla (r. 945-67) where he authorises someone to become *muḥtasib* (al-Ṣāḥib b. 'Abbād, *Rasā'il al-Ṣāḥib b. 'Abbād* [Cairo, 1948] pp. 39 ff.). Nevertheless, authority to employ the *muḥtasib* still lay in theory with the caliph, and his agreement sought before all else. In a communication from the Abbasid caliph al-Ṭā'ī (r. 974-91) to the amir Fakhr al-Dawla, the latter is instructed to appoint a *muḥtasib* for the eastern areas of the caliphate (*Ṣubḥ al-A'shā* 10:15 ff.). At other times, the wazīr made the appointments (see, for example, Tanūkhī, *Nishwār al-Muḥāḍara* [Beirut, 1971] 2:108, where the Buwayhid wazīr of Mu'izz al-Dawla employs Abū'l-Qāsim al-Juhnī as *muḥtasib* of Basra). In the Fatimid period both the caliphs and the wazīrs made the appointments, and many diplomas of investiture illustrating this are preserved in al-Qalqashandī's *Ṣubḥ al-A'shā*.

* *

The *muḥtasib* must diligently apply himself to all the norms and recommendations of Islamic law, as well as the habitual practices of the Prophet, such as trimming the moustache, plucking out the hair from armpits, shaving the pubes, clipping the nails, wearing clothes which are clean and not too long and perfuming with musk. In addition, he must uphold the religious duties and obligations. All this increases his honour and precludes attacks against his piety.

It is reported that a man came before Sultan Maḥmūd[12] requesting the *ḥisba* in Ghazna.[13] The Sultan looked at him and saw that his moustache was so long it had covered his mouth and that the hem of his clothes trailed on the ground. So he said to him: "O Shaykh, go and practise *ḥisba* over yourself, then you can return and ask for it over the people!"

**

When the *muḥtasib* orders and forbids the people let him be gentle and softly spoken, cheerful and good-natured. In this way it is easier to win over their hearts

---

[11] The *shurṭa* was a largely secular institution responsible for public security and order. Unlike the Islamic judge, the officers of the *shurṭa* were empowered to take action on mere suspicion and to threaten anyone with punishment without certain proof of a crime. While it may be presumed that the Islamic judge and the *muḥtasib* enjoyed a close institutional relationship due to the ostensibly religious nature of their various duties, there was also a certain resemblance between the subject matter of *ḥisba* and that of the *shurṭa* which also facilitated an association between them. Their independence from the strict rules of procedure may also have added to their common ground. It is therefore not surprising to find from time to time the investing of both these offices in the same individual. Under the Abbasid caliph al-Muqtadir (r. 908-32) a certain Muḥammad b. Ya'qūt was appointed to the *ḥisba* and the *shurṭa* (*Tajārib al-Umam* p. 209). The majority of such reports concern the Fatimid period, a circumstance which did not escape the attention of al-Qalqashandī who notes that "In Egypt in the days of the Fatimids, *ḥisba* was sometimes added to the *shurṭa*" (*Ṣubḥ al-A'shā* 5:453) and that "in some of their diplomas I have occasionally seen the *ḥisba* in Miṣr and al-Qāhira added to the two chiefs of the *shurṭa*" (*Ṣubḥ al-A'shā* 3:487). al-Qalqashandī's observations are corroborated by the extant record of five persons who combined within themselves the offices of *ḥisba* and the two chiefs of the *shurṭa* (see *Itti'āẓ* 2:83, 91, 100, 150-51; *Khiṭaṭ* 2:5). It is interesting to note that among the things which the Crusaders borrowed from the Arabs was the office of the *muḥtasib*, whom they called the master sergeant or chief of police.

[12] Sultan Maḥmūd (969-1030) was the ruler of Ghazna and Khurasan and one of the most famous of Muslim conquerors, sending many raids into India.

[13] A town in eastern Afghanistan, ninety miles west of Kabul.

and achieve the desired effect.[14] God said to His Prophet: "It is part of the mercy of God that you should deal gently with them. If you were severe and harsh-hearted, they would have broken away from you."[15] This is also necessary because to rebuke too severely will perhaps result in disobedience, and to exhort too harshly will be ignored.

It is related that a man came before al-Ma'mūn[16] and roughly ordered him to do good and forbade him from evil. al-Ma'mūn said to him: "God ordered those who are better than you to speak politely to those who are worse than me. To Moses and Aaron, He said: 'But speak to him mildly, perhaps he will take warning or fear God.'"[17] Then he dismissed the man and would have nothing to do with him.

This is also necessary because a man might achieve with gentleness what he cannot achieve by being harsh. As the Prophet remarked: "God is gentle and loves all gentle people. He rewards gentleness in a way that He does not reward harshness."

Let the *muḥtasib* be patient, not quick to give punishment or to chastise someone for the first sin they commit or the first slip they make. Only the prophets are infallible.

When he comes across someone giving short measure, tampering with the scales or adulterating his wares or his trade, as described in the chapters dealing with the different kinds of swindles, the *muḥtasib* should ask him to repent of his sin, admonish and intimidate him and threaten him with punishment[18] and *ta'zīr*.[19] Then,

---

[14] Indeed, al-Ghazālī points out that a good nature is more important for the *muḥtasib* than religious piety, because if he becomes angry knowledge and piety will not subdue him, but a good nature will. It will also ensure that he does not seek glory or renown (*Iḥyā' 'Ulūm al-Dīn* 2:292).

[15] Qur'ān 3:159.

[16] Abū'l-'Abbās 'Abd Allah (786-833). An Abbasid caliph and son of Hārūn al-Rashīd.

[17] Qur'ān 20:44.

[18] al-Ghazālī, while speaking on the subject of warnings and threats, cites a suitable admonition which he commends to the *muḥtasib*: "Stop that, or I'll break your head!" or "I'll cut your head off!" He does, however, admit that there is a justifiable amount of hyperbole involved. (*Iḥyā' 'Ulūm al-Dīn* 2:291).

[19] The *muḥtasib* was empowered to detect crimes and to inflict a suitable punishment. Generally speaking, the *ḥisba* manuals instruct him to make the severity of the punishment correspond to that of the transgression. The type of punishment he was allowed to administer was called *ta'zīr*. This was given at the *muḥtasib*'s discretion and was outside the strictly defined penalties of Islamic law which prescribes certain set penalties (*ḥadd*, plural: *ḥudūd*) for certain crimes.

if he does it again, he should administer *ta'zīr* to him in way which befits the crime but not too severely.

The *muḥtasib* should acquire a whip, a *dirra*, a *ṭurṭūr*[20] and servants and assistants, for this is more awe-inspiring and intimidating to the general public. He must assign his helpers to the markets and roads when he is absent, and also employ some scouts who will keep him informed of what the people are doing.[21]

* *

[20] Refer to Chapter 40 for details on the whip, the *dirra* and the *ṭurṭūr*.

[21] It seems clear that the *muḥtasib* often had an extensive range of duties and a vast field of jurisdiction. Thus, Ibrāhīm b. Batha (864-943) is reported to have been the *muḥtasib* for both sides of the river at Baghdad, which indicates that his authority extended to the two large markets on either side of the river Tigris (*al-Aḥkām al-Sulṭāniyya* p. 222). Similarly, large markets also came under the jurisdiction of individual *muḥtasib*s in such as Wāsiṭ, Kufa and Basra. During the Fatimid period we hear of a single *muḥtasib* being appointed to Miṣr, al-Qāhira and al-Jazīra simultaneously (*Itti'āẓ* 2:91). At the time of the Mamluks there were only three *muḥtasib*s in the whole of Egypt: the *muḥtasib* of al-Qāhira who had authority over all of Lower Egypt apart from Alexandria; the *muḥtasib* of Alexandria; and the *muḥtasib* of Fusṭāṭ/Miṣr whose jurisdiction included all of Upper Egypt (*Ṣubḥ al-A'shā* 4:37). All of this indicates that the *muḥtasib* cannot have undertaken even a small part of his duties without the aid of assistants. The *muḥtasib* was empowered to appoint his own assistants, who appear under a variety of names including *amīn* (trustworthy), *'awn* (helper), *ghalmān* (youth), *'ayn* (scout), *rasūl* (messenger), *nā'ib* (deputy) and *rajul* (man). It is, however, possible to distinguish two main types of assistants, each with his own particular status and functions. The first type was known by any of the above titles. These assistants would patrol the roads and markets, looking for any misdemeanour or contravention, and upon discovering anything would presumably report back to the *muḥtasib*. No mention is made of their being permitted to exact punitive measures, but no doubt they would put an errant merchant in his place if circumstances so dictated. In this, the *muḥtasib* may be seen as acting more as a director and ultimate arbitrator than in any other capacity. Regarding the specific functions of these assistants, al-Maqrīzī remarks that the *muḥtasib*

> May employ deputies representing him in all the regions of the state, like the representatives of the government ... His deputies go around the tradesmen and merchants, and he orders them to put a stamp on the cooking pots of the makers of *harīsa* and to inspect their meat and be acquainted with the butchers and the cooks. They must keep an eye on the public highways and forbid any nuisance on them, and must make the owners of ships not carry more than a safe load. This also applies to those who transport goods on animals. They must order the water-carriers to cover their skin vessels with cloth. They have a gauge which measures twenty-four buckets, each one being equal to forty *raṭl*s. They must also order the water-carriers to wear the short blue trousers which keeps their genitals covered. They must warn the school teachers not to beat the children violently nor on a vital part of the body. Similarly, the swimming instructors must be warned not to expose people's children to danger. They must also become acquainted with those whose behaviour is evil and forbid with deterrent and chastisement. They must inspect the weights and measures. (*Khiṭaṭ* 1:463-64)

The second type of assistant was called the *'arīf*. See Chapter 2 note 4.

Among the necessary conditions on the *muhtasib* is that he should refrain from accepting people's money and receiving gifts from salesmen and tradesmen. This is bribery, and the Prophet said: "May God curse those who give bribes and those who accept them." Refraining from this safeguards his honour and is more in keeping with his dignity. The *muḥtasib* must enjoin his servants and assistants to abide by these same conditions, for they are often the cause of accusations being levelled against him.[22] If he learns that one of them has accepted a bribe or a gift he should dismiss him so that he himself is no longer under suspicion or in doubt.

[22] There is an interesting anecdote concerning an assistant of the *muḥtasib*, an *'arīf*, who had jurisdiction over the bakers and who himself owned a bread shop. It would appear that the *'arīf* became somewhat angry because the price of his bread was being undercut by a competitor. So, using his influence, he put "two helpers from the *ḥisba*" in charge of the man and they fined him a number of dirhams. This coincided with the chief judge's visit to the mosque. The accused man asked the judge to intercede on his behalf so the *muḥtasib* was summoned and chastised for what he had done. The *muḥtasib* defended himself by saying that the *'arīf* was responsible for it all and that he himself had nothing to do with it. At this, the chief judge ordered the dismissal of the offending *'arīf* and decreed that he should be fined the same amount as he had unjustly taken from his competitor (*Itti'āẓ* 2:225). Elsewhere, al-Maqrīzī states that in 993 a proclamation was read out saying that "the assistants of the *muḥtasib* should not take anything from anybody" (*Itti'āẓ* 1:277). This could refer to bribe taking, or to the collection of a *ḥisba* tax, the *mukūs* (singular: *maks*). Under the Fatimids taxes were imposed on every kind of business, each store having to be in possession of a licence for which monthly dues were collected. As well as businesses just about every article bought and sold, every trade and occupation, were also taxed. These taxes were called *mukūs*. Later, under the Mamluks, the tax for the licensing of a business was known as *ḥisba*, and was a payment to the *muḥtasib*. It seems plausible that this later *ḥisba* tax was in fact identical to the Fatimid *mukūs*, in which case al-Maqrīzī's report could be an example of the caliph rescinding certain taxes; something which he occasionally found politically expedient to do. This suggestion is substantiated by another report which declares that in 1013 the *mukūs al-ḥisba* was abolished (*Itti'āẓ* 2:96).

CHAPTER TWO

Supervision of the Markets and Roads

The markets must be situated on an elevated and spacious site as they were in ancient Rome. If the market is not paved, there should be a pavement on either side of it for the people to walk on in winter. Nobody is permitted to bring a shop bench[1] from the roofed passageway[2] into the main thoroughfare as this obstructs passers-by.[3] The *muḥtasib* must remove and forbid this because of the harm it may do people. The people of every trade should be allotted a special market for which their trade is known, as this is more economically sound for them and will bring them better business. The *muḥtasib* should also segregate the shops of those whose trade requires the lighting of fires, like bakers and cooks, from the perfumers and cloth merchants due to their dissimilarity and the possibility of damage.

* *

When the *muḥtasib* is unable to understand the people's occupations, to each trade he may appoint an *'arīf*[4] who is a virtuous fellow tradesman, is experienced in their

---

[1] Arabic: *maṣṭaba*. "The shop (dukkan) is a square recess or cell, generally about six or seven feet high; and between three and four feet in width; or it consists of two cells, one behind the other; the inner one serving as a magazine. The floor of the shop is even with the top of the mastabah or raised seat of stone or brick, built against the front. This is usually about two feet and a half, or three feet in height; and about the same in breadth... The shopkeeper generally sits upon the mastabah, unless he is obliged to retire a little way within his shop to make room for two or more customers, who mount upon the seat ..." (E. W. Lane, *The Manners and Customs of the Modern Egyptians* [London, 1860] pp. 313-14).

[2] "Some of the [markets] are covered over with matting, or with planks, supported by beams extending across the street, a little above the shops, or above the houses" (*Manners* p. 313).

[3] The *muḥtasib*'s responsibility to ensure the clear passage of public highways receives treatment in all the *ḥisba* treatises, and is sometimes mentioned in the Buwayhid and Fatimid diplomas of his appointment. The writer of the Zaydī *Kitāb al-Iḥtisāb* states that

> It is necessary for the *muḥtasib* to prohibit the building of a shop or the fixing of a pole in the market street ... and not to permit either the non-Muslims or the Muslims to tie their riding animals in the Muslims' highways if there is harm in this for passers-by ... and it is incumbent on the *muḥtasib* to forbid the people from digging a well in the Muslims' highway, or building a mosque, except with the Imam's permission when the street is wide and there is no harm in this for the passers-by and the Muslims. This also applies to the making of a ditch ("A Zaidi Manual" p. 18).

[4] It is clear that the *'arīf* was employed primarily to inform the *muḥtasib* of that which the latter could not be expected to know by virtue of its technicalities, and it is in this function that the *'arīf* differs from the ordinary assistant. al-Shayzarī mentions nine occupations which had *'arīf*s attached to them,

trade, aware of their swindles and frauds, is well known for his trustworthiness and reliability and who will oversee their affairs and acquaint the *muḥtasib* with what they are doing. The *'arīf* must inform the *muhtasib* of all the commodities and merchandise brought into their market and the current prices, as well as other matters of which the *muḥtasib* ought to be aware. It is related that the Prophet said: "Over every trade seek the assistance of a virtuous fellow tradesman."

* *

The *muḥtasib* is not permitted to set the prices of merchandise over the heads of its owners nor to oblige them to sell it at a fixed price.[5] This is because during the time of the Prophet prices rose and the people said to him: "O Prophet, set the prices for us." But the Prophet replied: "God is the one who sets prices. I wish to meet God and want nobody to demand that I commit a transgression against a person or money."

If the *muḥtasib* comes across someone who is hoarding a certain foodstuff, that is, buying it when prices are low and waiting until they rise so that the food becomes more expensive, he should compel him to sell it.[6] This is because monopolising is

---

these being the butchers, fish fryers, makers of *harīsa*, sausage makers, confectioners, perfumers, weavers, dyers and surgeons. It is not likely, however, that only these occupations were controlled in this way. al-Maqrīzī mentions that "in every market in Miṣr and over all the craftsmen there was an *'arīf* who took control of their affairs" (*Itti'āẓ* 2:224).

[5] Although the *ḥisba* manuals expressly forbid the *muḥtasib* to set the prices on goods, this was sometimes not followed. For example, in 1024 the *muḥtasib* Bāqī al-Khādim al-Aswad ordered that the *khushkār* (poor quality bread) be one dirham for five *raṭl*s while the *ḥuwwārī* (fine quality) be one dirham for four *raṭl*s. The response to this was that the millers and bakers (making a healthy profit out of the current shortage) locked their mills and shops thus aggravating the situation even more. The unhappy Bāqī was dismissed that same day (*Itti'āẓ* 2:151). On the other hand, the bakers were at least on one occasion publicly pilloried for increasing their prices (al-Musabbiḥī, *Akhbār Miṣr* [Paris, 1978] pp. 15-16).

[6] While this injunction was no doubt of general applicability, it is possible that it was particularly addressed to the hoarding of grain. One of the main functions of the *muḥtasib* during the Fatimid period was the exercising of control over the bakers and grain merchants. Grain, and the bread which was made from it, was of crucial importance throughout the Islamic empire both prior and subsequent to the Fatimids. In no place is the utter dependence of the population on this commodity more easily seen than in the great efforts of the Fatimid caliphs to ensure an uninterrupted supply. Another illustration of its importance may be seen in the so-called Geniza records which exhibit a constant preoccupation with the prices and availability of wheat and bread (see *A Mediterranean Society*). Although whenever possible enough grain to last for a whole year was bought in one go and stored away, thus maintaining a regular supply, epidemics, a low Nile affecting agriculture or perhaps unscrupulous speculation on the grain market could disrupt the supply. At these times the government was obliged to act quickly and efficiently, and it seems that the *muḥtasib* was one of its chief agents of control. This is confirmed by the many references to the *muḥtasib* taking action in this field in our

unlawful and it is a duty to prevent what is unlawful. The Prophet said: "He who brings in merchandise is blessed, and he who monopolises it is cursed."

It is not permitted to meet a caravan, that is, for people to go outside the town and meet it as it approaches, telling them that the market is slow and thus buying cheaply from them. The Prophet forbade the meeting of a caravan and forbade selling merchandise until it is taken to the market. If the *muḥtasib* finds anyone intending to do this, he should chastise and prevent him.

It is also necessary to prevent bundles of firewood, sacks of straw, water containers, baskets of dung, sand and so on being taken into the market because of the damage they cause to people's clothes. When those who bring in firewood, straw and such like stop with it in the open squares, the *muḥtasib* should order them to take the loads off their animals. This is because the loads injure and hurt the animals when they stop walking, and the Prophet forbade the harming of all animals apart from those that are eaten. The *muḥtasib* must also order the market people to sweep the markets and keep them clear of dirt, mud and other things which harm people. This is because the Prophet said: "There should be no harm and no hurting."

* *

As for the roads and paths in the quarters, no one is allowed to extend the wall of his house or shop into the common thoroughfares. This likewise includes anything which is annoying or harmful to passers-by, such as waterspouts coming out of the walls in winter and drains coming out of the houses into the middle of the road in summer. Indeed, the *muḥtasib* must order those who have waterspouts to replace them with channels excavated within the walls and plastered with lime in which

---

records of the Fatimid caliphate. Thus, during one of the not infrequent shortages of grain, the *muḥtasib* Sulaymān b. 'Azza "collected all the grain merchants in one place and closed all the roads except for one. The selling only took place there, and no *qaddaḥ* [a dry measure] of grain came out of that place without him learning of it" (*Itti'āẓ* 1:122). At a later date, and in a similar crisis, another *muḥtasib* attempted to apply control over the selling of grain in Miṣr by closing some 150 granaries. But his actions had the opposite effect to that intended, which was presumably to ration grain supply, and the *muḥtasib* was summoned to the palace and chastised by the caliph with the following words: "You've killed the people through hunger and destroyed the country. It's your responsibility to make the country thrive with bread and wheat until there is another crop" (*Itti'āẓ* 2:165). Upon this, the granaries were again opened thus freeing the grain. The *muḥtasib* then ordered the selling of the grain and bread at a stipulated price and the situation is said to have improved somewhat.

water from the roof can flow. The *muḥtasib* must charge everyone who has in his house an outlet into the road for sewage to close it in summer and to dig himself a pit in his house into which the sewage can be put.

It is not permissible to stare at the neighbours from roof tops and windows. Nor is it permissible for men to sit without good cause in the roads which women take, or for women to sit by their doors in the roads which men take. The *muḥtasib* must chastise whoever does these things, especially if he sees an unrelated man and woman talking together in a secluded place, for this is even more suspicious. But God knows best.

CHAPTER THREE

*Qintār*s, *Raṭl*s, *Mithqāl*s and *Dirham*s

As these are the bases of commercial dealings and an integral part of sales, the *muḥtasib* has to be acquainted with them and verify their size so that transactions can take place without fraud and according to Islamic law.[1] The people of every region and country have adopted various kinds of *raṭl*s, especially the people of Syria. I will mention those things of which the muḥtasib must not be ignorant, so he will understand the disparity in prices.[2]

---

[1] Whatever variations there may have been in the responsibilities of the market inspector, his concern with correct weights, measures and scales always continued to be the primary one. The overriding importance of this area of his jurisdiction is readily attested by the great significance accorded to it by the *ḥisba* treatises. al-Māwardī declares: "The main subject of his jurisdiction insofar as it concerns the prohibition of niggardliness and deficiency is scales, weights and measures ... let the chastising against it be more manifest and the punishment for it greater" (*al-Aḥkām al-Sulṭāniyya* pp. 218-19). Indeed, control over weights and measures was an issue in the early days of Islam. The stress which was placed on this can be seen in numerous traditions ascribed to the prophet Muḥammad as it can in the many Qur'ānic references: "Do not give short weight or measure", "My people, give just weight and measure in all fairness" (Qur'ān 11:85-86. For other verses see 6:153, 7:83, 55:8, 83:1). There is even a chapter called "Those who give Short Measure". There are two reports of the *muḥtasib* during the Abbasid era actually dealing with affairs of this nature, both occurring during the reign of al-Mu'taḍid. In the first, a cotton merchant appears before the caliph complaining that he has just made a purchase from a man whose weights and scales proved to be defective. Mu'taḍid summons the *muḥtasib* and, rebuking him, orders him to attend to these matters (Ibn al-Jawzī, *al-Muntaẓam fī Tarīkh al-Mulūk wa'l-Umam* [Hyderabad, 1358 AH] 5 part II pp. 129-30). The second report, which may, however, refer to the same incident, has the *muḥtasib* rebuking the salesman and ordering him to standardise his scales like those of the other merchants (*Nishwār al-Muḥāḍara* 1:327). During the Fatimid period proclamations were made in the markets warning the merchants not to swindle in their measuring (*Itti'āẓ* 1:280), to put their weights and scales in order (*Itti'āẓ* 2:53), and on more than one occasion the *muḥtasib* beat and pilloried those guilty of infringements (see, for example, *Akhbār Miṣr* pp. 72, 78).

[2] Diversity of weights and measures called by the same name was common to all Muslim countries and different weights and measures were often used for different commodities. As can be seen from the text, almost every district had its own system. Studies on metrology have led to different values being assigned to them, and there are no generally accepted conclusions. The susceptibility to malpractice with weights and measures was no doubt largely attributable to their great variety. Indeed, the number and complexity of weights and measures at an early date receives ample confirmation: "Abū 'Ubayd said: 'We found that traditions had been related on the authority of the Prophet, his Companions and the Successors after them of eight kinds of measure'" (*Kitāb al-Amwāl* p. 514). The caliph 'Umar b. 'Abd al-'Azīz (r. 717-20) issued a proclamation in his so-called "Fiscal Rescript" which indicates the concern that the early authorities felt for this subject:

> Furthermore, in regard to standards of measure and weight, we see in both of them certain practices which those who adopt them themselves know to be injurious. Truly there is no deviation in measuring save from giving short measure, nor in weighing is there excess save from deficiency. Wherefore we hold that all standards of measure and weight in the land should be one and the same throughout the land ("The Fiscal Rescripts of 'Umar II", ed. H. A. R. Gibb, *Arabica* 2 [1955] p. 6).

As can be seen from al-Shayzarī's chapters on weights and measures, 'Umar's wish was not to be fulfilled.

As for the *qinṭār*, which God mentioned in the Qur'ān,[3] Mu'ādh b. Jabal[4] said: "It is equal to 1,200 *waqiyyas*", while Abū Sa'īd al- Khadari[5] said: "It is equal to the skin of an ox filled with gold." The common *qintār*, however, is equal to 100 *raṭls*,[6] while the *raṭl* equals 684 *dirhams*,[7] which in turn is equivalent to 12 *waqiyyas*, this being equal to 57 *dirhams*. This is the *raṭl* of Shayzar which the Banū Munqidh[8] prescribed.

As for the *raṭl* of Aleppo, this is 724 *dirhams*, and its *waqiyya* is 60 and one-third *dirhams*. The *raṭl* of Damascus is equal to 600 *dirhams*, and its *waqiyya* is 50 *dirhams*. The *raṭl* of Homs is 864 *dirhams*, while its *waqiyya* is 72 *dirhams*. The *raṭl* of Hama is equal to 660 *dirhams*, and the *waqiyya* is 55 *dirhams*. The *raṭl* from Ma'arra[9] is the same as the one from Homs. The Egyptian *raṭl* - may God protect it - is 144 *dirhams*, and the *waqiyya* is 12.

The *manna*[10] is equivalent to 260 *dirhams*, while the *raṭl* of Baghdad is equal to half a *manna*.

* *

Regarding the *mithqāl*, it is equivalent to one *dirham* and two and a half *dānaqs*,[11] that is, 24 *qīrāṭs*,[12] which is 85 *ḥabbas*.[13] The *dirham* from Syria is 60 *ḥabbas*. The weights of the people of Syria differ however, for the *mithqāl* in Shayzar is bigger

[3] Qur'ān 3:14, 75; 4:20.
[4] Mu'ādh b. Jabal b. 'Amr b. Aws (d. c. 640) was one of the Medinan supporters of the prophet Muḥammad and a transmitter of his traditions.
[5] Otherwise known as Sa'd b. Malik b. Sinnān (d. c. 696) who was one of the Companions of the Prophet and a transmitter of his traditions.
[6] The Arabic word *qintār* derives from the latin "centenarius". Regarding the *raṭl*, this was the most common weight. It was also a measure of capacity.
[7] A weight, to be distinguished from the coin of the same name.
[8] Shayzar is a town in northern Syria after which the author of this book is named. The tribe of Munqidh, a sub-section of the Banū Kināna, were granted Shayzar and the surrounding areas in c. 1025. They ruled the region for approximately two hundred years and were still in power when al-Shayzarī wrote this book.
[9] Also known as Ma'arrat Miṣrīn. Now a small town in northern Syria.
[10] A weight used in Egypt, particularly for weighing spices.
[11] A small weight and a coin.
[12] From the Greek, meaning the seed of a carob tree, whose weight equals one carat. It was also used to mean the twenty-fourth part of a thing, twenty-four being chosen because it is the first number which has an eighth, a sixth, a quarter, a third, and a half without a fraction.
[13] A barley grain.

than that of Aleppo by half a *qīrāṭ,* while the *mithqāl* of Hama is the same as that from Shayzar. The *mithqāl* of Damascus is bigger that the Shayzarī one, while the *mithqāl* of Ma'arra is the same as the one from Damascus.

* *

The measures of capacity, the *qafīz* and *makkūk,*[14] are likewise different. For the *qafīz* in Shayzar is equal to 16 *sunbul*s, which is the common measure of capacity containing one and a half *raṭl*s in Shayzar. The *qafīz* of Hama is 2 *sunbul*s less than that of Shayzar, while the *qafīz* of Homs is the same as that of Hama. The *makkūk* of Aleppo is larger than the *qafīz* of Shayzar by 3 *sunbul*s. This is also the case regarding the *makkūk* from Ma'arra, which is equal to 4 *marzubān*s, each *marzubān* equaling 4 *kayl*s[15] in Aleppo. The *ghirāra* from Damascus is equivalent to 3 *makkūk*s in Aleppo.

All the things I have mentioned are impermanent in all ages. The people adopt one thing during the reign of a sultan, and then it changes when the sultan does. But God knows best.

[14] These were used in northern Syria for measuring grains.
[15] Used for measuring grains.

CHAPTER FOUR

Scales, Measures, Standard of Coins,[1] *Raṭl*s and *Mithqāl*s

The most accurate scale is that in which the two sides are equal, the pans are balanced and the hole for the attachment on either side of the centre of the beam is one third of the thickness of the attachment. This hole should be one third of the way under the peg of the attachment, and two-thirds above it. This allows for the inclination of the scales by taking the tongue of the balance out of the beam of the attachment, and the pan will descend with the slightest weight. As for the scales from Damascus, the position of the hole for the attachment is different from what we have mentioned. Their inclination is allowed by putting the tongue into the beam of the attachment without the scale going down. The peg might be square, triangular or round. The best is the triangular one because it inclines with more sensitivity than the others.[2]

The *muḥtasib* must order those who use scales to wipe and clean them hourly of any oil or dirt, as a drop of oil may congeal on them and affect the weight.

The merchant must settle the scales before he begins to weigh and should place the merchandise on them gently, not dropping it into the pan from his raised hand, nor moving the edge of the pan with his thumb, as all of this is fraudulent.

Among the hidden swindles used with scales for weighing gold is for the merchant to put his hand in front of his face and to blow gently onto the pan containing the merchandise thus making it descend. The buyer will have his eyes on the scales and not on the mouth of their owner. The merchants also have ruses by which they give short weight when they hold the attachment for the scales. They also sometimes stick a piece of wax on the bottom of one of the pans and put the silver on it, then they put the weights on the other pan. In this way they take one or two *ḥabba*s out of

[1] Although coins appear in the title, al-Shayzarī does not actually deal with them here. For some information see Chapter 30 on money changers and the accompanying notes.
[2] See the article "al-Karasṭūn", *Encyclopaedia of Islam* first edition (Leiden, 1927) vol. 2 pp. 757-60 for details on the workings of the steelyard, which is being decribed here.

every *dirham*. The *muḥtasib* must always keep an eye open for this.

The Byzantine steelyards are more accurate than the Coptic ones, and the *muḥtasib* must occasionally examine them in case they have bent through use and become defective.

* *

The merchant should acquire *raṭl*s and *waqiyya*s made of iron and test their accuracy against the standard weights.[3] He must not use stone ones, as these chip when they knock against each other and thus become inaccurate. If stone weights have to be used because iron ones are unavailable, then the *muḥtasib* must order the merchant to bind them with leather and he must stamp them after testing their accuracy. He should re-examine them now and again in case the merchant has replaced them with wooden weights which look the same.

A single shop should not have a collection of different *raṭl*s, *waqiyya*s or other balance weights without good cause, as this is suspicious. Nor should the merchant use a third of a *raṭl*, a third of a *waqiyya* or a third of a *dirham* because they resemble the half, and he might mistake them for halves when he is busily weighing for a lot of customers.

---

[3] During the Fatimid and subsequent periods the standard weights and measures were housed in a building called the *Dār al-'Iyār*. Regarding this and the *muḥtasib*'s duties there, al-Maqrīzī states that

> The *muḥtasib* inspects the *Dār al-'Iyār* ... The standard measures were in a place known as the *Dār al-'Iyār* in which the accuracy of all the parts of the scales and all the weights were checked. He used to pay for the maintenance of this *Dār*, and for whatever copper, steel, wood, glass and other materials he needed, and for the wages of the workmen, overseers and such like, from the government *Dīwān* (*al-Dīwān al-Sulṭāniyya*). The *muḥtasib* or the deputies in his presence would go there to check the accuracy of what was produced in it. If it was correct, the *muḥtasib* endorsed it, and if not then he ordered that it should be re-made until it was correct. In this *Dār* were specimens against which he checked the standard measurement; for the weights, scales and measures would not be sold except from this *Dār*. All the merchants would go there every so often upon the *muḥtasib*'s summoning them, bringing their scales, weights and measures to be tested. If a deficiency was found, then the [scale etc.] was destroyed and its owner was taken to the *Dār* and compelled to purchase a replacement from those which were accurately manufactured there. Then he was forgiven. The *muḥtasib* compelled those whose scales or weights showed a defect only to repair that which was amiss in them and to pay a fee for that only. This *Dār* still remains in all the Fatimid states. When Ṣalāḥ al-Dīn took over the government he confirmed this *Dār* ... and it still remains (*Khiṭaṭ* 1:464, 1:110).

The *muḥtasib* must check the standard of the balance weights, the *ḥabba*s and so on, when their owners are not expecting it. This is because some of them take grains of wheat and barley, soak them in oil, bury the ends of needles in them and dry them in the shade. The grains come to look as they did before and show no sign of what has happened to them.

* *

The correct cubic measure is one whose top and bottom are equal in shape and size and which is not bent nor irregular, even though the bottom may have an iron ring around it for protection. It should be strengthened with nails so that it cannot expand and give over measure nor contract and give short measure. The best thing to gauge the measure is small seeds which are usually identical, such as coriander, mustard, fleawort and so on. Each shop should possess three sizes of measure - a full one, a half and an eighth - because the work demands having these.

The *muḥtasib* must continually inspect the measures and see that the merchants do not make them smaller, for some of them pour gypsum on the bottom, which so adheres to it that it can hardly be noticed. There are others who smear the dregs of oil extracted from grains on the sides and bottom. Yet others take some sap of the fig tree and knead it with oil until it becomes like a cream, then they stick this on the inside of the measures and it cannot be noticed. Some merchants have a ruse they employ when they hold the measure which makes it give less. The *muḥtasib* must therefore never cease to keep an eye on them. But God knows best.

CHAPTER FIVE

Grain and Flour Merchants

As we have already explained, it is unlawful for them to hoard grain. They should not mix bad wheat with good, nor old wheat with fresh, for this is swindling the people. If it is necessary to wash the grain, then it must be well dried afterwards and each type of wheat sold separately.

* *

Before the grain is milled, the flour merchants must sieve the dirt out of it and remove all the darnel and dust. They should also sprinkle a little water over the wheat while it is being milled as this makes it white and wholesome. The *muḥtasib* ought to keep an eye on the flour, for perhaps they have mixed sieved barley flour with it, bean or chick pea flour and such like. Or perhaps they have put flour in it that has been milled on an uneven millstone or mixed with darnel or the dust of the mill. If the *muḥtasib* has doubts about them he should make then swear an oath that they will do none of these things.

It is for the common good that the *muḥtasib* stipulates they produce a daily quota of flour and distribute it to the shops and bakeries.

CHAPTER SIX

Bakers

The bakers must raise the ceilings of their shops, open the doors and make wide holes in the roofs of their ovens for the smoke to come out so that the people are not harmed. When the baker has finished lighting the *tannūr*[1] he should first wipe inside it with a clean rag before baking the bread.

The *muḥtasib* writes the names of the bakers and the location of their shops in his register, because he needs to know these things. He should order them to clean and cover the water containers, to wash and clean the kneading troughs, what they cover the bread with and what they carry it on.

The dough kneader must not knead with his feet, knees or elbows, because this shows contempt for the food and perhaps some drops of sweat from his armpits or torso will fall into the dough.[2] Therefore, he must only knead while wearing a sleeveless robe or a woollen gown. He should also be veiled in case he sneezes or speaks and some drops of spittle or nasal mucus fall into the dough. He should tie a white band around his forehead so that no sweat falls from it into the dough, and also shave the hairs of his arms so that none of them fall. If he kneads during the day, there must be someone with a fly-whisk keeping the flies off him. He should abide by all these things after sieving the flour a few times with a close-textured sieve.

* *

The *muḥtasib* must take into account the way they adulterate the bread with vetch and beans, for these turn the crust red. Some bakers adulterate the bread with the flour of chick peas and rice because this makes it heavy, but under-cooked. Others make dough out of coarsely ground grain, barley flour or flour containing darnel and

---

[1] A kind of oven made of baked clay or bricks which is open at the top and has a fire at the bottom. The bread is in the form of flat cakes which are usually stuck to the sides of the *tannūr*.

[2] It is reported that in Egypt in 928 "it was prohibited to knead bread with the foot" (*Itti'āẓ* 2:53).

use this for the bread. All this leaves its traces on the crust and in the bread's appearance and hardness. The *muḥtasib* must forbid the bakers from adding borax to the bread because this also harms it even though it improves the crust. They should not bake the bread until it has risen, as unleavened bread is both heavy in weight and on the stomach. This is similarly the case when it has too little salt. The *muḥtasib* must prevent them from doing this as they only do it to make the bread weigh more.

They should sprinkle the crust with the appropriate wholesome seeds, such as white cumin, black cumin, sesame and seeds of the mastic tree. The bakers should not take the bread out of the oven until it is well baked but without burning. It is for the common good that the *muḥtasib* stipulates that each shop must bake a certain amount of bread every day so that the town will not be disturbed through lack of it. The *muḥtasib* must compel the bakers to do this if they refuse.

CHAPTER SEVEN

Oven Keepers

The *muḥtasib* should disperse them among the roads, quarters and outskirts of the town because of their utility and great importance for the people. He should order them to maintain the chimneys and to clean every hour the tiles of the oven of burnt seeds, cinders and scattered sand so that none of it sticks to the bottom of the bread. The oven keeper must have some water in a clean container with him, so that when he has finished baking the bread he can use it to swill out any debris left in the oven. If he leaves the debris there it will become smelly. On the following day he must wash the oven. He must also undertake to wash the board he uses to stack the dough on, because the dough sticks to it. If the people bring him many bowls of dough, whenever he finishes baking one of them he should separate it from the others by marking it so that they do not all become confused and indistinguishable.

The oven keeper must have two bakers working with him, one of them for bread and the other for fish. The fish should be kept apart in case any of its oils flow out onto the bread. The oven keeper should not take more of the dough than has been given to him as a fee.

The board used to stack the dough on might have a hole in it or be made of two sections with a gap between them. Then, when the oven keeper takes the people's dough and shapes it with his fingers some of it will fall between the two sections into another container. The *muḥtasib* must therefore keep an eye on him and prevent him from doing this.

The oven keeper's servants and hirelings should be immature boys because they enter the people's houses and meet their womenfolk. But God knows best.

CHAPTER EIGHT

Makers of *Zulābiyya*[1]

The frying pan for the *zulābiyya* must be made of fine red copper. First of all, some bran should be fried in it, then when the frying pan has cooled it is wiped with chard leaves[2] and returned to the fire. After this, a little honey is put in it and heated until it burns, then it is polished with crushed pot-sherds and washed out. It is then ready for use, as it will have been cleaned of dirt and verdigris.

* *

Zulābiyya should be made from one third finely ground flour and two thirds coarsely ground semolina. This is because if there is a lot of semolina, the *zulābiyya* will be too white, too light and will not cook sufficiently. Semolina should be used, however, even though it needs more oil than fine flour and so is disliked by the *zulābiyya* makers.

The best oil to fry with is sesame oil, and if this cannot be obtained then some other pure oil. The *zulābiyya* should not be fried until the dough has risen; the sign of this being that it floats to the surface of the oil, while when it has not risen it sinks to the bottom of the frying pan. Also, risen *zulābiyya* becomes like tubes which stick together when gathered in the hand, while unleavened *zulābiyya* becomes crushed and is not hollow in the middle. No salt should be put in the dough because *zulābiyya* is eaten with honey and it would make one nauseous if it contained salt.

As for when the *zulābiyya* turns black, this occurs due to the frying pan being dirty, or perhaps only fine flour being used and no semolina, or it being fried in old oil, or perhaps it was unleavened, or perhaps the fire was too hot. The *muḥtasib* must keep an eye on them regarding all these things.

---

[1] A kind of confection made with honey and almonds.
[2] Chard is a variety of beet with large succulent leaves.

Some small identical pieces should be made, forty of which weight one *raṭl*, and when the dough of these becomes sour, the *zulābiyya* maker can use them to make other dough sour. But God knows best.

CHAPTER NINE

Slaughterers and Butchers

It is desirable that the slaughterer be a Muslim, mature and sound of mind, invoking God's name and facing in the direction of Mecca when he slaughters. He should slaughter camels when they are hobbled and cows and sheep when they are lying on their left side. All this is mentioned in the Sunna on the authority of Muḥammad. He must not pull a sheep roughly by its leg nor slaughter with a blunt knife because this is cruel to the animal and the Prophet of God forbade cruelty to animals.

When he slaughters he must sever the two jugular veins, the gullet and the throat and not begin to skin a sheep until it has become cold and its spirit has departed. This is because 'Umar b. al-Khaṭṭāb[1] ordered the town crier to announce in Medina: "Do not skin a slaughtered sheep until it has become cold." It is permissible to slaughter with everything except teeth and nails because the Prophet of God forbade these things.

The *muḥtasib* should forbid the slaughterer from blowing onto the carcass of a sheep after it has been skinned, because the smell of a man's breath spoils and sullies the meat. Some of them cut the flesh away from the stomach and blow water in. They know places in the flesh in to which to blow water. Thus the *muḥtasib* must keep an eye on the slaughterers in the *'arīf*'s absence. There are others who parade fat cows in the markets then slaughter other ones. This is fraud.

* *

As for the butchers, the *muḥtasib* must prevent them from allowing rumps of the meat to hang over the edge of their shop benches. These must be put within the edge of the bench and the two corners so that they do not bother the people or touch their clothes. He should order the butchers to separate goat meat from that of sheep, not to mix them together, and to sprinkle goat meat with saffron so as to distinguish it from

[1] The second caliph in Islam. He was in office from 644 until his death in 655.

other kinds. The tail of the goat must remain attached to the carcass until all the meat is sold. Goat meat can be recognized by its white fat and thin ribs. It must not be mixed with the fat of sheep nor should fatty meat be mixed with lean. The fat of goat meat can be recognized by its whiteness and purity, and sheep fat by its bright yellowness. The *muḥtasib* must order the butchers to sell the tails separate from the meat, with no skin or meat mixed with them.

When the butcher finishes trading for the day and wishes to leave, he should take some ground salt and sprinkle it on the chopping block so that dogs do not lick it or any vermin crawl on it. If he cannot obtain any salt, then he may use ground plant ash[2] instead. It is for the common good that the butchers do not collaborate and thus do not agree together on one price.

The *muḥtasib* must prevent the butcher from selling meat by the live animal. That is, for him to buy a sheep which weighs a certain number of *raṭl*s and for the slaughter to give him an agreed amount of meat every day. This is because the Prophet forbade it.

If the *muḥtasib* has any doubts about an animal, whether it died of natural causes or was slaughtered, he should put it in water, because if it sinks it was slaughtered but if it does not it died of natural causes. This is the same for eggs when they are placed in water: they float when rotten and sink when they are sound.

The *muḥtasib* must keep an eye on the hunters of sparrows and other birds regarding what we have mentioned, for most of them have no religion and do not pray. The *muḥtasib* must therefore fear God in the exercise of his duties. He must not take a bribe nor accept a gift from any of them so that they cannot in this way get the better of the Muslims and sully their way of life. They might mix some birds which have died naturally with those which were slaughtered and sell them together.

[2] A mixture of sodium and potassium carbonates obtained by slow oxidation of certain plants burnt in a pit to ashes. In the ancient Near East plant ash used for washing was well known.

CHAPTER TEN

Sellers of Roast Meat

The *muḥtasib* must weigh the carcasses of lamb for them before they are put in the *tannūr* and record the weights in his register. He must weigh them again when they come out of the oven, because they are only properly cooked when they weigh a third less than before and must be returned to the oven if they weigh more than that. He should examine the meat when it is being weighed to make sure that the meat roasters have not hidden any iron or lead weights in it. An indication of when the meat is properly cooked is to pull quickly at the shoulder. If it comes away easily then it is cooked. It is also possible to break the thigh and if there are red veins in it and the juices of the meat come out then it is raw and not yet cooked. Some of the meat roasters smear the carcasses with honey and then put them in the oven. In this way they very quickly go brown and give off an aroma, so they must be examined to make sure they are properly cooked. Some of them slaughter a lot of lambs and take only some of them to the *muḥtasib* while hiding the rest. The roast meat must not be covered immediately upon removal from the oven nor put in lead or copper containers while it is still hot, as the physicians say that this makes it poisonous.

The *muḥtasib* must order them to coat their ovens with clean clay which has been kneaded with clean water, because they sometimes take clay from the floors of their shops which is mixed with blood and dung and this is unclean. Perhaps some of this clay will fall onto the roast meat when the oven is opened and taint it.

* *

As for the sellers of roast minced meat, some of them put water and salt in a container they have and add a little lemon juice to it, then they pass this around while the meat is being minced and the customers sprinkle it over the meat. There may be some of this left overnight in summer which turns rancid due to the oil which is poured on it, so the meat roasters mix it with fresh lemon to conceal its smell and taste from the customer.

Some of them buy a cooked sheep's head when these are cheap and put its flesh on the chopping block. They then gradually mince it along with the roast meat. They also occasionally mince kidney and liver along with the meat while the customer is not looking. All of these things are swindles and the *muḥtasib* must make sure that they are not doing them.

When the meat roasters have finished trading and wish to close for the day, they must sprinkle ground salt on their chopping blocks, as we said regarding the butchers. But God knows best.

CHAPTER ELEVEN

Sellers of Sheep's Heads

The *muḥtasib* should order them to scald the heads and trotters clean with boiling water, to clean the hair and wool thoroughly, and after that to wash them in cold water other than that which was used to scald them. The seller of sheep's heads must put his fingers in the noses after crushing the bridge, wash inside them and take out all the impurities, dirt and maggots if there are any.

They should not sell goats' heads alongside those of sheep and must put the goats' trotters in the goats' mouths to distinguish them from the sheep so that they do not confuse someone who cannot tell the difference between them. The sign of a sheep's head is that it has a hollow under each eye which is not present in goats. Similarly, the goat's snout is narrow from the bottom, unlike that of a sheep.

Perhaps one day they will not be able to sell all the heads and thus mix them with the fresh ones on the following day. The way to identify stale heads is to take out the small bone in the throat, called the fork, and smell it. If it smells unpleasant, then the head is old.

Some of them buy the oil which has dripped off the roast meat, mix it with oil from the trotters and put it in the *tharīda*.[1] The *muḥtasib* must keep an eye on them regarding all these things. The heads should not be taken out of the cooking pots until they are properly cooked and the seller must have some ground salt and sumach[2] to sprinkle over them before they are sold. But God knows best.

---

[1] A broth made of wheat and sopped bread.

[2] A preparation of the dried and chopped leaves and shoots of plants of the genus *Rhus*.

CHAPTER TWELVE

Fryers of Fish

They must be ordered to wash daily the baskets and trays with which they carry the fish and to sprinkle ground salt in them every night after washing them. They must do likewise with their palm leaf weighing pans, because if they neglect to wash them they will give off an offensive smell and become increasingly dirty. Then when fresh fish is put in them its smell will be tainted and it will taste unpleasant. They must thoroughly wash the fish after slicing it open, cleaning it out and scraping off its skin and scales. After this, they should sprinkle salt and flour on it; for every ten *raṭl*s of fish, one *raṭl* of flour. After drying the fish they fry it. They must not mix stale fish with fresh. The sign of a fresh fish is that the gills are red, whereas those of a stale fish are not.

When the *muḥtasib* is absent, the *'arīf* should check the frying pan every hour in case they fry the fish with oil mixed with the fat coming from the fish's stomach. The best thing to fry fish with is sesame oil. They must not fry it with used oil whose smell has become rancid nor remove the fish from the frying pan until it is properly cooked, but without overcooking or burning.

* *

As for the fish which is imported into the town or remains unsold in the shops, the scales must not be scraped off but they should be protected with salt, especially their heads and gills where maggots appear first. Whenever fish which has not been sold and is unwanted becomes rotten it must be thrown on the rubbish heaps outside the town. But God knows best.

CHAPTER THIRTEEN

Cooks

They must be ordered to cover their vessels and protect them from flies and crawling insects after washing them with hot water and plant ash. They should not cook goat meat with that of sheep, nor camel meat with that of cows, in case someone recovering from an illness should eat it and it become the cause of a relapse. The *muḥtasib* must keep a watch on them so that they do not give too much fat and too little meat, as most of them extract the oil and pour it into the cooking pot so that it floats on the surface and deceives the people into thinking it is because there is a lot of meat. The sign of goat when it is in the cooking pot is its dark colour, unpalatable smell and small bones.

The *muḥtasib* must be aware of the way they adulterate the food. They add flour to *maḍīra*[1] and thus make it heavier and thicker. Some of them thicken it with rice flour and fine semolina. Others adulterate *bahaṭa*[2] with taro.[3] The sign of all these things is that the food tends to be brown in colour. Some cooks thicken *labaniyya*[4] with the dregs of oil extracted from grains or with cornstarch.

If I was not afraid of instructing the irreligious in the methods of adulterating food I could write much about the way foods may not contain their proper ingredients. But I avoid mentioning them for fear of who will learn them and teach them to the people.

In a treatise known as *The Alchemy of Cooking*, Ya'qūb al-Kindī[5] mentioned the meat dishes which are cooked without meat, fried liver without liver, brains without

[1] Meat cooked with sour milk.
[2] Rice cooked with milk and clarified butter.
[3] Also called elephant's ear. An Asian aroid plant grown for its large edible root.
[4] A dish made with rice and milk.
[5] Abū Yūsuf Ya'qūb b. Isḥāq al-Kindī (c. 801-c. 866), "the philosopher of the Arabs". An eminent scholar and philosopher who is credited with numerous books. These embrace all the sciences of the time, and include the manufacture of perfume, glass, jewellery and armour (see *Fihrist* 2:615-26).

brains, sausages and *turdīn*[6] without meat, omelettes without eggs, *jūdhāb*[7] without rice, sweets without honey or sugar and so many dishes without their ingredients that they would take a long time to describe and which the cooks have not discovered. For this reason I have refrained from mentioning them. The *muḥtasib* must keep an eye on the cooks concerning this so that no one should learn about it. But God knows best.

---

[6] A certain kind of food eaten by the Kurds.
[7] A kind of food made of sugar, rice and meat.

CHAPTER FOURTEEN

Makers of *Harīsa*[1]

The usual recipe for *harīsa*, without dictating to its makers and without making it difficult for the people, is one *ṣā'*[2] of wheat for eight *waqiyya*s of mutton and one *raṭl* of beef. The meat used for *harīsa* should be lean and young, free of dirt and tubercles, veins and muscles. It should be tender, not scrawny, and its smell should not be tainted. It must be soaked in salt water for an hour until all the blood has come out of it. It is then taken out and washed in some other water, put in the cooking pot in the presence of the *'arīf* and stamped with the *muḥtasib*'s seal. In the early morning the *'arīf* will come and break the seal and they will make the *harīsa* in his presence. This is in case they remove some of the meat and put it back the following day, for most of them do this if the cooking pot is not stamped.

Some of them adulterate the *harīsa* with prepared taro, while others buy cooked sheep's heads when they are cheap, strip the meat off them and put it in the *harīsa*. Others boil the meat of cows or camels, dry it and store it away, then when they have the opportunity they soak it in hot water for an hour and put it in the *harīsa*. Sometimes they may have some meat left over in the cooking pots, so they mix it in with the *harīsa* on the following day. The *muḥtasib* should control all these things with his seal.

* *

The oil used for the *harīsa* should be pure and with a pleasant smell, and should have mastic and cinnamon added to it. The *muḥtasib* must watch out for the methods of adulterating the oil. Some of them take the bones and skulls of cows and camels and boil them thoroughly in water until a lot of oil comes out of them, then they mix this with the oil used for the *harīsa*. The way to identify this is to drop a little of it onto a tile; if it does not congeal or is transparent, then it has been adulterated with

[1] A kind of thick pottage made of cooked wheat and meat pounded together.
[2] A cubic measure which varied in magnitude.

the things we have mentioned. The *muḥtasib* must order them to wash, clean and salt the oil containers so that their smell and taste are not affected, for maggots multiply in them, and if the oil is returned to the dirty containers, it becomes stale in both smell and taste. But God knows best.

CHAPTER FIFTEEN

Sausage Makers

The most important thing is that the premises in which they make the sausages should be near to the *muḥtasib*s booth[1] so that he can keep a special watch on them, for their frauds are so many they can hardly all be known. The *muḥtasib* must order them to use only pure, good, lean meat and to mince it finely on clean chopping blocks. When they mince the meat there should be someone with them with a fly-whisk to keep the flies away. They should only mix the meat with onions, spices or seasonings in the presence of the *'arīf* so that he may know their quantities by weight. After this, they stuff it into clean intestines.

They must be watched for their methods of adulterating the sausages. Some of them adulterate the sausages with the meat of cooked heads, some with liver, kidneys and hearts. Others adulterate the sausages with tough and scrawny meat or mix in the tough meat of camels and cows. Some sprinkle water over the meat when they are mincing it and the *muḥtasib* must forbid them from this. Others fill *sanbūsak*[2] with grilled fish and seasonings, while some adulterate it with shelled beansprouts and onion.

The *muḥtasib* learns of all these frauds by looking into the sausages and seeing what they contain before they are fried. It is difficult to know once they are in the frying pan because the makers skewer them when they are almost ready and the adulterants come out and are cooked over the fire.

The oil in which the sausages are fried should not be old or rancid and should have a wholesome flavour and smell. After they have fried the sausages, they should sprinkle wholesome and appropriate ground spices and seasonings over them. But God knows best.

---

[1] Arabic: *dikka*. It is uncertain what this was exactly. The only information regarding the *muḥtasib*'s headquarters in the market is a remark by al-Maqrīzī who says that it was next to the *Dār al-'Iyār* (see Chapter 4 note 3).

[2] A kind of meat pie.

CHAPTER SIXTEEN

Confectioners

There are many kinds and different varieties of confectionery and it is impossible to understand all the characteristics and measures of the ingredients, such as cornstarch, almonds, poppy seeds and so on. Sometimes there may be much of one thing in one kind of confection, and little in another. Knowledge of all this falls under the *'arīf*'s jurisdiction. The confection should be well cooked, neither raw nor burnt, and the maker should always have a fly-whisk in his hand to keep the flies away.

The *muḥtasib* must watch out for the ways they adulterate the confection, for there are many. One of them is for the makers to mix the honey of bees with grape pulp. The sign of this is that when it is cooked it gives off the smell of grapes. Some of them mix the juice from sugar cane, which they call *qaṭṭāra*, with syrup. The sign of this is that it settles at the bottom of the vessel. There are varieties of confectionery which are adulterated with flour and cornstarch, rice flour, lentil flour and the husks of sesame seeds. The sign of this is that when put in water it floats on the surface. They adulterate the poppy seed *nāṭif* [1] with semolina, the sign of this being that it floats on the surface of the water and also that it becomes hard. Sometimes they adulterate the *hiyājī nāṭif* [2] with semolina fried with *kishk*.[3] At other times they might adulterate the yellow *nāṭif* with breadcrumbs. The sign of all these frauds is that the confectionery floats on the surface of water. Some of them adulterate *basandūd* [4] with breadcrumbs or perhaps make it with lentil flour.

Some confectioners adulterate gazelle's ankle[5] and *mashāsh*[6] with crystallised sugar cane juice. The sign of this is that the colour tends to be brown or black. Some of them adulterate *zulābiyya* with dissolved sugar cane crystals instead of honey.

---

[1] A kind of confection made of honey, sugar, pistachios and hazelnuts. See the editor's note in *Nihāyat al-Rutba fī Ṭalab al-Ḥisba* (Cairo, 1946) p. 40.

[2] Unidentified.

[3] *Kishk* (or *kashk*) is made of crushed cereal grains mixed with sour milk and left to dry in the sun.

[4] Unidentified.

[5] Unidentified.

[6] A decoction of honey poured on a plate to harden.

Similarly, they might adulterate soft and juicy *khabīṣa*[7] and *ṣābūniyya*[8] with more cornstarch than is necessary. The sign of this is that it crumbles, and rises if left overnight. Some adulterate *nūbiyya*[9] with flour, while others adulterate *kishkanānij*[10] which is baked in the *tannūr*. If it is so adulterated it falls off the side of the oven. All the adulterations of confectionary can be seen in its appearance and taste and the *muḥtasib* must keep an eye on the makers regarding all these things. But God knows best.

---

[7] A mixture of wheat flour, almond or sesame oil, after the cooking of which sugar and honey are added.

[8] This is made with flour which has been fried with clarified butter, sugar and milk. It is formed into cakes resembling soap (*ṣābūn*) and put on a tray in the oven until it is cooked. See editor's note *Nihāya* p. 41. Elsewhere, Ibn al-Ukhuwwa remarks that for every ten *raṭl*s of sugar, *ṣābūniyya* should contain two *raṭl*s of cornstarch, two *raṭl*s of unripe dates and a good quality aromatic (*Ma'ālim al-Qurba* Arabic text p. 114).

[9] Unidentified.

[10] A kind of confection made from ground semolina which is kneaded and rolled out and to which is added sugar, ground almonds, camphor and a little rose water. See editor's note *Nihāya* p. 41. Ibn al-Ukhuwwa states that for every *qinṭār* of sugar it should contain fifty *raṭl*s of flour, a *mithqāl* of Iraqi musk, five *raṭl*s of Syrian rose water and pistachio nuts (*Ma'ālim* Arabic text p. 114).

CHAPTER SEVENTEEN

Apothecaries

The swindles contained in this and the following chapter are so numerous that it is impossible to know all of them. So may God have compassion for the one who inspects the apothecaries and must learn how to uncover their frauds. The *muḥtasib* should make a note of them in the margins of his register and rely on the favour of God, for they are more harmful to people than anything else; drugs and potions being of various natures, mixtures and purposes depending on their ingredients. Some of them are suitable for an illness or physical condition but when other ingredients are added to them the drugs change their nature and inevitably harm the sick person. It is the duty of apothecaries to have fear of God in this matter.

The *muḥtasib* must intimidate them, exhort them and warn them of punishment and chastisement. He must inspect their drugs every week, for one of their well-known frauds is to adulterate Egyptian opium[1] with horned poppy.[2] They also adulterate it with the sap of wild lettuce leaves[3] and with gum. When it has been adulterated with the horned poppy, if dissolved in water it gives off a smell like that of saffron. If it has been adulterated with wild lettuce sap, it is coarse and its smell is faint. When it tastes bitter, has a pure colour and is without strength, it has been adulterated with gum. Sometimes they adulterate Chinese rhubarb[4] with a plant called *rawānd al-dawābb*[5] which grows in Syria. The sign of this is that good rhubarb is red, has no smell, is light in weight and the superior type of it is free of worms. When it is soaked in water it turns slightly yellow. Whatever does not have these characteristics is adulterated with what we have mentioned.

---

[1] At this time the best opium was prepared in Abū Tīj in Upper Egypt (see Moses Maimonides, *Glossary of Drug Names*, trans. F. Rosner [Philadelphia, 1979] p. 27). It is the dried milky juices of the black poppy, and had celebrated virtues.
[2] A plant of the species *Glaucium*, distinguished by its large horn-like capsules.
[3] This is probably escarole, which has slightly bitter edible leaves and which is considered the origin of the garden lettuce.
[4] *Rheum officinale*. Its dried roots have been important medically in China since c. 2700 BC. (See *The Medical Formulary of al-Kindī*, trans. M. Levey [Madison, 1966] p. 337.)
[5] Literally, "animal rhubarb", and so called because it was used by the veterinarians. It is a black wood with many powers and is sometimes referred to as Khurasanian rhubarb.

Sometimes they adulterate bamboo concrete[6] with bones burnt in a furnace. The sign of this fraud is that when it is put in water bone sinks while bamboo concrete floats. At other times they adulterate frankincense[7] with rosin[8] and gum. The sign of this is that when thrown into a fire the rosin burns, emits smoke and a smell. They sometimes adulterate tamarind[9] with the flesh of plums, or adulterate juice of lycium[10] with dregs of oil and the gall bladders of oxen[11] when they cook it. The sign of this latter fraud is that when some of it is thrown on a fire the pure lycium juice flares up, then when it is extinguished its cinders are the colour of blood. Also, the genuine substance is black with green inside. That which neither sets on fire nor turns into cinders is adulterated with the things we have mentioned.

Sometimes they adulterate costus[12] with elecampane roots.[13] The way to know this is that the costus smells and has a taste when put on the tongue, whereas elecampane is otherwise. They adulterate the down of nard[14] with that of taro. The sign of this is that when put in the mouth it makes one feel nauseous and burns. They also adulterate euphorbia resin[15] with dry ground beans, and mastic with resin from the savin juniper bush.[16] Some of them adulterate the resin of the mukul tree[17] with hard resin. The way to recognise this adulteration is that the Indian variety gives off a smell when burnt and is not bitter. They adulterate Cretan bindweed[18] with that from

---

[6] A kind of "lime" as a secretion in the knots of a particular species of bamboo. It is used, among other things, in prescriptions for mouth pustules, for the throat, for fever, epilepsy and for the eyes (*Medical Formulary* p. 300).

[7] Also called olibanum. An aromatic gum resin obtained from trees of the genus *Boswellia*.

[8] Also called colophony. A translucent brittle amber resin substance.

[9] A tree indigenous to India. Among other things, the pulp of the fruit was used as a laxative. Eye salves were made from the leaves, while internally it was used for jaundice (*Medical Formulary* p. 251).

[10] The juice extracted from the leaves and branches of the shrub box-thorn. Among other things, this was used for scrofula, lesions, the eyes and to hold back a foetus (*Medical Formulary* p. 259).

[11] Gall bladders of various animals were used to treat a number of ailments (see *Medical Formulary* p. 334).

[12] A kind of aromatic wood used as a remedy for the stomach, kidneys and bladder, in a drug for the throat, for canker and for ulcers (*Medical Formulary* p. 316).

[13] A perennial flowering plant, having large hairy leaves and narrow yellow petals. The roots are bitter and aromatic. It had various medicinal uses (*Medical Formulary* p. 270).

[14] An aromatic Indian plant of various varieties. It was used as a cure for pustules in the mouth, as a cure for insanity and to strengthen the breathing (*Medical Formulary* pp. 286-87; *Glossary* p. 178).

[15] Also known as spurge resin. An aromatic growing at the southern border of the Atlas mountains in Morocco (see *Glossary* p. 20).

[16] A small evergreen spreading bush. Oil is obtained from the shoots and leaves of the plant.

[17] The balsamodendron mukul tree from India. The resin was used to remove phlegm, moistness and heat from the body, as a kidney remedy, as a dentifrice and for haemorrhoids (*Medical Formulary* p. 329; *Glossary* pp. 158-59).

[18] A kind of convolvulus with various medicinal applications (see *Medical Formulary* pp. 233-34).

Syria, but there is no harm in this. They also adulterate it with the down of common polypody.[19] Some of them adulterate scammony[20] with the hardened sap of latex plants.[21] The way to know this is to put it on the tongue and if it stings then it is fraudulent. Some of them also adulterate it with ground horn which is kneaded with resin water into the shape of scammony. Yet others adulterate it with bean and chick pea flour. The way to recognise all these is that the genuine is pure in colour like *gharī*,[22] whereas the adulterated is not. They sometimes adulterate myrrh[23] with resin soaked in water. The indication of this is that pure myrrh is light in weight and has a uniform colour. When it breaks, some things the shape of smooth finger nails can be seen in it similar to pebbles and it has an agreeable smell. If the myrrh is heavy and has the colour of pitch it is no good. Some of them adulterate the bark of frankincense with that of the pine.[24] An indication of this is to throw it in a fire and if it burns and gives off a pleasant smell then it is pure, but if does the opposite it is adulterated. Some adulterate marjoram[25] with melilot seeds.[26]

They adulterate wax with goat's tallow and with rosin, and sometimes when it is being shaped they sprinkle bean flour, soft sand or ground kohl[27] in it. This is then put inside the candle and covered with pure wax. The way to discover this is to light the candle and see the inside of it. They adulterate verdigris with marble and green vitriol.[28] The way to recognise this fraud is to wet your thumb and put it in it, then rub it between the thumb and index finger. If it is soft and becomes creamy, it is pure. But if it turns white and granular, it is fraudulent. It is also possible to put some between your teeth and if you find it like sand then it is adulterated with

[19] A fern, *Polypodium vulgare*, used for diarrhoea among other things (*see Medical Formulary* p. 243; *Glossary* p. 52).
[20] A convolvulvus which grows on the coasts of the Mediterranean, Asia Minor and Persia. It was probably used as a purgative (see *Glossary* pp. 187-88).
[21] Any of the various plants which exude a milky fluid when they are cut. The fluid coagulates when exposed to the air.
[22] A certain red dye.
[23] An aromatic resin obtained from several trees and shrubs and used, among other things, for boils, cankers, abscesses, toothache, eye disease, and in a remedy to cure insanity and nosebleeds. It was also used as a constituent of perfumes, ointments and incense (*Medical Formulary* pp. 333-34).
[24] Pine was used for its resin in fumigation.
[25] Used in an application for the liver and stomach, and in a remedy for the kidneys and bladder etc. The juice was also used in eye remedies (*Medical Formulary* p. 335; *Glossary* pp. 162-63).
[26] Or sweet clover. Used as an aromatic.
[27] A cosmetic powder used to darken the area around the eyes and usually made from powdered antimony sulphide.
[28] Ferrous sulphate.

marble. One can also heat a plate of metal in the fire and sprinkle some of it on. If it turns red it is adulterated with green vitriol, but if it turns black it is pure. They sometimes mix yellow myrobalan[29] with black myrobalan and sell this along with Kabuli myrobalan. They also mix choice yellow myrobalan with different kinds of myrobalan from Kabul and sell it along with Kabuli. They sprinkle water on the pods of the cassia tree[30] while they are wrapped in cloth when being sold and the weight increases from one *raṭl* to one and a half. Some of them take lac,[31] melt in over the fire and mix it with powdered baked brick and red clay. Then they let it congeal and flatten it out into disks. When it is dry they break it into pieces and sell it as dragon's blood.[32] Some of them coarsely grind mastic then put some opopanax[33] in it and cook it with some bees' honey and saffron. When it boils and froths they add some more mastic and stir it until it congeals. Then when it has cooled they make it into tablets, break it, mix it with opopanax and it cannot be detected.

As for all the medicinal oils and others, they adulterate them with vinegar after it has been boiled on the fire and ground walnuts and almonds have been added to remove its smell and taste. Then they mix it with the oils. Some of them take apricot stones and sesame seeds, grind them, knead and press them, and sell the oil as almond oil. Others adulterate the oil of the balm of Gilead tree[34] with that of the lily. The way to identify this is to put a few drops of it onto a piece of wool and wash it. If the oil disappears without a trace then it is pure, if not, it is adulterated. Similarly, when the pure oil is dropped in water it dissolves and assumes the consistency of milk, while the adulterated oil floats like ordinary oil and remains in drops on the surface.

[29] A dried plum-like fruit of various tropical trees of the genus *Terminalia* and used as an intestinal astringent (*Medical Formulary* p. 342).
[30] A well-known drug. The brown-blackish, long and cylindrical pods are used. They are divided into compartments by partitions and filled with a pulp which is sweetish and slightly purgative.
[31] The dark-red resinous encrustation produced on certain trees by the puncture of an insect, the *Coccus* or *Carteria lacca*. It was used as a scarlet dye.
[32] A resin from various plants of the lily family. It was used as a cure for haemorrhoids and canker, among other things (*Medical Formulary* p. 268; *Glossary* pp. 74-75).
[33] A gum-resin acquired from the root of the *Opopanax chironium*. It is a native of southern Europe and is a yellow-flowered umbelliferous plant resembling a parsnip. It had various medicinal applications (see *Medical Formulary* pp. 254-55; *Glossary* p. 60).
[34] Considered good for the stomach. The seed is used today in Iran and Iraq as an expectorant, a stimulant, for stomach disorders and to expel flatulence (*Medical Formulary* p. 245).

There are many things we have avoided mentioning in this chapter because the way they are adulterated and blended with other ingredients is secret, and we are afraid that someone with no religion will learn them and swindle the Muslims with them. In this chapter and others we have only mentioned the well-known and popular frauds, and have said nothing about those which are not well known. Most of these have been mentioned by the writer of *The Alchemy of Perfume*.[35] May God have mercy on anyone who gets hold of this book, and may they tear it up and burn it seeking the favour of God.

[35] The author referred to could be al-Kindī, who is mentioned by Ibn al-Nadīm as having written a book with this name (*Fihrist* 2:625).

CHAPTER EIGHTEEN

Perfumers

The frauds associated with perfume are many and various due to its different kinds and varieties and the resemblance between the medicinal ingredients and their similarity in scent. I will only mention those whose adulterations are well known and which are often prepared, and will not refer to those whose adulteration and preparation is a secret and which few of the perfumers occupy themselves with.

Some of them fill musk bags[1] with the bark of emblic myrobalan[2] and Indian pepperwort, and also *shādūrān*.[3] They knead it with diluted pine resin and for every four *dirhams* of this they add one *dirham* of musk. Then they fill the musk bags with it, seal them with resin and dry them on the top of the oven.

The way to recognise this and all other frauds regarding musk bags is for the *muḥtasib* to open them and put them to his lips like someone wanting to know what is inside a substance. If the musk is sharp like fire to his mouth then it is genuine and unadulterated, but if it is not, it is adulterated. Some of them fill the musk bag with emblic myrobalan, sarcocol[4] and *shādūrān* whose resin has been extracted with hot water. They knead this with diluted resin and treat it. Then they add three *dirhams* of it to every *dirham* of the musk from Sughd,[5] crush it all together, fill the musk bag with it and dry it on top of the oven. The way to know if it is so adulterated is as we have already mentioned. Some of them fill the musk bag with oak bark treated with fire. For every three *dirhams* of this they add one *dirham* of musk then they put it in the bag. The way to know if it is so adulterated is as we have already mentioned. Some of them make musk without a bag from aristolochia,[6] *rāmik*[7] and dragon's

---

[1] A musk bag is simply a bag into which musk is placed. Musk is the strong-smelling glandular secretion of the male musk deer.

[2] A drug having a number of medicinal uses, and also employed in musk recipes. It is the fruit of the *Phyllanthus emblica* which grows in most parts of Lower India (see *Medical Formulary* p. 235).

[3] Uncertain. Perhaps the gum of an old oak, or the gum found in the roots of walnut trees.

[4] The gum of a Persian tree resembling frankincense.

[5] Sugh is a district in central Asia, to the east of Bukhara.

[6] A genus of aromatic shrubs.

[7] A medicinal paste made of oak apple with aromatic drugs (see *Medical Formulary* pp. 270-71).

blood all kneaded together. They add one *dirham* of this for every *dirham* of musk. Others make musk from spikenard, filings of aloes-wood,[8] cinnamon and cloves mixed with an equal amount of musk. Yet others make it from cloves, *shādūrān* and saffron. They knead them all together with rose water, mix this with an equal amount of musk and put it all in ambergris.[9]

The way to identify these and all other kinds of adulteration of the varieties of musk is to put a little of it in your mouth, spit it out onto a piece of white cloth and shake it off. If it can be shaken off and does not stain then it is not adulterated with dye or anything else. But if it cannot be shaken off and stains, then it is adulterated.

Some of them put dragon's blood or young goat's blood[10] on the pure musk, while others crush the musk with gazelle's blood, put it in its intestines, bind it with thread and dry it in the shade. Then they take it out and blend it with other substances in retorts. Some of them adulterate musk with burnt liver. The way to recognize all these frauds is as we have already mentioned. Some of them also mix the musk with lead pellets the same size as peppercorns or smaller dyed with ink. This cannot be noticed until it is crushed.

* *

As for ambergris, some of them make it from cuttlefish bone, black resin, beeswax, sandarac[11] and nutmeg. They blend these together and add the mixture to an equal amount of ambergris. Others make it from cuttlefish bone, sandarac, aloes-wood, spikenard and lizard droppings. They mix these and leave it for a while in a horse's stomach, then they take it out and blend it with an equal amount of ambergris. Sometimes it is moulded into shapes or formed into necklaces and other things. They sometimes make ambergris out of musk, wax and ambergris. The pieces of ambergris are occasionally sprayed with sandarac, so it is necessary to burn the tops

[8] A fragrant wood and resin from the East African *Aloexylon* and *Aquilaria*.
[9] A secretion from the intestines of the sperm-whale and found floating in tropical seas. It is much used in perfumery.
[10] Blood from various animals was used in drugs and preparations.
[11] A resin from the sandarac tree. The tree is pinaceous and comes from north west Africa. The resin is brittle, pale yellow and transparent. It is obtained from the bark of the tree and used in the manufacture of incense.

of them to find out whether they are free of this or other substances. At other times the pieces of ambergris are hollowed out and bits of lead are put inside. The way to recognize all the frauds we have mentioned is to put some on the fire and all the added substances will have their own smell. Also, it does not dry out, and if it has got sandarac in it the ambergris will crumble.

* *

As for camphor,[12] some of them manufacture it with the waste marble from the marble trimmers, while others knead the camphor with diluted white resin and work it through sieves. Some of them make it from sal ammoniac[13] which they break into small pieces and mix with it. Others make it from unpowdered *dharīra*,[14] unbaked gypsum and white resin added to an equal quantity of camphor. Some make it with the decaying wood of the castor-oil plant[15] and prepared rice, while others make it from date stones ground to a paste until it resembles cuttlefish bone and mixed with an equal amount of camphor. Then they knead it with camphor juice and spread it out thinly so that it looks like camphor. The way to identify the adulterations we have mentioned, and those we have not, is to put some of it in water. If it sinks it is adulterated, but if it floats it is pure. It is also possible to put some on a rag and place this in the fire. If it completely dissipates it is pure, but if it burns and turns to ash it is adulterated.

* *

Some of them adulterate hairy saffron with chicken breasts and beef after boiling them in water. They take off whatever meat they want, cut it into strips, dye it with saffron, dry it and mix it in the baskets. The way to identify this fraud is for the *muḥtasib* to soak some of it in vinegar. If it contracts it is adulterated with meat. It will also change its colour when put in vinegar, whereas pure hairy saffron retains the same colour as before.

---

[12] A whitish, crystalline aromatic from the wood of the camphor tree.
[13] Ammonium chloride. A hard white opaque crystalline salt.
[14] A kind of perfume made from *Calamus aromaticus* from India. When powdered it is a whitish perfume. Also called *qaṣab al-dharīra*.
[15] A tall Indian and tropical African plant.

Some of them cut *akshūt*[16] like the hair of hairy saffron and cook it with cooked brazilwood. They then add something to it dyed with saffron water and sprinkle a little ground sugar on to make it become heavy and coagulate. After this they mix it with an equal amount of saffron and put it in the baskets. The sign of this adulteration is to put some in your mouth; if it is sweet it has been adulterated with what we have indicated. Some of them take fenugreek plants[17] and soak them for a certain number of days in old wine containing saffron, sieved pepper and turmeric. Then they spread this out in the shade and mix it in the baskets. The indication of all these adulterations of saffron is that the hairs are dry. Take some from the middle of the basket and you will identify it by its dryness.

Some of them finely mill the adulterated saffron so that the fraud cannot be detected, and while it is being milled they mix in dragon's blood so that its colour remains as it was. Adulterated saffron turns white when it is milled so they put dragon's blood in it. To uncover this fraud put some in a glass container of water; if it sinks it is adulterated, but if it floats it is pure. Some adulterate saffron with ground glass. This fraud can be uncovered by doing as we have already mentioned. Others adulterate it with ground cornstarch. The way to detect this is to put it in a pot of water on the fire and it will thicken and become sticky. Some of them adulterate the saffron with *khalūq*.[18] The way to recognize this is that when it is put in vinegar and mustard it turns red and stains. A number of them think it permissible to divide a clay vessel with a sheet of paper and to fill one side of it with *khalūq* and the other with ground saffron. Then they deal it out according to the gullibility of the customer.

* *

As for *ghāliyya*,[19] some of the perfumers use molten tar[20] as a basis for it. Then for every two *dirhams* of this they add one *dirham* of fine musk, one *dirham* of ground

[16] A certain plant that clings to the branches of trees, having no root. A species of *Cuscuta* or *Dodder*.
[17] A heavily scented Mediterranean leguminous plant.
[18] A kind of reddish-yellow perfume.
[19] A perfume made of ambergris and musk kneaded with ben tree oil.
[20] Tar was obtained from various conifers.

aloes-wood, one *dirham* of *sukk*,[21] ladanum[22] melted over the fire and half a *mithqāl* of ambergris. All of this is then mixed with four *mithqāl*s of ben tree oil[23] and becomes barely distinguishable from *ghāliyya*. Some of them make its base out of the sieved residue of soft marble and prepared *shādūrān*, and to every two *dirham*s of this they add the good *ghāliyya* we have mentioned. Others make it from pistachio nuts in equal proportions to the *ghāliyya*. Some others make its base from husked fresh sesame seeds and burnt papyrus paper and mix it with *ghāliyya*. Some make its base from the wax and stems of *shādūrān* and mix it with *ghāliyya*. All these varieties of fraudulent *ghāliyya* are not hidden from the *muḥtasib* and the *'arīf* because of their colour, smell and appearance. So the *muḥtasib* must personally examine them all as most of those who sell them are hawkers and people who sit on the roads who have no religion.

As for civet,[24] it is the same as *ghāliyya* in the manner and numerous ways of its adulteration. The only difference between them is the weight of their constituents, but we have not mentioned this because it is well known.

* *

Some of them adulterate aloes-wood. They acquire sandalwood, file it in the same way as aloes-wood, soak it in old cooked grapes and mix it with aloes-wood. The way to uncover this fraud is to throw some of it on the fire and it will smell like sandalwood. Others make it from the bark of a wood called *al-iblīq*.[25] They soak this for a few days in rose water treated with musk and camphor, then bring it out, boil it and roll it all together. Others do the same using bark of the olive tree, and the way to uncover this fraud is to throw some on the fire and the adulteration will be obvious.

---

[21] A perfume probably made from *rāmik*, oak apples, dates, aloes-wood, sandalwood etc.

[22] A gum resin which exudes from plants of the genus *Cistus* and which is employed in perfumery and fumigation.

[23] Probably *Moringa pterygosperma* and also used medicinally for a variety of purposes (see *Medical Formulary* p. 241).

[24] The yellowish fatty secretion of the civet cat from Africa and south Asia which is used as a fixative in the manufacture of perfumes.

[25] Unidentified. A plant which is coloured black and white.

* *

Some of them adulterate the oil of the ben tree, for they manufacture it from cotton seed oil or apricot stone oil and make this stronger with some musk from Sughd and other aromatics. Others also make it from *anfāq* oil.[26] They let this stand for a while, put some pieces of myrtle[27] in it and it acquires a green colour and approximates the musk from al-Madā'in.[28] Some of them sublimate nodes of pine and thc bark of frankincense and nobody doubts that it is camphor juice. The way to detect this fraud is for the *muḥtasib* to put a few drops of it on a white rag and then to wash it. If it sticks to the rag and leaves a trace then it has been adulterated with what we have described in this book. The only people who are impudent enough to make it like this and sell it are foreigners, non-Arabs and those who wander the roads. The *muḥtasib* must not neglect to expose all these things and to administer *ta'zīr* to the perpetrator as previously described.

---

[26] The oil extracted from olives before they have ripened.
[27] A south European shrub with pink or white flowers and aromatic blue-black berries.
[28] A medieval Arab town in Iraq, which lay some twenty miles south east of Baghdad on either side of the Tigris.

CHAPTER NINETEEN

Makers of Syrups

No one shall thicken syrups and prepare the pastes and *jawārshanāt*[1] unless his skill is well known, his knowledge is obvious, he has wide experience and has witnessed the testing of drugs and their quantities by their masters and those with experience of them. The syrup maker must only prepare the syrups from recognised treatises and pharmacopoeia, such as the pharmacopoeia of Sābūr,[2] the *Malakī*,[3] the *Qānūn*[4] and other trustworthy ones.

The maker of syrups must fear God and the Day of Judgement in his negligence regarding these drugs and their measures and when he adds that which is incompatible with them and deprives them of their particular characteristics, such as prepared sugar cane juice with cow's milk, and vinegar with white lead. Many of them do this. They take what is pure in colour with a wholesome smell and taste and prepare the syrups and pastes from it in place of sugar and honey. The *muḥtasib* must therefore make them swear that they will not do this, because it harms, corrupts and impairs the mixture.

The way to detect the adulteration of sugar cane juice is that it necessarily turns black when added to another type of syrup and smells of vinegar when left for a period of time. The *muḥtasib* can also put some of it in the palm of his hand, pour a few drops of water on it and rub it between his fingers. If it is adulterated the honey will turn white like *fānīd*.[5]

---

[1] Drinks which help the digestion of food.

[2] Sābūr b. Sahl (d. 869) was a Christian physician from Jundishapur. He later moved to Baghdad and worked for the Abbasid caliph al-Mutawakkil. He wrote an important pharmacopoeia called *Kitāb al-Aghrabadhīn al-Kabīr*.

[3] This refers to the *Kāmil al-Ṣināʿa al-Ṭayyiba* by ʿAlī b. ʿAbbās al-Majūsī (died between 982 and 995). He is only known for this book which was his magnum opus. It was recognised as a masterpiece when it was written and became the main textbook for students of medicine. One hundred years later it was largely superseded by Ibn Sīnā's *Qānūn*.

[4] Written by Ibn Sīnā (980-1037), a philosopher and physician who is known in the West as Avicenna. His *Qānūn* maintained its authority until modern times and served as a basis for seven hundred years of medical teaching and practice.

[5] A sort of confection made from concrete juice of sugar cane and starch.

The *muḥtasib* must examine their syrups at the beginning of every month. The maker of syrups may not re-cook those ingredients which the *muḥtasib* finds to be sour and rancid due to the time they have been kept, because they will be impaired and corrupted. This does not apply to rose water and violet water because even though they go rancid very quickly re-cooking them makes them stronger, longer lasting and more beneficial for the stomach. When the colour of spiced oxymel[6] tends towards black it is adulterated with the sugar cane juice already mentioned. Similarly the pastes, when they deteriorate in the clay vessels and turn sour or begin to smell they have been adulterated with the ingredients we have referred to.

The makers of syrups must thicken all the syrups so that they have body. If they thicken a syrup from jujube,[7] they should give it body by preparing it from a lot of the fruit, because this refines the blood. Some of them knead the dregs of vinegar with date juice and *shādūrān*, then they shape it into pastilles and sell it as barberry juice.[8]

---

[6] A medicinal drink or syrup made of vinegar and honey, sometimes with other ingredients.
[7] The dark red edible fruit of trees of the genus *Ziziphus*.
[8] From the plant *Berberis vulgaris*, having orange or red berries (see *Glossary* pp. 14-15).

CHAPTER TWENTY

Sellers of Clarified Butter[1]

The *muḥtasib* must inspect their measures, *raṭl*s and scales, in accordance with what we mentioned previously in the relevant chapter. They must be forbidden from mixing poor and good merchandise together when they have bought them separately for a different price. They must also be forbidden from mixing old and fresh dates together and old dried grapes and new, and must not sprinkle water on the dates and the dried grapes to moisten them and make them weigh more. Neither must they pour oil on the dried grapes to make their colour purer and their appearance more attractive.

Some of them mix sugar cane juice with hot water and sprinkle it on the dates, while others adulterate oil when it has become stale with that of the safflower.[2] The way to uncover this fraud is that when the oil is put on a fire it gives off a lot of choking smoke. Some of them adulterate sesame oil when it has become rancid. Yet others mix pure oil with oil in which cheese has been left in casks. The sign of its adulteration in this way is that it is greasy and crackles and spits when held over the flame of a lamp. Most of them adulterate vinegar with water. The way to know this is that when pure vinegar is poured on the ground it bubbles and froths, whereas it does not when it is mixed with water. Similarly, a sprig of water moss put in it will soak up the water and leave the vinegar. When this water moss is put in milk that has been mixed with water it separates them. The adulteration of milk with water can be discovered by the *muḥtasib* dipping a hair in it then taking it out. If none of the milk sticks to it, it has been adulterated with water, but if the milk sticks to it in droplets, then it is pure.

The *muḥtasib* must keep an eye on them regarding the various kinds of pickles, especially when they have put melon skin in them. For whenever this is very dry and hard it should be put back into strong vinegar, and whenever it is soft it should be

---

[1] It is clear from the following passage that these traders dealt with much more than clarified butter.
[2] A thistle-like Eurasian plant with large heads of orange-yellow flowers having an oil. Also called false saffron.

thrown away because it has gone rotten. When their pickles become sour, the *muḥtasib* must order that they are disposed of outside the town, because they are no good after this.

They are not permitted to sell any unsold cheese in casks, nor fat and oils which have gone rancid, putrefied or become maggot-infested because of the harm they cause to people. This also applies to capers which have become maggot-infested in their jars. The *muḥtasib* must prevent them from preparing pickling brine by boiling it over a fire because this causes leprosy. Among them are those who make pickling brine and sell it on the same day. That is, they take a lot of carob beans or sugar cane juice and cumin, caraway seeds and sumach and pound them all with barley flour. This is also very harmful, so the *muḥtasib* must stop them from doing it.

They occasionally mix spices together. Some of them mix caraway seeds with those of a plant called snake's eye which are similar in colour but a little larger and odourless. The *muḥtasib* should keep an eye on them in this matter. Sometimes they adulterate syrup from Baalbek[3] with a pure wheat flour and *kaddān*.[4] The method to uncover this fraud is that when some of it is put in water the wheat flour sinks to the bottom of the container, and perhaps the water will become foamy.

The majority of them mix bees' honey with water. The sign of this adulteration is that in winter it becomes granular like semolina, while in summer it turns into a thin liquid. Some of them grind pomegranate skins and use this to adulterate turmeric. They sometimes put sand and marsh mallow in henna, but this adulteration is easy to notice. At other times they adulterate pitch with cane ash or sand, and adulterate bitumen in a similar way.

* *

Their merchandise must be kept in clay vessels and jars so that no flies or vermin get to it, nor dust, dirt and such like fall on it. It may be put in palm leaf baskets as long as these are covered with cloth. They should also have fly-whisks in their hands to

---

[3] Baalbek is a small town in the Bekaa valley in Lebanon.
[4] The meaning of this word is unclear, but it seems to refer to "dry pieces of clay".

keep the flies away from the merchandise. The *muḥtasib* must order them to keep their clothes clean, to wash their ladles, containers and hands and to wipe their scales and measures in the way we have mentioned.

The muḥtasib should inspect the owners of the isolated shops in the quarters and on the roads outside the markets. He must examine their merchandise and scales every week when they are not expecting it, for most of them swindle in the ways we have described.

CHAPTER TWENTY-ONE

Cloth Merchants

No one should trade in cloth unless he knows the laws of selling, the contracts of business transactions, what is lawful for him and what unlawful. If he does not know, he will be unaware of what he is doing and commit what is forbidden. 'Umar b. al-Khaṭṭāb said: "No one will trade in our market except he who knows the laws of his religion. Otherwise, he will take usurious interest whether he intends to or not." During the present time I have seen most of the cloth merchants in the markets acting unlawfully in their transactions. God willing, we shall mention these things.

One of them is collusion. This is for a man to offer a high price for a commodity while not wanting to buy it, in order to entice someone else to pay more. This is unlawful, because the Prophet forbade collusion in selling. Abū Hurayra[1] related that the Prophet said: "Do not bid against each other, nor hate each other, nor envy each other, nor collude against each other. Be brothers and servants of God." Do not offer a higher price for a commodity than it is worth in order to deceive the people, for this is unlawful.

Another of these things is "sale against a brother's sale". This is when someone buys a commodity at a fixed price with the stipulation that he can annul the agreement, and then another man says to him: "Give it back and I will sell you a better one than that for the same price, or a similar one at a lower price." This practice is also unlawful, because the Prophet said: "A man may not sell against his brother's sale, nor ask for a girl's hand in marriage when she has already promised another."

Some of them "offer a commodity for sale against their brother's offer". This is for someone to buy a commodity from a man and then for another man to say to him: "I will give you a better one than that for the same price, or a similar one at a lower price." He then shows him the commodity and the buyer considers it. This is also unlawful, according to what the Prophet said: "A man must not offer a commodity

[1] A Companion of the Prophet and a prolific narrator of traditions, c. 600-78.

for sale against his brother's offer." Some of them say to the buyer: "I will sell you this garment for the same price as such and such sold his", or "I will sell you this commodity for the same price."

Some say to the merchant: "I will sell you this garment as long as you sell me yours", or "I will sell you this gown for 10 dirhams in cash or for 20 dirhams on credit."

Others sell the commodity with payment after an unspecified period, or sell it with payment on an unspecified future event. That is, they say: "You don't have to pay for this until the Meccan pilgrims come", or "until the grain is threshed" or "until the sultan makes his gift" and such like.

Some of them buy a commodity from a merchant like themselves, then sell it to another man before taking possession of it. All these things are unlawful, and it is not allowed to do them because the Prophet forbade them.

Selling by "touch" is also impermissible.[2] That is, for the seller to say to the buyer: "If you touch the garment with your hand, you are obliged to buy it whether you want to or not." Nor is selling by "throwing at one another" permitted. That is, for the seller to say to the buyer: "I will sell you this garment I have for the one you have." Then when each of them throws his garment to the other the transaction is obligatory. Selling by "a pebble" is also impermissible. That is, for the seller to say to the buyer: "I will sell you whatever land or garment the pebble falls on." This is because of what Abū Sa'īd al-Khadrī related regarding the Prophet forbidding selling "by touch", "by throwing at one another" and "by a pebble", by which he intended what we have mentioned.

* *

The *muḥtasib* must make sure that they are truthful in the terms of purchase and concerning the original price in a resale with a stated profit, for most of them do

[2] This and the following two prohibitions were designed to prevent buying "by chance", that is, these rules are aimed at preventing gambling, which is prohibited in Islamic law.

what is impermissible. One of these things is for someone to buy a commodity for a definite price payable after a specified period, and then to bargain for an amount which will bring them a profit if paid in cash immediately. This is not allowed because the deferred period is allowed for by a portion of the price.

Some of them buy a commodity at a stated price, then when the contract is concluded and the seller asks for the price, the buyer reduces it a little. This is not allowed once the contract has been concluded. Others buy a commodity at a stated price, but if they find it has a defect and then return to the seller asking for a discount, they firstly bargain about the original price which they paid for it without the discount.

Some of them come to an agreement with their neighbour or servant to sell them a garment for 10 dirhams, for example, then they buy it back from him for 15 dirhams so that they can say: "I bought it for 15 dirhams". All these things are unlawful and impermissible. If a merchant buys a piece of cloth for 10 dirhams then has it bleached at a cost of one dirham, embroidered for one dirham and repaired for one dirham, then he does not say that he bought it for 13 dirhams because he would be a liar. Rather, he says that it cost him 13 dirhams. And if he himself is the one who embroidered it, bleached and repaired it, then he cannot say that it cost him 13 dirhams because he has not paid for someone else to do it. Neither can he say that its price was 13 dirhams because he would be a liar. Rather, he must say that he bought it for 10 dirhams and worked on it to the value of 3 dirhams.

The *muḥtasib* must watch them in all we have mentioned and forbid them from doing these things. He must examine their scales and their cubits,[3] and prevent them from forming a partnership with the bazaar criers and brokers. He must make sure that they deal fairly with the customers and the importers of merchandise and that they are truthful in all situations.

---

[3] Arabic: *dhirāʿ*. This was originally the part of the arm from the elbow to the tip of the middle finger. Then it came to be the measure of the cubit, then the name of the instrument for measuring it, as here. Ibn al-Ukhuwwa refers to seven kinds of cubits, then states that the legally established cubit mentioned by al-Ghazālī is twenty-four fingers long, each finger being the length of six barleycorns placed back to front, and each barleycorn being the width of six mule hairs (*Maʿālim al-Qurba* Arabic text p. 88). In general, however, it varied in length.

CHAPTER TWENTY-TWO

Brokers and Bazaar Criers

They should be virtuous and trustworthy, from among the religious, those of integrity and the truthful. This is because they take responsibility for the people's goods and are entrusted with selling them. None of them is allowed to raise the price of a commodity on his own account, to be the partner of a cloth merchant, to buy the commodity for himself, or to state the price of a commodity without its owner authorising him to do so.

Some of them approach the makers of clothes and weavers and lend them gold on condition that nobody sells their wares apart from them. This is unlawful as it is a loan for profit. Others buy a commodity for themselves and deceive its owner into believing that some people have bought it from them. Then they later find someone to buy it.

Some of them own the commodity themselves and advertise it, increasing the price on their own behalf and making the people believe that it belongs to one of the merchants. Others agree with a cloth merchant on a certain sum, then when another merchant comes to the cloth merchant with goods, the cloth merchant recommends that the bazaar crier should sell them. When the goods are sold and the money is taken the bazaar crier gives the cloth merchant the money agreed upon. The cloth merchant is acting unlawfully when he does this.

Whenever the bazaar crier learns that a commodity is defective, it is his duty to inform the buyer and draw his attention to it.

The *muḥtasib* must keep an eye on them regarding all the things we have mentioned and examine their circumstances regarding these.

CHAPTER TWENTY-THREE

Weavers

The *muḥtasib* must order them to weave a length of cloth well and closely textured, make it to the full length and width agreed upon, to use fine yarn and to take the black crust off the cloth with a rough black stone. He should prevent them from sprinkling the cloth with flour and roasted gypsum while it is being woven, because this conceals its coarseness and makes it appear closely textured. This is swindling the people. When one of them weaves cloth from poor quality and knotted yarn he must sell it separate from the rest of the cloth. If not, this is swindling.

Some of them weave the surface of the cloth out of good and uniform yarn, then weave the rest of it from thick knotted yarn. The *'arīf* must therefore watch and keep an eye on them regarding this. If one of them takes yarn from someone to weave them cloth, he must take it by weight. Then, after weaving, he should wash the cloth and return it to its owner by weight so as to remove any suspicion regarding him. If the owner of the yarn claims that the weaver has replaced his yarn for another, the *muḥtasib* should send the weaver before the *'arīf*. If he submits to the *'arīf*'s decision then that is the end of it, but if not, the *muḥtasib* must have the issue judged according to Islamic law.[1]

Some of them have a stone basin in front of their shops in which to rub the cloth. Then when they leave, the dogs come and lick it. The *muḥtasib* must therefore charge the weavers to put wooden covers over the cloth or to wash it seven times a day if necessary, once with dust. He must prevent them from stretching out their

[1] In this context we may note that while being generally advised to be aware of the rulings of Islamic law, the *muḥtasib* was not expected to be qualified in its interpretation. That is, strictly speaking, he was not permitted to exercise his personal opinion in any case not clearly defined, in the way that a judge could. He only had jurisdiction in "obvious objectionable actions". In theory, however, once the judge had exercised his judicial prerogative and had reached a decision regarding a particular case, the *muḥtasib* was empowered to put that decision into effect on the judge's behalf. For example, the *muḥtasib* may not impose the amount of maintenance (*nafaqa*) upon a man for his divorced wife, but once the judge has decreed that it should be paid the *muḥtasib* is permitted to ensure that it is forthcoming (*al-Aḥkām al-Sulṭāniyya* p. 213). Similarly, Ibn al-Ukhuwwa remarks that the *muḥtasib* may enforce the repayment of debts as long as the fact of debt has been established (*Ma'ālim al-Qurba* p. 26). One of the few dissenting voices regarding this was al-Iṣṭakhrī who held that the

cloth in the Muslims' roads because this inconveniences passers-by. He must also stop them throwing the flour and other edible matter which is in the cloth under the feet of the Muslims. But God knows best.

---

muḥtasib may, like the judge, exercise his personal opinion in deciding cases. al-Iṣṭakhrī was himself both a judge and a *muḥtasib* (*al-Aḥkām al-Sulṭāniyya* p. 209).

CHAPTER TWENTY-FOUR

Tailors

They must be ordered to cut the cloth out well, to make the neck opening properly, to make the gussets wide, to make the sleeves and cuffs to the same length and to sew the hems evenly. It is best that the stitches are tight, not loose and big, and that the needle is fine. The thread in the needle should be short because if it is too long it will fray and weaken. It will also weaken when the tailor pulls it through the cloth.

The tailor must not cut out a valuable piece of cloth for anyone until he has measured it. He may cut it after that. If it is an expensive material such as silk or brocade, he must weigh it before taking it. Then, when he has sewn it, he must return it to its owner at the same weight.

The *muḥtasib* must keep an eye on them because of the people's property which they steal. For when some of them sew a silk garment, for example, they put sand and glue in the lining and steal a corresponding weight of material. He must stop them from keeping the people waiting for their clothes to be sewn, inconveniencing them by making them repeatedly come back and by withholding their property. They should not keep the people waiting for a job longer than one week unless they have stipulated to the customer that it will take longer. They must not break this agreement.

The *muḥtasib* must make the repairers swear that they will not repair a torn garment for the dyers and the cloth-beaters unless its owner is present. The embroiderers and ornamental stitchers must not transfer embroidery from one garment to another which the bleachers or cloth-beaters have given them. Many of them do this with the people's clothes.

As for the makers of *qalansuwas*,[1] the *muḥtasib* should order them to make these out of new pieces of cloth, silk thread and dyed linen, not out of old dyed pieces of cloth

[1] A kind of headgear or cap.

stiffened with glue and starch. This is fraudulent and the *muḥtasib* must stop them doing it. But God knows best.

CHAPTER TWENTY-FIVE

Cotton Carders

They must not mix new cotton with old nor red cotton with white. They must card the cotton many times until the black husks and broken seeds are removed from it. This is because if any seeds remain it will affect the cotton's weight, and if they are left in a blanket, a *jubba*[1] or a *qabā'*[2] the mice will nibble at them.

They must not mix the finest cotton at the bottom of the carding box nor the pure cotton at the sides of the walls with anything else. Some of them card bad red cotton, put it at the bottom of the pile and cover it with pure white cotton. This does not show until it is spun.

The *muḥtasib* must forbid them from allowing women to sit by their shop doors waiting for the carding to be completed, and from talking with them.

They must not put the cotton in a damp place after it has been carded because this makes it heavier and it becomes lighter when it dries. This is a fraud which they all practise, so the *muḥtasib* must stop them doing it. But God knows best.

---

[1] A long outer garment, open in front with wide sleeves.
[2] A luxurious seamed robe, apparently of Persian origin, slit in the front with buttons and made of fabrics such as brocade.

CHAPTER TWENTY-SIX

Flax Spinners

The finest flax is from Giza in Egypt, and the best of this is the soft leafy variety, while the worst is the short rough variety which breaks without warning.

They must not mix good flax with bad, nor flax from Nablus[1] with that from Egypt. Some of them mix unspun cotton with soft flax after it has been combed. All these things are fraudulent.

They must not allow women to sit by their shop doors, as we mentioned regarding the cotton carders. But God knows best.

[1] A town in west Jordan.

CHAPTER TWENTY-SEVEN

Silk Makers

They must not dye raw silk before it has been bleached lest it should deteriorate later. They sometimes do this to make it weigh more. Some of them make the silk heavier with starch while others make it heavier with clarified butter or oil. Some of them mix the silk with a quantity of other material.

The *muḥtasib* must therefore keep an eye on them concerning all these things. But God knows best.

CHAPTER TWENTY-EIGHT

Dyers

Most dyers of red silk, and other kinds of thread and material, dye with henna instead of madder[1] in their shops. The dye appears good and bright, but when it is exposed to the sun its colour changes and its brightness fades. Some of them darken cloth with oak apples and vitriol when they want to dye it the colour of kohl. They put it in large containers and it comes out a uniform jet-black. But the colour changes after only a short time and the dye wears off. All this is fraudulent and the *muḥtasib* must stop them doing it.

They must write the people's names on their clothes in ink so that none of them get confused. During holidays, festivals and other celebrations, most dyers and *marandajūn*[2] alter the people's clothes and rent them out to those who want to wear them at that time and dress themselves up. This is a breach of trust and wrong and the *muḥtasib* must prevent them from doing it. He must keep an eye on them regarding the way they make and adulterate the dye and he must show it to their *'arīf*. But God knows best.

[1] A dark reddish-purple dye obtained from the madder plant.
[2] Those who dye cloth black by using *yarnadaj*, which is a kind of vitriol.

CHAPTER TWENTY-NINE

Shoemakers

They should not use too many old pieces of cloth as padding between the inner and outer linings, nor between the inner sole and the outer. They may stitch the padding for the heels, but must not stitch a sole which has split during tanning nor new leather nor any leather which has not been tanned. They must twine the thread well and make it no longer than a cubit, because if it is longer than this it will fray and be too weak to pull through the leather. They should not sew with pig's hair, but should rather use palm fibres or fox whiskers, as these are better.

They must not keep someone waiting for his shoes except when they have stipulated a certain day in advance. This is because the people are inconvenienced by repeatedly having to return to them and by the withholding of their property.

They should not use paper, felt and such like to make women's slippers so that these squeak when the women walk, as the women of Baghdad like to have them. This is shameful, and is a disgrace which does not befit free-born people. The *muḥtasib* must therefore stop them being made and worn. But God knows best.

CHAPTER THIRTY

Money Changers

To make a living out of money changing is dangerous to the religion of those engaged in it. Indeed, the money-changer will transgress against his religion if he is ignorant of Islamic law and unaware of the rules concerning usury. Thus a person should not engage in it until he has acquainted himself with the law, so as to avoid committing any of the various categories of prohibitions.

The *muḥtasib* must inspect their market and keep an eye on them. If he comes across anyone practising usury, or doing anything while changing money which is not permitted in Islamic law, he should chastise him and evict him from the market. He should do this after acquainting him with the basic principles of usury.

It is not permitted for anyone to sell gold coins for gold, nor silver for silver, except in the same quantities and by taking immediate possession. For if the money changer makes a profit when he is exchanging the same metal, or if he and the customer part before possession is taken, this is unlawful.[1] As for selling gold for silver, profit is permitted here, but credit and concluding the sale before delivery is made are unlawful. It is not permitted to sell pure coinage for that which is adulterated, nor to sell adulterated gold and silver coins for other adulterated ones, such as selling Egyptian dinars for those from Tyre,[2] or those from Tyre for the same, or *Aḥadī* dirhams[3] for those from Qairouan[4] because of ignorance as to their value and the lack of similarity between them.[5]

---

[1] Islamic law states that gold can only be exchanged for gold, and silver for silver, in equal quantities. This is regardless of whether the gold or silver has been worked or not. Thus, if profit is to be made, gold must not be sold for gold, and silver not for silver.

[2] A town in south Lebanon.

[3] Perhaps this indicates those coins which were struck by al-Ḥajjāj b. Yūsuf in Iraq at the order of the caliph ʻAbd al-Malik b. Marwān (r. 685-705). On them was engraved *qul huwa Allahu aḥad* ("Say that God is One").

[4] A town in north-east Tunisia.

[5] Just as the units of weights and measure suffered from a lack of uniformity and thus lent themselves to fraud and swindling, so the coinage suffered from the same disadvantage. During the Umayyad and Abbasid periods the minting of specie was centrally controlled by the government. Later, there was a move towards decentralisation and regionalism which was perhaps inaugurated by Hārūn al-Rashīd (r. 786-809) who appointed a subordinate official, the *nāẓir al-sikka*, to supervise the mints. As a result of this development, together with an increase in the number of mints due to the

It is likewise not permitted to sell whole dinars for cut pieces of a dinar because of their difference in value. Nor is it permitted to sell dinars from Qashan[6] for those from Sabur[7] due to the difference in their composition.

It is also not permitted to sell a dinar and a garment for two dinars. Some money changers and cloth merchants occasionally practise this usury in another way. They give the buyer a dinar as a loan and then sell him a garment for two dinars, so that he owes them three dinars for a specified period when they will ask him for it all back. This is unlawful and it is not permissible to do it with this condition because it is a loan bringing profit. If they had not loaned him the dinar, he would not have bought the garment for two dinars.

---

largely monetary character of the economy, a situation arose in which different mints were producing coins which only satisfied local standards of fineness and which bore only a general resemblance to the products of other mints. Unlike the copper *fals* (plural: *fulūs*) which had a limited distribution, dirhams and dinars were in use over a very wide area, despite their being of different qualities and thus purchasing power. Nevertheless, because of the general rarity of specie the situation was allowed to continue unchecked. A similar circumstance also existed regarding old coinage which was left in circulation. The fact of the coins becoming thinner and therefore less valuable led to products of the self-same mint having different values at the same time. The various governments, provinces and even cities within the same province were from an early date concerned with minimising the effects of this unsatisfactory situation. It was only natural that the *muḥtasib*, whose jurisdiction was concerned primarily with the market, should be charged with some responsibility for currency control. An obvious target for the *muḥtasib*'s attentions was the money changers who were a common feature in the markets, exchanging the various kinds and qualities of dirhams and dinars in circulation. The first explicit mention of this in the *ḥisba* treatises is found in the Zaydī manual from the early tenth century AD:

> The muḥtasib must order the money-changers to adjust correctly the weights and scales and forbid them from smearing the dinars with kohl [so that they weigh heavier], and from taking coins which have been coated with mercury and those which are counterfeit ("A Zaidi Manual" p. 24).

There are some indications that at certain times and in certain places the *muḥtasib* was connected with the workings of the mint itself. The first indication is found in a passage by al-Māwardī written under the Buwayhids which, while not ascribing any supervisory capacity to the *muḥtasib*, states that he has the authority to select assayers of coins if the town becomes large enough to warrant their employment (*al-Aḥkām al-Sulṭāniyya* p. 219). Likewise, Tāj al-Dīn al-Subkī, writing somewhat later, states that one of the *muḥtasib*'s important duties is the checking of the fineness of coinage and the careful consideration of minting (*Mu'īd al-Ni'am wa Mubīd al-Niqam* [Cairo, 1948] p. 66). Similarly, in a Fatimid diploma of investiture it says

> Regarding the mint and the coins which are dispersed from it, there may be counterfeit among these which only come to light after some time. So let [the *muḥtasib*] apply himself to this with his breast which knows no anguish and let him submit to a test that which does not succeed in confusing him insofar as he is able (*Ṣubḥ al-A'shā* 11:214-15).

Elsewhere, it is remarked that the chief judge had responsibility over the mint (see *Khiṭaṭ* 1:445, 450; *Ṣubḥ al-A'shā* 3:482) or alternatively the ordinary judge (see *Ṣubḥ al-A'shā* 10:384, 433).

[6] The chief town of Khurasan in central Iran.

[7] An old Persian town on the road from Shiraz to the sea.

Some of them buy dinars with silver dirhams or with the *qarāṭīs* of the Franks.[8] Then they say to the seller: "Pay your creditor with these so that you can get rid of them or take them from me a few at a time", and the man will agree with him in this due to his great ignorance. All these things are unlawful and may not be done. The *muḥtasib* must therefore keep an eye on them concerning all we have mentioned and not mentioned of this sort.

Some people have said that when a four *mithqāl* piece is divided its weight is clearly reduced. Because of this many money changers hate to take them.

If one of the money changers has to pay someone more than four dinars they pay him four and promise him the rest at a later date.

As for the examination of their scales and weights, this has been mentioned previously. But God knows best.

[8] This was the silver money used by the Crusaders in Syria and was sometimes worth more than a dinar, sometimes less.

CHAPTER THIRTY-ONE

Goldsmiths

They must not sell vessels and trinkets of gold and silver except for coins of a different metal, so that the increment is lawful. If the goldsmith sells them for their like, then increment, credit and concluding the sale before delivery is made are unlawful, as we mentioned in the chapter on money changers.

If the goldsmith sells any trinkets which have non-precious metals in them, he must tell the buyer the extent of the adulteration so that he is aware of it. And if he wants to make a trinket for someone, he must only smelt it in the furnace in the presence of the customer and after ascertaining its weight. When it has been smelted it should be weighed again. If it needs to be soldered, the goldsmith must weigh the solder before putting it on.

He must not set any stones or jewels in a ring or trinket except after weighing them in the presence of their owner.

In general, the frauds and adulterations of goldsmiths are secret and are difficult to detect. Nothing deters them from this apart from their honesty and piety, for they know tinctures and pigments which no one else does. Some of them colour silver in a way which does not leave the metal except after it has been smelted a long time in a smelting pot. For two parts of this they then mix in one part of gold.

One of their frauds is the way they make silver yellow. They take *sădhanj*[1] which has been roasted and oiled separately, haematite[2] which has been roasted with prepared *maranj*[3] sap seven times, and vitriol and cinnabar[4] roasted with eagle water[5] solution in a retort. Then they grind them all together, roast two cups of the

[1] Also known as bloodstone. It is a dark red stone which also has medicinal properties.
[2] One of several minerals known by this name.
[3] A kind of wood.
[4] A heavy red mineral, the chief ore of mercury. Also a red form of mercuric sulphide used as a pigment.
[5] Liquid ammonia.

mixture seven times with the aforementioned *maranj* water, then seven times with the eagle water solution. After this it will solidify into a red stone the colour of blood. They mix one *dirham* of this with ten *dirham*s of silver and it becomes gold with a standard of sixteen. If this hard red amalgam of precious metal and adulterants is dissolved then allowed to harden again the silver acquires a standard of twenty from which dinars and jewellery may be made.

Some of them take haematite and roast it seven times with an ox's gall bladder. They then add a similar quantity of gold coated with sulphur which has been extracted from quicklime and alkaline ashes.[6] After this, it is all roasted with eagle water solution seven times and oiled with wild saffron oil seven times. It hardens into a stone like the previous one. If it is dissolved then allowed to harden again it becomes stronger than the previous one, similar to metal. They mix one *qīrāṭ* of this with one *dirham* of silver.

They can produce so many things from alchemy and tinctures that it would take a long time to describe them, and if I was not afraid that the irreligious might learn of these secrets I could explain many of them which a lot of goldsmiths have not discovered. Every Muslim must fear God and not swindle the Muslims in any way whatsoever. If the *muḥtasib* comes across anyone doing this, he must chastise and publicly condemn him, as has been explained previously.

As for the dust and sand from the goldsmiths' shops, it should only be sold for copper coinage or a similar equivalent, for it has gold and silver in it and may thus lead to unlawful profit.[7] But God knows best.

---

[6] That is, the ashes of alkaline plants, such as saltwort and kali.

[7] Ibn al-Ukhuwwa further remarks that the dust belongs to the public as its individual owners are unknown. It must be sold and the proceeds given away as charity on behalf of its owners (*Ma'ālim al-Qurba* Arabic text p. 147).

CHAPTER THIRTY-TWO

Coppersmiths and Blacksmiths

They are not allowed to mix copper with the *ḥabaq*[1] which the goldsmiths and smelters of silver extract when they smelt, for this hardens the copper and makes it less malleable. Then if a drinking vessel or a mortar is moulded from it, it will break easily like glass. They must not mix pieces of broken copper containers and such like with unused copper, rather, each must be smelted separately and worked separately.

* *

As for the blacksmiths, they must not hammer out knives, scissors, pincers and the like from soft iron and sell it as steel. This is fraudulent. They must not mix straightened-out nails with those which are newly forged, and must only use pure steel for knives, scissors and razors. But God knows best.

[1] This substance cannot be identified.

CHAPTER THIRTY-THREE

Veterinarians

Veterinary science is an honourable one which philosophers have written about in their books and on which they have composed numerous treatises. It is more difficult to treat the illnesses of animals than it is those of men, because an animal cannot speak and tell of its sickness and pain. It is only possible to get information about their ailments by touching and looking. The veterinarian thus needs skill and understanding of the illnesses of animals and their treatment.

No one should practise veterinary science unless he has a religion to stop him harming the animal with inexperienced blood-letting, cutting or cauterization and such like, thus leading to the death or injury of the animal.

* *

The veterinarian must examine the animal's ankle and inspect its hoof before paring it. If it is distorted or crooked, he should pare the opposite side of the hoof so that he makes it even. If the animal's foot is straight, he should use small nails at the back and large nails at the front. But if it stands in the opposite way, he should use small nails at the front and large nails at the back. The veterinarian must not pare the hoof too much and thus go into the animal's flesh. He should not put the nails in too loosely so that the shoe moves letting in small stones and sand and hurting the animal. Nor should he put the shoes on the hoof too tightly and thus cause terrible suffering to the animal. Know that hammered shoes stick better to the hoof, that soft shoes take hard nails better and that thin nails are better than thick ones.

If the animal is in need of having a vein opened, the veterinarian should hold the scalpel between his fingers with the handle in his palm, leaving half a finger nail length of the scalpel exposed. He should then delicately and gently cut the vein on its upper side. The veterinarian must not cut the vein until he has stopped it with his finger, particularly the jugular veins for these are potentially dangerous as they lie next to the oesophagus. If he wants to open any of the jugular veins he must firmly bind the animal's neck so that they stand out, then he may do as he intends.

* *

The veterinarian must be experienced in the illnesses of animals, be aware of what animals require and the defects which occur in them. The people must resort to him when they cannot agree on what the illness is.

Some learned people have stated in the books on veterinary science that there are 320 illnesses which animals may have. These include tightness in the oesophagus, disease of the nostrils with a discharge, disease of the nostrils without a discharge, madness, weakness of the brain, headache, *al-ḥamir,*[1] *nafakha,*[2] tumours, violent fits, *al-dība,*[3] *al-khushshām,*[4] pain in the liver, pain in the heart, worms in the stomach, *al-maghal,*[5] cholic, *rīḥ al-sawas,*[6] gripes, *al-ṣidām,*[7] a cold cough, a hot cough, an eruption of blood from the anus and penis, *al-baḥal,*[8] throat disease, difficulty in urinating, pain in the joints, stones caught in hooves, swelling of the foot, whitlows, split hooves, *al-nakab,*[9] *al-khalad,*[10] facial paralysis, watering eyes, limp ears, toothache, and other things which would take a long time to explain. The veterinarian needs to know how to treat the animal and the reason behind these illnesses, for some of them cause permanent damage to the animal which contracts them, while others do not cause permanent damage. If it did not take so long I would give a detailed account. The *muḥtasib* must not neglect to test the veterinarian concerning what we have mentioned and to observe what he does with the people's animals. But God knows best.

---

[1] A stomach complaint afflicting horses and caused by eating too much barley.
[2] A disease attacking horses and making their testicles swell.
[3] A swelling on the animal's chest which prevents it from eating.
[4] A certain disease in the nose stopping the breath.
[5] A disease of the head.
[6] A disease which afflicts horses and similar animals on the rumps, between the hip and the thigh, causing weakness in the back legs.
[7] A certain disease which affects the heads of horses and similar animals.
[8] A disease which afflicts the penis.
[9] A disease of the shoulder joints which causes the animal to halt.
[10] A certain ailment which causes suppurating sores on the animal.

CHAPTER THIRTY-FOUR

Traders in Slaves and Animals[1]

The slave-trader must be trustworthy, reliable and honest, well known for his integrity and respectability. This is because he is responsible for the people's male and female slaves and is occasionally alone with them in his house.

The trader must not sell a female or a male slave to someone unless he knows the seller or can find someone who knows him. He must write the seller's name and description in his register in case the person sold is a freeman or has been stolen.

Anyone who wants to buy a female slave may look at her face and palms, but if he asks to examine her in his house and be alone with her the trader must not allow it unless there are other women present. These may see her whole body. Whoever wants to buy a male slave may look at what is above the navel and below the knees. All this may be done before the contract of sale. After the contract, the man may look at all the body of a female slave.

It is not permitted to separate a female slave and her child before seven years have elapsed. Nor it is permitted to sell to a *dhimmī*[2] a female or male slave who might be

---

[1] Regarding the relationship of the *muḥtasib* to the slave market. It is stated that in 1033 Dāwūd b. Ya'qūb al-Kutāmī was appointed to the *ḥisba*, the ports and the *aswāq* (markets) (*Itti'āẓ* 2:135; *Akhbār Miṣr* p. 14). At first sight it appears somewhat enigmatic that as the *muḥtasib*'s duties were largely concerned with the markets that he should have yet another distinct office called *aswāq*. There is no information concerning this function but it could have been a forerunner of the Mamluk position of the *nāẓir aswāq*, the jurisdiction of whom was over the horse and slave markets only. This hypothesis becomes more attractive when we see *ḥisba* and the supervision of the slave markets distinguished from each other elsewhere. In the time of the caliph al-Mu'taḍid (r. 892-902), al-Sarakhsī "took the office of *ḥisba* in Baghdad, the inheritances (*al-mawārīth*) and the slave market (*sūq al-raqīq*)" (*Mu'jam al-Mu'allifīn* 2:157). During the Buwayhid period also, a Buwayhid amir is entrusted with *ḥisba* and the slave markets (*Ṣubḥ al-A'shā* 10:15). The *ḥisba* treatises of al-Shayzarī and al-Māwardī do not mention any authority of the *muḥtasib* over the slave markets, although they both state that he must ensure that slaves are correctly treated. This omission indicates the independent nature of the two jurisdictions. But Ibn al-Ukhuwwa, writing during the Mamluk period, devotes a chapter to the *muḥtasib*'s responsibilities in the slave market, in the course of which he outlines the general practices of that market and indicates some of the tricks and deceptions which the *muḥtasib* must be on his guard against (*Ma'ālim al-Qurba* pp. 152-53). The conclusion would appear to be that on occasion the *muḥtasib* looked after the slave market and, while not strictly being under his aegis, was required to know something of its working.

[2] A non-Muslim protected person. See Chapter 39 for a brief explanation of the term.

a Muslim. The trader must be absolutely certain that the slave is not a Muslim. Whenever the trader knows that a person for sale has a defect, he must reveal this to the buyer, as we mentioned at the beginning of the book.

* *

The slave-trader must be well acquainted with defects and experienced in incipient illnesses and diseases. If he wants to sell a male slave, he must first examine all his body except for his genitals. He does this so that if the slave has a defect or an illness he can inform the buyer of it. The first thing he should look at is his face, for if it is somewhat yellow or ashen this indicates haemorrhoids or a disease or illness in the liver or the spleen.

A broker must not sell an animal unless he knows the seller or can find someone who knows him. He must write the seller's name in his register, as we have already said, in case the animal is defective or stolen. But God knows best.

CHAPTER THIRTY-FIVE

Baths and their Attendants

In this chapter and the preceding one we mention things which have nothing to do with *ḥisba*.[1] We refer to them only for the general benefit knowledge of them brings and because they are relevant in this place. Indeed, wisdom is the cherished goal of every wise person, and the benefit is wonderful wherever it is found.

Some wise man said that the best kind of bath is that which has been built a long time, is roomy and has sweet water.

The one who heats the water for the baths assesses the amount of fuel needed according to the temperament of those who wish to use it.

Know that the physical effect of the bath is to warm with its air and to moisten with its water. The first room cools and moistens, the second room warms and relaxes, while the third room warms and dries.

The bath has both advantages and disadvantages. As for the advantages, these are to open the pores and remove extraneous matter, to dissipate odours, to restrain the body when it is loosened with dysentery, to clean away the dirt and sweat, remove itching, scabies and weariness, refresh the body, improve the digestion, bring colds and catarrh to a head, and to be useful against fevers which last for only one day,

---

[1] Ibn al-Ukhuwwa states that the baths (*ḥammām*) do come under the jurisdiction of the *muḥtasib* (*Ma'ālim al-Qurba* Arabic text pp. 154-58). Indeed, this was one of the most obvious arenas for immoral behaviour, not least because of the absolute prevalence of such amenities. Public baths were one of the most conspicuous aspects of social life. al-Baghdādī (d. 1071) tried to achieve a demographic study of Baghdad by enumerating the number of baths there from the third to the fifth century AH. His count varied from sixty-six thousand in the time of the caliph al-Muwaffaq (r. 870-91), through a steady decline until the amirate of the Buwayhid Bahā' al-Dawla (r. 989-1012) in which he enumerated three thousand; while al-Ya'qūbī informs us that there were some ten thousand public baths in existence in Baghdad not long after its foundation. Even allowing for a good deal of exaggeration, and any possible confusion between private baths and public ones, there still must have been an enormous number. This abundance is understandable in the light of the baths' importance to the community, where they were used for achieving ritual purification and for fulfilling the laws of general hygiene, as well as serving as one of the few means of social recreation. The life of the community revolved around them. The majority were mixed baths for men and women; men being admitted on one day while women used the facilities on the next. Some, however, were set aside for the exclusive use of women.

hectic fever[2] and quartan fever[3] after these have matured. As for the disadvantages, the bath saps the body's energy, weakens enthusiasm when too long is spent in it, spoils the appetite for food and reduces sexual potency. The greatest danger is to pour hot water on weak limbs.

Sometimes people use the bath before breakfast or while they are fasting and this causes serious dehydration and emaciates and weakens the body. Sometimes people use the bath just after eating their fill and this fattens the body. It does cause poor circulation however. The best time to use the bath is after the first digestion having eaten one's fill. This refreshes the body, fattens it and improves the complexion.

* *

The *muḥtasib* must order the attendants to wash, sweep and clean the bath a few times each day with fresh water, not water that has been used for bathing. They should scrub the tiles with a rough material so that no soap, leaves of the lotus tree or marsh mallow[4] sticks to them causing people to slip.[5] Once a month they should wash the supply tank of the dirt which has collected in its channels and the sediment settled at the bottom. This is because if it is left for more than a month the water in it will both taste and smell unpleasant.

If the caretaker wants to climb up to the supply tank to let the water flow into the baths he must do so only after first washing his legs in case he has been in water

---

[2] A kind of fever which accompanies consumption or other wasting diseases, and is attended with flushed cheeks and a hot dry skin.

[3] A fever recurring every fourth day inclusively.

[4] Ibn al-Ukhuwwa describes lotus leaves used for washing (*Ma'ālim al-Qurba* Arabic text p. 158). Edward Lane also notes that the dried and crushed leaves of the lotus tree were often used by poor Egyptians as a substitute for soap (*Manners* p. 513 note 2). Presumably marsh mallow leaves were used for a similar purpose.

[5] al-Ghazālī remarks that

> Leaving lotus leaves for washing and slippery soap on the floor of the bath are also objectionable practices. When someone leaves such a thing in a place where it is difficult to see and thus avoid it, and then departs and someone slips on it and breaks one of his limbs - then the responsibility for this is shared between the one who left it and the bath attendant, as it is the latter's duty to keep the bath clean (*Iḥyā' 'Ulūm al-Dīn* 2:297).

used for bathing. The pipes must not be closed with the hair from combings, rather, they should be closed with palm fibres and clean rags so that there is no controversy.

Incense should be burnt in the baths twice a day, especially when the attendants start to wash and sweep them. When the baths are cold the caretaker should fumigate them with lavender as its fumes make the air circulate and the bath smell pleasant.

The water used for bathing must not be allowed to remain in the baths lest it should smell. The shoemakers and others must not be allowed to wash any leather in the bath because the smell of the tanning is unpleasant for people. Lepers and those afflicted with elephantiasis are not permitted to enter the bath. The owner of the bath must have some bath robes to hire out or lend to the people, because strangers and poor people need this.

The *muḥtasib* must order them to open the bath at dawn because people require it for the ritual ablutions before prayer. The attendant must look after the people's clothes and is responsible if any of them are lost, according to what the Shāfiʿī school of law[6] correctly says.

* *

The barber, that is, the bathhouse attendant, should have a light touch, be nimble and proficient in shaving, and his razor should be wet and sharp. He should not stand directly in front of the head and the places where the hair is, nor should he eat anything which makes his breath smell, such as onions, garlic and leeks, lest he offend the people when he is shaving them. He must cut hair on the forehead and the temples as is required, not cut a young boy's hair without his guardian's permission and not cut the first growths of a beard nor the fully-grown beard of an effeminate man.

The *muḥtasib* must order the masseur to rub his hand with pomegranate skin to make it rough, remove the dirt and thus please the people. The use of beans and

---

[6] Muḥammad b. Idrīs al-Shāfiʿī (767-820). The founder of the Shāfiʿī school of law. This was the prominent school in Egypt under Ṣalāḥ al-Dīn when this book was written.

lentils to rub with in the bath must not be permitted, because these are foodstuffs and should not be treated with contempt.

* *

The *muḥtasib* should inspect the bath a few times each day and take into account what we have mentioned. He should chastise anyone he sees who reveals his nakedness, because it is unlawful and the Prophet cursed both those who see it and those who are seen.[7] But God knows best.

---

[7] In 1005 in Egypt a public order was issued that nobody should enter the bath without a cover. This was proclaimed in the streets to the accompaniment of bells (*Itti'āẓ* 2:54). Some time later, and thanks to a watch being put on the baths (by the *muḥtasib*'s assistants?), a group of persons were apprehended for appearing without a cover and were beaten and publicly pilloried (*Itti'āẓ* 2:54). After a further proclamation in 1009 the same scene was again repeated, the offending persons meeting an identical fate (*Itti'āẓ* 2:76). Whether the same group was involved, the source neglects to inform us.

CHAPTER THIRTY-SIX

Phlebotomists and Cuppers[1]

No one should practise phlebotomy unless he has an attested knowledge of the anatomy of limbs, veins, muscles and arteries, and fully understands their locations and nature. This is so that the scalpel does not cut the wrong vein or a muscle or an artery and thus lead to injury of the limb or destruction of the part bled, for many limbs have been destroyed due to this.

Whoever wants to learn phlebotomy must practise on chard leaves, that is, the veins which are on the leaf, until his hand is steady. The phlebotomist must not allow himself to do any manual work which causes the ends of his fingers to become calloused and insensitive and hence renders the examination of veins difficult. He must also treat his eyes with invigorating eye salve and compound ointments if he is one of those who needs such things.

He should not bleed a slave without the permission of the owner, a child without the permission of the guardian, nor a woman who is pregnant or menstruating. The phlebotomist should only bleed someone in a well-lit place and using a sharp instrument, and not when he is feeling uneasy.

In general, the *muḥtasib* must exact a pledge and a covenant from them that they will not bleed anyone under ten physical conditions, that they will be very cautious in these cases and only bleed after consultation with the physicians. These ten conditions are: when the patient is under fourteen years old, is very old, emaciated, obese, shaking, white and flabby, pale with anaemia, has chronic diseases, has an extremely cold temperament and is in great pain. The phlebotomist must recognise these conditions when they are present. The physicians have forbidden the bleeding of someone under a further five conditions, but these are not as harmful as the previous ten. These are bleeding someone immediately after sexual intercourse, after

[1] Phlebotomy is a surgical incision into a vein. Cupping is the process of applying a cupping glass to the skin, this being a glass vessel from which air can be removed by suction or heat to create a partial vacuum. It is used to draw blood to the surface of the skin for slow bloodletting.

a bath for ritual ablution, when they are full of food, when their stomach and bowels are heavy, and when they are either extremely hot or extremely cold. The phlebotomist must be very careful in these circumstances as well.

Know that there are two situations regarding bleeding: when it is optional, and when it is obligatory. As for when it is optional, this is done in the morning after digestion and emptying of the bowels. As for when it is obligatory, this is done at the time of need, when there is no room for delay and when no obstacle is allowed to stand in the way.

The person bled must not fill himself with food afterwards, rather he should eat slowly and lightly. He should not exert himself afterwards, but should lie down. He must be careful not to sleep immediately after being bled, as this causes the limbs to weaken. If someone's hand swells after being bled, they should have the other hand bled if possible.

* *

The phlebotomist must have a number of scalpels, those for capillaries and others. He must also have a ball of silk or wool and silk or something else to cause vomiting made of wood or feather. He must have rabbit fur and the medicament from the aloe plant and storax.[2] He takes one part of storax, aloe, myrrh and dragon's blood, and half a part of burnt vitriol[3] and ordinary vitriol and mixes them all together into a cream. The phlebotomist then keeps this next to him for when he needs it.

He must also have a musk bag and musk pastilles and equip himself with all we have mentioned in case the patient has a fainting fit. In this case, the phlebotomist should immediately make the patient swallow the emetic ball of silk, make him smell the musk bag and eat some of the pastilles. This will revive him. If any haemorrhaging of a vein or artery occurs, the phlebotomist should stem it with the rabbit fur and the storax medicament mentioned previously.

---

[2] Storax was considered to have a number of medicinal purposes (see *Medical Formulary* pp. 329-30).

[3] An impure iron sulphate which was used medicinally (see *Medical Formulary* p. 318).

The phlebotomist must not make an incision with a blunt scalpel. This is very harmful because it errs and does not follow the vein, thus causing swelling and pain. He should rub the point of the scalpel with oil so that it does not hurt when an incision is being made, even though this stops the incision from healing quickly. He should hold the scalpel between the thumb and middle finger and leave the forefinger to feel with. The scalpel should be held no further than half way down its length so that it is not insufficiently controlled. He should not use the scalpel in a sudden movement, but rather carefully so that he puts its tip into the veins.

I have never witnessed anyone more proficient in phlebotomy than two men I came across in Aleppo, each of them boasting that he was more skilful than his colleague. One of them wore a thin undershirt and bound his hand outside of this. Then he immersed himself in a pool and bled his hand on the bottom of the pool. As for the other, he held the scalpel in his left foot, between the big toe and the next, and then bled his hand.

Know that the phlebotomist must make the incision wider in winter so that the blood does not congeal, and must make it narrower in summer so that the patient does not faint easily.

Repeated bleeding keeps the one bled strong. Whoever wants to be bled again on the same day must have the vein cut obliquely so that it does not heal quickly. The best practice for repeated bleeding is to do it only every two or three days. Whenever the colour of the blood changes or the patient faints and has a weak pulse, the phlebotomist should immediately press on the vein and pinch it.

* *

Know that there are many veins which are bled. Among these are those in the head, in the hands, in the body, in the legs and the arteries. The *muḥtasib* must test the phlebotomist's knowledge of these as they are sometimes next to muscles and arteries. I will mention the ones which are best known. As for the veins in the head which are bled, there is that of the forehead which goes up between the eyebrows, the bleeding of which is good for heavy eyes and chronic headache. There is the vein which lies on top of the head, the bleeding of which is good for migraine and head wounds. There are the two meandering veins on the temples, the bleeding of which is good for ophthalmia, watery eyes and itches and pimples on the eyelids. There are the two veins behind the ears, which are bled to stop the begetting of children. The *muḥtasib* must make them swear that they will not bleed either of these veins because it stops procreation and this is unlawful. There are the veins in the lip, the bleeding of which is good for sores and canker in the mouth and pains and tumours of the gums. Finally, there are the veins under the tongue, the bleeding of which is good for quinsy and tumours on the tonsils.

* *

There are six veins of the hand and arm. These are the vena cephalica, the medial, the vena basilica, the exterior cubital, the vena salvatella and the axillary. When the phlebotomist is working, he must push the end of the muscle onto a soft place and make his incision wide if he wants to repeat it. As for the medial vein, it is very dangerous to bleed this because of the muscle which lies beneath it. Sometimes this vein lies between two nerves, and sometimes there is a delicate round nerve like a string above it. The phlebotomist must therefore be acquainted with this, avoid it when he does his bleeding and be careful that his incision does not hit it and cause chronic numbness. As for the vena basilica, this is also extremely dangerous due to the artery under it. The phlebotomist must be careful of this, for if the artery is cut the blood will not cease to flow. As for the vena salvatella, the correct way to bleed it is lengthwise, while the exterior cubital should be bled obliquely. The more the phlebotomist inclines towards the arm in bleeding the vena basilica, the safer it is.

* *

As for the veins of the body, two of them are on the stomach. One of these is situated over the liver and the other is situated over the spleen. The bleeding of the one on the right is good for dropsy, while the one on the left is good for the spleen.

* *

As for the veins of the legs, there are four of them. Among these is the vein of the sciatic nerve, which is bled on the outer part of the ankle. If it is hidden, then the branch between the little toe and the next is bled. The benefits of this are great, especially for gout, varicose veins and elephantiasis. Then there is the vena saphena which is situated on the left side of the leg and is more obvious than the sciatic nerve. Bleeding it is good for haemorrhoids, causes menstruation to occur and benefits the organs below the liver. Also among them is the vein situated behind the Achilles tendon like a branch of the vena saphena, and the benefits of bleeding it are the same as with this latter vein.

* *

As for the veins and arteries which are generally bled and which it is permitted to bleed, these are the small ones and those situated far from the heart, because blood from these will stop flowing when they are bled. As for the large arteries situated near the heart, blood from them will not stop flowing when they are bled. Among those which it is permitted to bleed are mostly the arteries of the temples and those between the thumb and the index finger. Galen[4] instructed that they should be bled during sleep.

* *

Cupping is of great benefit and is less dangerous than phlebotomy. The cupper must be delicate, nimble and experienced in the work, for his hand must be gentle and quick in making incisions and attaching the cupping glass. The first cupping should be light and the cup quickly removed. Then it should be gradually slowed down and prolonged. The *muḥtasib* must test the cupper by asking him to make an incision in a leaf stuck to a baked brick. If the cut goes through the leaf then the cupper has a heavy hand and is not proficient. The sign of a cupper's skill is a light touch and his not hurting the patient.

[4] Galen (129-c. 199) was the last great medical writer of Greek antiquity. Ḥunayn b. Isḥāq (see Chapter 37 note 1) listed well over a hundred of his major and minor works which were translated into Arabic and/or Syriac (*Fihrist* 2:685-86). But even this list is incomplete.

* *

The learned have mentioned that cupping is bad at the beginning and end of the month. This is because at the beginning of the month the humours[5] will neither be excited nor roused, while at the end of the month they will be without vigour and cupping will be of no benefit. It is best to cup in the middle of the month when the moon is full, because the humours will be excited and the brain growing in the cranium. The best time of day for cupping is the second and third hours after daybreak.

* *

As for the benefits of cupping, these ensue firstly from cupping the hollow at the back part of the neck, which is a substitute for bleeding the medial arm vein. This is good for heaviness of the brows, itchy eyes and bad breath, although it does cause forgetfulness. As the Prophet said: "The rear part of the brain is the seat of the memory, and cupping weakens it." Cupping of the medial vein is a substitute for bleeding the vena basilica and is good for pains in the shoulder and the throat, although it does weaken the opening to the stomach. Cupping of the two occipital arteries is a substitute for bleeding the vena cephalica, and is good for the face, the teeth, the eyes, the ears, the nose, the throat and trembling of the head, although it does cause trembling of the head for those who did not have it previously. Cupping under the chin is good for the face, the teeth, the throat and for clearing the head. Cupping the crown of the head is good for dizziness and slowing down the greying of hair, although it does impair the intellect and cause imbecility. Cupping the front of the thighs is good for pain in the testicles and tumours on the thighs and legs. Cupping the back of the thighs is good for swellings and tumours erupting on the buttocks. Cupping the legs is a substitute for bleeding. It cleans the blood and induces menstruation. But God knows best.

---

[5] In ancient and mediaeval physiology, the four humours were considered to be the principle fluids of the body. They were phlegm, blood, choler and melancholy or black choler. The relative proportions of these were thought to determine a person's disposition and physical and mental qualities.

CHAPTER THIRTY-SEVEN

Physicians, Eye Doctors, Bone Setters and Surgeons

Medicine is both a theoretical and a practical science. Islamic law allows its study and practise because it maintains the health and removes illnesses and diseases from the noble frame of the body.

The physician is the one who knows about the body's anatomy, the physical constitution of the organs and the diseases which afflict them, their causes, symptoms and characteristics and the medicines which benefit them. He knows the substitutes for medicines which are not available, the manner of extracting them and the way they act, so that he can give the correct kind and dosage of medicine for the disease. It is unlawful for anyone who does not have this knowledge to treat sick people, nor is such a person allowed to embark upon any treatment in which there is a risk, or to meddle in any of the things we have mentioned which he does not fully understand.

It is related that the kings of Greece used to appoint to every city a physician famous for his wisdom. Then they would assemble all the other physicians before him so he could test them. He ordered any whose knowledge he found deficient to study and to read science and forbade them from practising. When a physician visited a sick person he asked him the cause of his illness and what pain he was feeling. Then he prescribed some medicaments and such like. After this, the physician made a note of what the patient had told him and what he had prescribed for him during the consultation, and submitted this to the patient's relatives, along with the testimony of the patient and those who were with him. On the following day, the physician returned, checked the progress of the illness and wrote another prescription according to the circumstances. He made another record of this and once again submitted it to the patient's relatives. He did likewise on the third day, the fourth day, and so on until the patient either recovered or died. If he recovered from the illness, the physician received his fee and the patient's gratuity. If, however, the patient died, his relatives went before the head physician and gave him the copies of the prescriptions which the original physician had written. If the head physician considered that they met the requirements of wisdom and the practice of medicine, without negligence or carelessness on the part of the physician, he would tell them so. But if, on the other hand, he held the contrary opinion he used to tell the relatives: "Take blood money for your relative from the physician, because he is the one who killed him with his malpractice and negligence."

In this distinguished manner, the Greek kings took precautions to such an extent that no one could practise medicine who was not a physician, and no physician could be negligent concerning any of it.

The *muḥtasib* must make them take the Hippocratic oath as he does with all physicians, make them swear not to administer harmful medicine to anyone, not to prepare poison for them, not to describe amulets to anyone from the general public, not to mention to women the medicine used for abortions and not to mention to men the medicine preventing the begetting of children. They must avert their eyes from the women's quarters when they visit their patients, and they must not disclose secrets nor lift up veils.

* *

The physician should have a complete set of medical instruments to hand. These are pincers for extracting molar teeth, cauterisering irons for the spleen, tweezers for removing blood clots, syringes used to treat cholic and for the penis, a clamp for holding haemorrhoids prior to removal, an instrument for removing excess flesh from the nostrils, a probe for fistulas, an instrument for lifting up the eyelid, a piece of lead for weighting, a key for the womb, an instrument for detecting pregnancy, a poultice for the intestines, a vessel for removing air from the chest, and other things which he needs to practise medicine, apart from the instruments of the eye-doctor and the surgeon which will be mentioned in the appropriate place.

The *muḥtasib* must examine the physicians on what Ḥunayn b. Isḥāq wrote in his well-known book *The Trial of the Physician.*[1] As for the book *The Trial of the Physician* by Galen,[2] no physician can be expected to perform what he stipulated for them in it.

Regarding the eye-doctors, the *muḥtasib* must also test them on a book by Ḥunayn b. Isḥāq, namely, *The Ten Treatises of the Eye.*[3]

* *

The *muḥtasib* must allow only those doctors to treat people's eyes whom he finds in the test know about the seven layers of the eye, the three humours, the three diseases of the eye and their ramifications, and those who are acquainted with the preparation of eye salves and the various drugs. The eye-doctor must not neglect any of the instruments of his profession, such as hooks for removing films and pellicles[4] on the eyes, a scour for removing scabs,[5] scalpels for bleeding, a container for eye salves and so on.

As for the itinerant eye-doctors, most of them cannot be trusted as they have no religion preventing them from assailing people with incisions and eye salves and have no experience of diseases and defects. No one should depend on them to treat their eyes, nor trust their ointments and salves, for some of them make salves out of a base of starch and gum and dye it different colours. They dye the red one with red chalk, the green one with turmeric and indigo, the black one with acacia and the yellow one with saffron. Some of them make salves from the horned poppy and make its base from the ben tree which they make into a paste with dissolved gum.

---

[1] Ḥunayn b. Isḥāq (808-73) was the most important mediator of ancient Greek science to the Arabs. It is largely as a result of his accurate translations of Hippocrates and Galen that the Arab physicians of the Middle Ages became worthy successors to the Greeks. He did an immense number of translations. He also composed his own books, mainly medical, having had a particular interest in ophthalmology. The book referred to in the text is mentioned by Ibn al-Qifṭī as *Kitāb Miḥnat al-Ṭabīb* (*Tarīkh al-Ḥukamā'* [Leipzig, 1903] p. 131). It is also mentioned by Ibn al-Nadīm under the title *Catechism of Medicine for Students* (*Fihrist* 2:693).

[2] Also known as *De Medici Tentione*. This book was translated by Ḥunayn b. Isḥāq (*Fihrist* 2:685).

[3] This book is mentioned by Ibn al-Nadīm as *Treatment for the Eye in Ten Sections* (*Fihrist* 2:693).

[4] A film growing from the side of the eye next to the nose on the white of the eye, and extending to the black.

[5] A certain growth resembling rust on the inner side of the eyelids.

Others make ointments out of burnt myrobalan stones and pepper. It is not possible to know fully all their frauds regarding eye salves, so the *muḥtasib* must make them swear that they will not resort to them if he is unable to stop them treating people.

* *

As for bone setters, no one may practise bone-setting until they have mastered the sixth book of the *Kunnāsh* of Paul[6] on this subject. They must also know the number of bones in the human body, which is 248, the shape of every one of them, their kinds and sizes, so that if one of them should be broken or dislocated they will be able to put it back as it was. The *muhtasib* must test them on all these things.

* *

As for the surgeons, they should be familiar with Galen's book known as *Qāṭājānus* [*Kata Genos*][7] on wounds and ointments, and the book of al-Zahrāwī on wounds.[8] They must also know human anatomy and the organs, the muscles, veins, arteries and nerves, so that the surgeon can avoid these when he opens abscesses and removes haemorrhoids.

The surgeon must have a set of scalpels with him, including some with rounded ends and some with oblique ends, lancets, a forehead hatchet, an amputating saw, an ear-piercer, a wen-cutter, a strip of cloth to wrap up ointments and a medicament made from storax which stops the flow of blood and which we have described previously.

Sometimes they deceive the people with a bone which they surreptitiously insert in a wound. Then they bring it out in front of the people and claim that it was their

---

[6] The Byzantine physician Paul of Aegina (c. 625-90) who studied in Alexandria and practised in Rome. His *Kunnāsh fī 'l-Ṭibb* (*Thesaurus on Medicine* or *De Medica Syntagma*), referred to here, was composed of seven books dealing with dietetic hygiene, general pathology, diseases of the nervous system and sense organs, leprosy, skin diseases and burns, poisons, surgery and pharmacology. The sixth book on surgery was a standard work for centuries. It is mentioned by Ibn al-Nadīm as being translated into Arabic by Ḥunayn b. Isḥāq (*Fihrist* 2:689).

[7] Also known as *De Compositione Medicamentorum Secundum Genera*. The book referred to was translated by Ḥubaysh b. al-Ḥasan al-Ā'ṣim, a student and nephew of Ḥunayn b. Isḥāq, under the title *Kitāb Tarkīb al-Adawiya* (*Tarīkh al-Ḥukamā'* p. 131).

[8] Abū'l-Qāsim Khalaf b. 'Abbās al-Zahrāwī (d. c. 1009), a Spanish surgeon born near Cordoba and credited with several books. The book referred to is his *al-Taṣrīf li man 'ajiza 'an al-Ta'līf*.

cutting medicines which extracted it. Some of them make ointments out of lime washed in oil, then dye it red with red clay, green with turmeric and indigo or black with powdered charcoal. The *'arīf* must keep an eye on them regarding all these things. But God knows best.

CHAPTER THIRTY-EIGHT

Educators of Boys

They must not teach the boys to write in the mosques, because the Prophet ordered that mosques should be kept free of boys and the insane as they scribble on the walls and soil the floor, not bothering about urine and other kinds of dirt. Rather, they should acquire teaching premises on the roads or on the outskirts of the markets.

* *

The first thing that the educators should teach the boy is the short chapters of the Qur'ān. This should be done after he is well versed in the letters of the alphabet and their vowelling. He should gradually guide the boy in these until he accustoms him to how they look. Then he ought to acquaint him with the orthodox articles of faith, the basics of arithmetic and whatever letter writing and poetry is considered appropriate, excluding the foolish and depraved varieties. In the holidays, the educator should order the boys to improve their handwriting according to a prescribed model, and ask them to write down what he has dictated to them from memory and without looking.

The educator should order any boy who is over seven years old to pray with the congregation, because the Prophet said: "Teach your children to pray when they reach seven, and when they are ten, beat them if they neglect it." The educator must also order the children to honour their parents and to obey them without hesitation, to greet them and kiss their hands when they come into their presence.

The educator should beat them when they are ill-mannered, use bad language, and do other things against Islamic law, such as playing with dice, eggs,[1] backgammon and all other kinds of gambling. He should not beat a boy with a stick so thick that it will break a bone, nor with one so thin that it will cause too much pain. Rather, the

[1] al-Maqrīzī relates that during the Fatimid period on a festival day called *Khamīs al-'Adas*, the Christians used to cook lentils (*'adas*) and made multi-coloured eggs in the market of Cairo. The slaves, riff-raff and youths would gamble with these eggs (*Khiṭaṭ* 1:266).

stick should be of middling size. The educator should use a wide strap and aim at the buttocks, the thighs and the lower part of the legs, because there is no fear of injury or harm happening to these places.

* *

The educator must not use any of the boys for his own needs and concerns nor for anything which will dishonour their parents, such as moving dung, stones and such like. Nor must he send them to his house when it is empty, lest they be open to accusations. Nor must he send a boy with a woman to write a letter or for anything else, for there is a group of godless people who deceive boys in this way.

The one who escorts the boys to and from the place of learning should be reliable, trustworthy and suited to the task, because he is in charge of them in their comings and goings, is alone with them in deserted places and comes into the presence of the women. Thus, he has to have these qualities.

The educator must not teach a woman or a female slave how to write, because this makes a woman worse, and it is said that a woman learning to write is like a snake made more venomous by being given poison to drink.

The educator must stop the boys from memorising or reading any poetry of Ibn al-Ḥajjāj,[2] and should beat them if they do. This also applies to the poetry of Ṣarī‘ al-Dilā’[3] as there is nothing good about it. The educator must similarly not acquaint them with any of the poetry composed by the Ṭalibī *Rawāfiḍ*.[4] Rather, he should teach them the poetry which eulogises the Companions[5] so that he fixes this in their hearts.

---

[2] See Chapter 8 note 1 for information on him.

[3] Abū'l-Ḥasan Muḥammad b. 'Abd al-Wāḥid (d. 1021). He was born in Basra, Iraq, and later lived in Baghdad. He is known for his eulogies, humorous and mocking verse.

[4] A general name of opprobrium for those considered to be Shi'ites.

[5] Arabic: *ṣaḥāba*. That is, those who had personal contact with the prophet Muḥammad. They are highly regarded in Sunni Islam as the traditions of Muḥammad are transmitted from them.

CHAPTER THIRTY-NINE

Ahl al-Dhimma[1]

The covenant of protection is only valid from the Imam, or from someone whom the Imam authorises. No one shall be given a covenant of protection unless he has a holy book or similar belonging to the unbelievers, such as the Jews, the Christians and the Magians. As for anyone else who does not have a holy book or similar, like the polytheists, idol worshippers, apostates from Islam or atheists and heretics, they are not permitted to have the covenant of protection nor to be confirmed in their beliefs. Nothing should be accepted from them apart from submission.

* *

The *dhimmīs* must be made to observe the conditions laid down for them in the treatise on *jizya*[2] written for them by 'Umar b. al-Khaṭṭāb, and must be made to wear the *ghiyār*.[3] If he is a Jew, he should put a red or a yellow cord on his shoulder; if a

---

[1] Literally, "people of the covenant/obligation". Also called *dhimmīs*. They were the non-Muslims living in Muslim states who were given protection, liberty, property and the right to practise their religions on condition that they formally recognised the domination of Islam. One feature of the *muḥtasib*'s responsibilities was the enforcement of those discriminatory measures which ensured the differentiation between Muslim and non-Muslim. Most of the *ḥisba* treatises deal with this. It is probable, however, that as was the case with the other functions, this one varied much according to place and time and cannot have been performed throughout the *muhtasib*'s history with the same amount of conscientiousness and zeal as the treatises would have us believe.

[2] *Jizya* was the poll tax which was occasionally levied on non-Muslims in Muslim states. This payment of a poll tax was probably the only universally applicable and essential discriminatory measure against the non-Muslim minorities. The source of the institution may be found in the Qur'ān:

> Fight against such of those to whom the Scriptures were given as believe neither in Allah nor the Last Day, who do not forbid what Allah and His Apostle have forbidden, and do not embrace the true faith, until they pay tribute out of hand and are subdued (9:27 ff.).

Traditionally, the caliph 'Umar b. al-Khaṭṭāb is credited with inaugurating this and other regulations for non-Muslim subjects. For a translation of the so-called "Covenant of 'Umar I" see A. S. Tritton, *The Caliphs and their Non-Muslim Subjects* (London, 1930). An interesting parallel with the *muḥtasib*'s collection of the *jizya* is a report concerning al-Sā'ib b. Yazīd, an *'āmil al-sūq* for 'Umar b. al-Khaṭṭāb, which quotes him as saying "I was an *'āmil al-sūq* in Medina ... we used to take the *'ushr* [tithe] from the Nabateans" (*Kitāb al-Amwāl* p. 533), thus indicating that the precursor of the *muḥtasib* also had some connection with the collection of taxes from the non-Muslim population. It is not known what this particular tax refers to, but it could perhaps be identified with the taxes which 'Umar is credited with establishing on certain trades, in this case maybe the trade in which the Nabateans were principally employed.

[3] Sometimes used as a synonym for *zunnār* and meaning "distinction", a term denoting a compulsory distinctive mark in the dress of a *dhimmī*. It is described as a "piece of cloth, a patch of stipulated

Christian, he should tie a *zunnār*[4] around his waist and hang a cross around his neck; if a woman, she should wear two slippers, one of which is white and the other black. When a protected person goes to the baths, he must wear a steel, copper or lead neckband to distinguish him from other people.

The *muḥtasib* should stop them from riding horses and carrying weapons and swords. When they ride mules, they should do so with side saddles.[5] Their buildings should not be higher than those of the Muslims nor should they preside over meetings. They should not jostle Muslims on the main roads, but should rather use the side streets. They should not be the first to give a greeting, nor be welcomed in meetings. The *muḥtasib* must stipulate that they offer hospitality to any Muslim who passes by and give him lodging in their houses and places of worship.

They must not be allowed to display any alcoholic drinks or pigs, to recite the Torah and the Bible openly, to ring the church bells, to celebrate their festivals or to hold funeral services in public. All this was stipulated by 'Umar b. al-Khaṭṭāb in his treatise, so the *muḥtasib* must keep an eye on their affairs regarding these things and force them to comply.

* *

The *muḥtasib* must take the *jizya* from them according to their social status. Thus, at the beginning of the year a poor man with a family pays one dinar, while someone of middling wealth pays two dinars and a rich man pays four dinars. When the *muḥtasib* or his agent comes to collect the *jizya*, he should stand the *dhimmī* in front

---

colour (red, blue or yellow) placed over the shoulder". Sometimes it is taken to mean the kind of dress distinction imposed on the *Ahl al-Dhimma*, and sometimes the garment itself.

[4] A distinctive girdle worn by *dhimmī*s.

[5] Whatever the situation may have been under previous regimes, there is ample evidence that at least under certain of the Fatimid caliphs such discriminatory measures were enforced. This is particularly the case during the reign of al-Ḥākim bi Amr Allah. As an example, we may quote the following account, which relates that in the year 1013:

> The Christians were ordered to wear black turbans and black *ṭaylasān*s [a shawl-like garment], to hang wooden crosses around their necks, and that their saddle stirrups should be wooden. None of them must ride a horse but rather they should ride only mules and donkeys, nor should they ride with embellished saddles and bridles, and the belts of these must be black. They should tie the *zunnār* around their waists, and not employ a Muslim,

of him, slap him on the side of his neck and say: "Pay the *jizya*, unbeliever." The *dhimmī* will take his hand out of his pocket holding the *jizya* and present it to him with humility and submission.

Along with the *jizya*, the *muḥtasib* should stipulate that they abide by the laws of Islam, for if the *dhimmī* does not do this, wages war against Muslims, fornicates with a Muslim woman or acquires her in the name of marriage, entices a Muslim away from his religion, robs a Muslim on the highway, shelters polytheists or shows them the vulnerable points of any Muslims or kills a Muslim, then his status as a protected person is annulled, he is immediately executed and his wealth is confiscated. This is because it is stipulated that the *dhimmī*s do none of this. The *muḥtasib* must be acquainted with these things and compel the *dhimmī*s to abide by all of them. But God knows best.

---

nor buy a slave girl ... The situation become harder for them and a number of Christian scribes and others embraced Islam (*Itti'āẓ* 2:93-94).

CHAPTER FORTY

The Affairs of *Ḥisba* in General and Particular

In this book we have mentioned matters of *ḥisba* over some well-known tradesmen and how to uncover some of their frauds and swindles. This is sufficient for the *muḥtasib* and provides a basis on which to judge the other things which we have not referred to. In this chapter I will mention some particulars relating to what has preceded in this book and what the *muḥtasib* must do in *ḥisba* for the welfare of the general public. Among these things are the whip, the *dirra*[1] and the *ṭurṭūr*.

As for the whip, the *muḥtasib* should choose one of middle thickness, neither too thick nor too thin and soft but rather something between the two. This is so that it does not harm the body and there is no fear of injury. As for the *dirra*, it should be made of ox or camel hide and filled with date stones. As for the *ṭurṭūr*, this should be made of felt, variegated with coloured pieces of cloth, adorned with onyx, sea-shells, bells and the tails of foxes and cats. All these instruments should be hung on the *muḥtasib*'s booth for the people to see, so that the hearts of the wicked will tremble and swindlers are restrained.

---

[1] There are many instances of the *muḥtasib* administering beatings in the Fatimid sources. It is stated, for example, that a certain Dawwās b. Ya'qūb the *muḥtasib* went into Miṣr in 1024 along with his men and helpers and summoning the carriers of wheat and the brokers "beat some of them with the *dirra* and threatened them" (*Akhbār Miṣr* p. 74). Again, a further report of the same year says that the *muḥtasib* "beat a group of bakers severely because he found their scales for *raṭl*s giving short weight and their weights with which they weigh *dirham*s made heavier" (*Akhbār Miṣr* p. 72). In the hands of cruel *muḥtasib*s this punishment could occasionally prove much harsher than it was intended to be, as in the following instance which took place in Damascus during a period of Fatimid control of Syria. In 1015, the *muḥtasib* Ibrāhīm b. 'Abd Allah died, a man noted for the energetic execution of his responsibilities. One day

> he chastised a man; and when he beat him with a *dirra* the man said "That was on the back of Abū Bakr's head." When he struck him again, he said "That was on the back of 'Umar's head." Then he struck him again and he said "That was on the back of 'Uthmān's head." Then he struck him again and the man did not know what to say. The *muḥtasib* said to him "You don't know the order of the Companions. I will teach them to you; and the best of them are the people of Badr. Let me beat you their number." So he beat him 316 *dirra* strokes. Then the man was carried away and died a few days later (*al-Nujūm al-Zāhira* 4:236).

The conclusion was that when the caliph al-Ḥākim heard about this he sent the *muḥtasib* a message thanking him and saying "Such is the reward of he who disparages the pious ancestors."

If the *muḥtasib* comes across anyone drinking alcohol he should give him forty lashes with the whip. If he thinks that public interest will be served by giving him eighty lashes, then he may do so. This is because 'Umar b. al-Khaṭṭāb gave eighty lashes to someone drinking alcohol, in accord with the formal legal opinion of 'Alī b. Abī Ṭālib.[2] The *muḥtasib* should strip off the man's clothes, lift the hand holding the whip until the white of his armpit can be seen and distribute the lashes on the man's shoulders, buttocks and thighs. If the man committed adultery while being a *bikr*,[3] the *muḥtasib* should whip him in public, as God said: "and let a party of believers witness their punishment".[4] If it is a woman, he should whip her while she is wearing her covering and clothes. As for the adulterer who has consummated a marriage, the *muḥtasib* should gather the people around him outside the town and order them to stone him, as the Prophet did with Mā'iz.[5] If it is a woman who has consummated a marriage, the *muḥtasib* should dig a hole for her in the ground, sit her in it up to her waist, and then order the people to stone her, as the Prophet did with the woman from Ghāmid.[6] If the evildoer has committed sodomy with a boy, the *muḥtasib* should throw him off the highest point in the town. This should all be done when the crimes have been proven by the Imam, after which the *muḥtasib* takes charge.

* *

As for the *ta'zīr*, this should be in proportion to the people's circumstances and commensurate with the crime. For there are some people who can be chastised verbally and reprimanded, others who should be flogged, but not severely, and yet

[2] The cousin and son-in-law of Muḥammad, and the fourth caliph in Islam (d. 660).
[3] Ibn al-Ukhuwwa defines this term as "someone who has not had sexual intercourse with a wife in legal marriage" (*Ma'ālim al-Qurba* Arabic text pp. 185-86).
[4] Qur'ān 24:24.
[5] Mā'iz b. Mālik is mentioned in a number of traditions related about the Prophet. He is reported to have admitted committing adultery, and as a result to have been stoned to death on Muḥammad's orders (see *Ṣaḥīḥ Muslim* [Lahore, 1976] 3:914-26).
[6] The woman from Ghāmid features in a tradition concerning the above Mā'iz. She is said to have approached the Prophet and to have admitted being pregnant through adultery. Muḥammad ordered her to give birth to the child and then to wean it. After this she was put in a ditch up to her waist and stoned to death (see *Ṣaḥīḥ Muslim* 3:916).

others who should be whipped with the *dirra*, made to wear the *ṭurṭūr* and to ride a camel or donkey.[7]

If the *muḥtasib* sees anyone carrying alcohol or playing a musical instrument, such as a lute, a *mi'zafa*,[8] a *ṭunbūr*,[9] a *barbaṭ*[10] or a *mizmār*,[11] he should chastise him according to the extent that public interest will be served, after pouring the alcohol away and breaking the instruments.[12] The *muḥtasib* must do likewise if he sees an unrelated man and woman consorting together, either in private or on the road.

---

[7] The *ṭurṭūr* was worn by the convicted man to add further humiliation to his public pillory. Ibn al-Ukhuwwa, commenting on the guilty man having to ride a camel or a donkey, remarks that it was common for the culprit to ride backwards on the animal (*Ma'ālim al-Qurba* p. 194). Public pillory was indeed a very common form of punishment, with or without the *dirra* and the *ṭurṭūr*. The following report, however, contains all three elements as well as others of a more bizarre nature:

> There was in Miṣr an elderly man known as al-Abzarī, and one of his habits was that if a Kharijite came out in rebellion he would dye a large *ṭurṭūr* with coloured dyes and hang different kinds of coloured rags on it. Then he would buy a monkey and teach it to whip the *ṭurṭūr* with a *dirra* which he acquired for it. If the caliph al-Ḥākim seized the Kharijite and wanted to have him publicly reviled he put him on a camel and called for al-Abzarī. Then he ordered him to put the *ṭurṭūr* on the rebel and to place the monkey behind him beating him with the *dirra*. al-Abzarī would then ride with him on the camel and shout to the right and to the left so that people would look at the spectacle (Ibn Ẓāfir, *Akhbār al-Duwal al-Munqaṭi'a* [Cairo, n.d.] p. 47).

The main elements of this story are also contained in an account by Ibn Taghrībirdī where the rebel is named as Abū Rakwa (*al-Nujūm al-Zāhira* 4:216-17). There is a similar but later account (1127) containing many of the above elements, with the addition of "torch-bearers in the guise of angels". For other examples of beatings and pillorying by the *muḥtasib* see *Akhbār Miṣr* p. 14, where he beats a group of flour merchants and bakers and pillories them, also p. 78, where in the year 1024 a *muḥtasib* of Miṣr beats a dishonest merchant and takes him around the town on a camel, also *Itti'āẓ* 1:120 where in the year 970 the Fatimid *muḥtasib* beats twenty-one millers and parades them around the town. See also *Itti'āẓ* 3:119; *al-Nujūm al-Zāhira* 5:6-7; and in Baghdad under the Abbasid caliph al-Mustanṣir see *Itti'āẓ* 2:254.

[8] A stringed instrument, probably a lyre. Accounts vary as to its actual nature.

[9] A stringed instrument played with a plectrum, like the old English bandore.

[10] A lute-like instrument.

[11] An instrument of the woodwind family. A reed pipe.

[12] The *muḥtasib* was enjoined to enforce the ruling of Islamic law concerning the censure of singing and of musical instruments (see "A Zaidi Manual" pp. 17, 19; *al-Aḥkām al-Sulṭāniyya* p. 217; *Iḥyā' 'Ulūm al-Dīn* 2:290, 296). This was similarly the case during at least part of the Fatimid period as is testified by a proclamation announcing that "singing and games are forbidden" (*Itti'āẓ* 2:87). One point of interest which the *ḥisba* treatises took up was the permissibility of the *muḥtasib*'s breaking the musical instruments which he came across. Thus, al-Mārwardī states:

> As for openly displaying forbidden musical instruments, according to the regulation it is the *muḥtasib*'s duty to break them into pieces of wood so that they no longer resemble their former shapes. He should also chastise anyone who displays them. But he should not break them if their wood is suitable for anything other than musical instruments (*al-Aḥkām al-Sulṭāniyya* p. 217).

The *muḥtasib* also had to censure the drinking of alcohol. Once again, the *ḥisba* treatises describe the pros and cons of the *muḥtasib*'s breaking the wine jars and his pouring away the offending liquor (see, for example, *al-Aḥkam al-Sulṭāniyya* pp. 216-17; *Iḥyā' 'Ulūm al-Dīn* 2:290-91).

The *muḥtasib* must inspect the places where the women gather, such as the yarn and flax market, on the banks of rivers, at the doors of the women's baths and other places. If he sees a young man alone with a woman or speaking to her about something other than a commercial transaction, and looking at her, the *muḥtasib* should chastise him and forbid him from standing there. Many wicked youths stand in these places and they have no need to except to dally with the women.

The *muḥtasib* must also inspect the preachers' gatherings. He must not let the men mix with the women and should put a screen between them. When the gathering disperses, the men should leave first and go on one road, then the women should leave and take another road. The *muḥtasib* must chastise any youth who stands in the women's road without good cause.

He must inspect the funeral ceremonies and the graveyards and if he hears any woman wailing or lamenting he should chastise and prevent her, because lamenting is unlawful. The Prophet said: "The lamenting woman and all around her are in hell."

The *muḥtasib* must stop women from visiting the graves, because the Prophet said: "May God curse women who visit graves." If a funeral procession takes to the streets the *muḥtasib* should order the women to walk behind the men and not to mix with them. He must also order them not to bare their faces and heads when they are walking behind the dead, and instruct the town crier to announce this in the town. The most important thing, however, is to prohibit women from attending the burial.

Whenever the *muḥtasib* hears of a woman who is a harlot or a singer he should call her to repent of her sin. But if she returns to it, he must chastise her and banish her from the town. He must do likewise with effeminate men and those who have no beard, well known for their perversions with other men. The *muḥtasib* should forbid an effeminate man from shaving off or plucking out his beard and from going amongst women. This also applies to anyone who could have a fine beard and yet goes without one, for when he shaves his beard off this is a sign of his depravity and the *muḥtasib* must chastise him for doing it.

* *

The *muḥtasib* should superintend the Friday prayer mosques and the ordinary mosques[13] and order the attendants to sweep and clean them of dirt every day, to shake dust off the mats, to wipe the walls down and to wash the lamps and light them every evening. He must also instruct the attendants to close the doors after every prayer and to keep the mosques free of boys, the insane and those who eat food or sleep in them, practise a trade or sell goods in them, search for strayed animals or sit talking to the people about worldly affairs in them. Islamic law states that the mosques are above such things and that they are repugnant. The *muḥtasib* must direct all those who live in the neighbourhood of a mosque diligently to pray the Friday prayer when they hear the call to it, in order to show the characteristic outward forms of the religion and the sign of Islam.

This is especially important in this time of many innovations, differing sects, various forms of the Bāṭiniyya[14] and those who have declared the destruction of Islamic law and the abolition of the norms of Islam. It is therefore the duty of every Muslim to display the basic principles of Islam and to proclaim Islamic law, in order to counter these things so that the beliefs of the people gain ascendancy.

* *

No one should call to prayer from the minaret unless they are honest, trustworthy, reliable and aware of the times of the prayers. This is because the Prophet said: "The muezzins[15] are to be relied upon and the Imams are responsible. So may God have mercy on the Imams and grant forgiveness to the muezzins."

---

[13] This responsibility to ensure the correct maintenance of the mosques and the ordering of seemly behaviour in them is a recurrent theme, found not least in the Fatimid diplomas of investiture.

[14] Bāṭiniyya was a name given in medieval times to the second largest Shi'ite sect, the Ismā'īlīs. It refers to their emphasis on the "inward" (*bāṭin*) or "inner" meaning behind sacred texts, especially the Qur'ān, to the disregard of the evident literal meaning. The term was also used to describe other thinkers who were not necessarily Ismā'īlīs but who upheld such an allegorical or symbolic interpretation.

[15] Arabic: *mu'adhdhin*, the official of the mosque who calls the faithful to prayer five times a day from the minaret. In general, the *muḥtasib* had to take care that the particular forms of Muslim worship and ritual purity were adhered to. Connected with this is a function which receives particular emphasis in the various *ḥisba* treatises, that is, the *muḥtasib*'s concern for the muezzin and the correct performance of the call to prayer. Bearing in mind the attention paid to the muezzin, it is perhaps not

The *muḥtasib* must test them on their knowledge of the times for the prayers, and forbid those who do not know from calling to prayer until they do know. This is because they may call at the wrong time and the people will hear them and perhaps pray too early, thus rendering their prayer invalid. In this case, the muezzin will have spoiled the people's prayer, so it is his duty to know the times and read the chapter on calling to prayer and the function of the prayer leader in books of Islamic law. The muezzin should preferably be a youth with a good voice.

The *muḥtasib* should prohibit wailing in the call to prayer, that is, singing and stretching out the sounds. The *muḥtasib* must also order the muezzin not to look into people's houses when he climbs up the minaret, and make him swear an oath to this effect. No one but the muezzin should climb up the minaret at the times of prayer.

The muezzin must be acquainted with the mansions of the moon[16] and the shape of the constellations in these mansions so that he knows the times of the night and the passing of the hours. There are twenty-eight mansions and these are: *al-sharaṭān*, *al-*

---

surprising that we should come across a couple of accounts of the *muḥtasib* dealing with him in the historical sources. The first account concerns a certain Abū'l-Qāsim al-Juhnī, about whom there is little information but who can be inferred from associated references to have been a *muḥtasib* during the time of the first Buwayhid amir Mu'izz al-Dawla. The account relates that Abū'l-Qāsim chastised a muezzin and made him swear on oath that he would not enter the mosque while wearing shoes that he had worn to the toilet, nor remain in the mosque or give the summons to prayer while in a state of major ritual impurity (*Nishwār al-Muḥāḍara* 2:108). This must be the same story that al-Māwardī refers to in a vague fashion. While talking about the *muḥtasib*'s duty only to chastise for what is clearly at fault, he remarks:

> He does not punish on the basis of insinuations or suspicions, as was the case in what was related about a *muḥtasib*. He asked a man who was entering the mosque with shoes: "Are you taking them into the House of His Holiness?" When the man denied that he was, the *muḥtasib* wanted to make him swear an oath to that effect. This is a stupidity from he who does it. The same applies if he suspects that a man is neglecting to cleanse himself from a major ritual impurity (*al-Aḥkam al-Sulṭāniyya* p. 214).

The second report probably also took place during the Buwayhid amirate and concerns an unnamed *muḥtasib* who had a disagreement with a muezzin. The narrator says:

> I heard some of our shaykhs telling a story about a man, a muezzin, who fell out with a *muḥtasib*. The *muḥtasib* summoned him and the muezzin said: "What is there between us that necessitates your summoning me?" The *muḥtasib* replied: "I want you to inform me of the times of the prayers. If you know them, all well and good, but if you don't then I won't allow you to call to prayer among the people on any other but the correct time." He found him unable to do that so he prohibited him from it (*Nishwār al-Muḥāḍara* 2:293).

[16] Muslim commentators differ in their identification of these mansions or houses. They are the twenty-eight divisions of the moon's path occupied by the moon on successive days. For a description of all the following terms see E. W. Lane, *Arabic-English Lexicon* (Cambridge, 1984).

buṭayn, *al-thurayya*, Aldebaran, *al-haq'a*, *al-han'a*, *al-dhirā'*, *al-nathra*, *al-ṭarf*, *al-jabha*, *al-kharatān*, *al-ṣarfa*, *al-'awwā'*, *al-simāk*, *al-ghafr*, *al-qalb*, *al-shawla*, *al-na'ā'im*, *al-balda*, *al-zubānān*, *al-iklīl*, *sa'd al-dhābiḥ*, *sa'd bula'*, *sa'd al-su'ūd*, *sa'd al-akhbiya*, *al-fargh al-muqaddam*, *al-fargh al-mu'akhkhar* and *baṭan al-ḥūt*, which is *al-rishā'*. These are all the mansions of the moon.

The dawn breaks regularly in each of these mansions for thirteen days, then it moves to the following mansion. If the muezzin knows in which mansion the dawn breaks, he only has to look to the mansion in the middle of the sky to know what is in ascendant and what descendant and how long there is between him and the dawn. In this there is both science and mathematics which would take a long time to explain. Whoever wishes to know these things should refer to the *Kitāb al-Anwā'* [*The Book of the Heavens*] by Ibn Qutayba al-Dīnawarī.[17] This book is indispensable for the muezzin so he can know about the dawn.

The muezzin may receive payment for calling to prayer. The Imams, however, may not be paid for prayers and for their function as prayer leaders, and the *muḥtasib* should forbid them from accepting payment as this is unlawful. If, on the other hand, something is presented to the Imam without any preconditions, he may accept it as a donation or a charitable gift.

The *muḥtasib* must instruct the Qur'ān reciters to recite it in the proper manner, as God ordered, and forbid them from making it musical and reciting it in a singing voice used for songs and poems. Islamic law has forbidden this.

The reciters should not attend a funeral service without the next of kin sending for them. If they are given anything freely by way of a gift without preconditions they may accept it, but if there are obligations attached they may not. The *muḥtasib* should keep an eye on them regarding this.

No one should wash corpses unless they are trustworthy and honourable, have read about funeral rites in Islamic law and are acquainted with the relevant ordinances.

---

[17] One of the great polygraphs of Islam (828-89). The book referred to is a treatise on practical astronomy and meteorology. It is still extant.

The *muḥtasib* must question them on these matters and whoever knows should be allowed to remain, but whoever does not know should be sent away to learn.

The *muḥtasib* must forbid the blind and the beggars who attract people around them from reciting the Qur'ān in the markets in order to beg, for Islamic law has prohibited this. He must also stop them reciting the poetry which the *Rawāfiḍ* have composed about the Ṭālibīs[18] and from speaking about the death[19] and such like, because all this incites the general public and it is therefore wrong to do it.

* *

The *muḥtasib* must frequent the sessions of the judges and arbiters and forbid them from sitting in the Friday prayer mosques and ordinary mosques to judge between the people.[20] This is because a man in a state of ritual impurity, a menstruating woman, a *dhimmī*, a young boy, a madman, someone barefooted or not careful about dirt and who thus sullies the mosque and soils the mats sometimes appear before the judges. When there is a crowd of people and they contest the opposing parties, voices are sometimes raised and it becomes very noisy. Islamic law has said that all these things are prohibited.

I saw something written in the treatise by Abū al-Qāsim al-Ṣaymarī[21] saying that the caliph al-Mustaẓhir billah,[22] the Commander of the Faithful, appointed one of al-Shāfi'ī's followers to the *ḥisba* in Baghdad. The man stopped at the mosque of al-Manṣūr and found the chief judge judging between the people in it. He said to the judge: "Greetings. God said: '[He will assuredly help] those who, if We establish them in the land, will establish prayer, give alms and order good and forbid evil. With God rests the end of all affairs.'[23] And God has given His caliph al-Mustaẓhir

[18] 'Alī b. Abī Ṭālib and his descendants who are revered by the Shi'ites.
[19] This is a reference to the tragic death of al-Ḥusayn, the second son of 'Alī b. Abī Ṭālib. He is considered by the Shi'ites to be one of their Imams. His martyrdom had, and continues to have, a profound effect on Shi'ite consciousness. This is shared to some extent by the Sunnis.
[20] Despite this injunction, the traditional place where the judge's courts were held was in the mosque. This was also the case regarding the Fatimid *muḥtasib*, who also held his tribunals in one or other of the two great mosques of the Egyptian capital, either that of Ibn Ṭūlūn or that of 'Amr b. al-'Āṣ (*Khiṭaṭ* 2:463; *Ṣubḥ al-A'shā* 3:487).
[21] Unidentified.
[22] The Abbasid caliph Abū'l-'Abbās Aḥmad al-Muqtadir (r. 1094-1118).
[23] Qur'ān 22:41.

billah, the Commander of the Faithful, power on the Earth and he has stretched out his hand with the ordering of good and the forbidding of evil. He has made us his representatives in this, carrying out the ordinances of God with regard to his subjects. Whoever violates the ordinances of God wrongs himself. It is most important for us to act according to His divine statutes, adhere to what God ordered and avoid what He forbade so that the people follow our example. We are the salt of the town. We restore the people's affairs when they become corrupted, but if the salt becomes corrupted, who will restore it? This session of yours is not appropriate in the mosque. Haven't you heard the words of God: '[His light is found] in temples which God has permitted to be raised for the celebration of His name in them. In them He is glorified, in the mornings and in the evenings, by men whom neither trade nor profit can divert from the remembrance of God, nor from prayer or alms.'[24] But there is nothing of this in what you are doing. Here, a woman comes in to you with her husband for you to pass judgement, and she has her baby with her that urinates on the mats. Then a man who has been walking in the dirt and filth steps on the mats with his shoes. The voices are raised in a clamour outside your circle, and sometimes a man in a state of major ritual impurity or a menstruating woman comes to see you. Our Prophet ordered that all these things should be avoided. So hold your sessions in the middle of the town so that it isn't difficult for someone to see you. And let that be an end to it!"

al-Ṣaymarī said: "So the judge immediately rose and never again sat in judgement in the mosque."

Whenever the *muḥtasib* sees a man acting insolently in a court session, contesting the judge's verdict or not complying with the judgement, he should chastise him for it. As for if he sees the judge furious with a man, cursing or exasperated with him, the *muḥtasib* should prevent him from it, admonish and put the fear of God in him. For the judge may not pass judgement while he is angry, nor use obscene language, nor be uncivil and coarse. The judge's assistants and helpers should be likewise. If there is a handsome youth among them, the judge should not send him to bring the

[24] Qur'ān 24:36.

women. The judge should hold his sessions in the middle of the town so that it is not difficult for the people to appear before him.

* *

As for the representatives who appear before the judge, there is no good in them nor do the people benefit from them at the present time. This is because most of them have little religion. They take money from the opposing parties and hold on to it for some legal reason. They obstruct the litigation, and justice is therefore lost and slips from the hands of the one who seeks it and has a right to it. If two opposing parties appear in person before the judge the truth quickly comes to light from what they say without them needing representatives. It is as if not having representatives at the present time is preferable to appointing them, except in the case of a minor or a woman who does not appear in public. In this situation, the judge should appoint representatives for them.

* *

The *muḥtasib* must visit the audiences of the governors and princes, order them to do good and forbid them from evil and admonish and remind them. He should order them to be compassionate and charitable with their subjects, and he should remind them of what the traditions of the Prophet have to say on this subject. When the *muḥtasib* admonishes them and prevents them from being unjust he should be courteous and polite, softly spoken and amiable, not overbearing and stern. God said to His Prophet: "If you were severe or harsh-hearted, they would have broken away from you."[25] Indeed, the story about al-Ma'mūn has already been related at the beginning of the book.

* *

The *muḥtasib* is fully aware of the particulars of *ḥisba* over all that resembles the above-mentioned tradesmen and the well-known crafts in this book of mine, and he

[25] Qur'ān 3:159.

knows how to uncover their swindles. This is easy to know by inspection and seeing with one's own eyes, such as *ḥisba* over the greengrocers and sellers of vegetables. The *muḥtasib* should order them to sell their produce washed of manure and free of grass and weeds. He should also instruct them to cut the roots off lettuce and radishes. He should forbid them from washing fresh onions and garlic because the water increases their pungency and offensive smell. If any vegetables remain overnight in their shops, they must not mix them with the fresh ones picked during the day. The *muḥtasib* should forbid them from selling any melon, cucumber or fresh figs which are worm-eaten and anything which is so over-ripe that its skin has split.

The *muḥtasib* must prohibit such as the sellers of pulses from selling beans and chick-peas which are worm-eaten and from mixing those they have left over from the previous day with those they have freshly boiled. He should order them to sprinkle ground salt and wild thyme over the pulses so as to make them harmless. The *muḥtasib* must also check their measures, for they take a piece of wood which is a span long, for example, and hollow out a measure from it only four fingers deep. The people are then deceived by the wood's size and length, not realising how much has been hollowed out. This is a fraud which cannot be concealed.

Similarly, the sellers of earthenware, small clay jugs and vessels, for they plaster those that have a hole or are cracked with lime made into a paste with fat, the white of eggs and ground red earthenware.

The *muḥtasib* must also forbid the washermen from washing people's clothes in water in which alkali, lime or natron[26] have been boiled, for these harm the clothes, make them wear out quickly and encourage lice and nits in them.

There are also the water carriers, owners of leather water bags and waterskins. The *muḥtasib* should order these to wade into the river until they are far from the bank and the dirty places. They must not draw water from somewhere on the river near an animal watering place, nor from a public drinking place or the outlet of a bath.

[26] A mineral consisting of hydrated sodium carbonate.

Rather, they should go upstream or a long way downstream. If one of them acquires a new water bag, the *muḥtasib* must instruct him to use it for a few days to carry water to the places where building clay is being made. He must not sell the water for drinking, because it will taste and smell unpleasant due to the effects of tanning and pitch. Once the unpleasantness has gone, however, the *muḥtasib* will give him permission to sell the water to people for drinking and general use.

The *muḥtasib* must order the water carriers to tie bells or clappers of iron or brass around the necks of their animals so that they make a noise when they pass through the market or a quarter, and thus blind people, children and the inattentive will be put on their guard. This also applies to donkey-drivers and those who carry firewood on their animals. The *muḥtasib* should compel them to do this because it is in the public interest. They must not burden their animals with more than they can bear, drive them too fiercely when they are carrying loads, beat them too severely nor leave them standing in a courtyard with their loads on their backs. For the immaculate Islamic law has forbidden all these things. It is also their duty to fear God regarding the feeding and foddering of the animals; they should be given enough food to satiate them, not a trifling or negligible amount.

If I began to mention everything that the *muḥtasib* must do concerning the affairs of *ḥisba* there would be no end to this book. But I have set down the basic rules and principles from which the *muḥtasib* can draw analogies in similar situations. Indeed, the regulator of the affairs of *ḥisba* is the immaculate Islamic law, for all that Islamic law forbids is prohibited and the *muḥtasib* must put a stop to it and prevent it happening, and all that Islamic law permits the *muḥtasib* must maintain as it is. For this reason, we mentioned in the first part of the book that the *muḥtasib* should be a *faqīh* knowing the rules of Islamic law. When the *muḥtasib* is ignorant he becomes confused and falls into what is forbidden and what he should guard against.

We ask God for help, protection and success. He is our Sufficiency and the Best Disposer of Affairs.

Appendices

APPENDIX I

al-Ghazālī on *Ḥisba*

The following is a translated abridgement of al-Ghazālī's treatise entitled *al-Amr bi'l-Ma'rūf wa'l-Nahī 'an al-Munkar* (*The Ordering of Good and the Forbidding of Evil*). Abū Ḥāmid al-Ghazālī (1058-1111) is generally considered by both Muslim and western scholars to be the greatest and most influential figure in Islamic religious thought. The work from which the present translation is taken is his *Iḥyā' 'Ulūm al-Dīn* (*The Revival of the Religious Sciences*. Cairo, n.d. vols. 5-8 pp. 1186-1275) which is thought to be al-Ghazālī's greatest work. In the *Iḥyā'* al-Ghazālī describes his notions of what it is to be a good Muslim and how the latter should live his life.

Some liberties have been taken regarding the ordering of the text so as to make al-Ghazālī's exposition and arguments more systematic and accessible to the modern reader.

**

The Ordering of Good and the Forbidding of Evil

In the Name of God the Compassionate the Merciful

Praise be to God without praise of Whom books cannot commence, and without the mediation of Whose magnanimity and assistance favours are not granted. And blessings upon the foremost of the prophets, Muḥammad the Prophet and servant of God, and upon his noble family and the virtuous Companions who came after him.

The ordering of good and the forbidding of evil is the hub of religion. It is the momentous concern with which God sent all the prophets. If it came to an end and its learning and practices were forgotten, then prophethood would cease, religion would vanish, civil strife would prevail, transgression would spread, ignorance would proliferate, corruption would become commonplace, folly would stretch far and wide, countries would be destroyed and the servants of God would be doomed and not know of this until the Day of Resurrection.

If this were to happen (God forbid that it should), if the learning and practices of *ḥisba* were obliterated and its truth and characteristics totally destroyed, people would be consumed with adulation of physical things, lose all fear of the Creator and abandon themselves to their cravings and carnal appetites as do the animals. On the surface of the Earth there would scarcely be found a true believer who is beyond reproach. Whoever strove to reinstate the signs of religion and to remedy these defects, either commissioned to do so or taking it upon himself, who restored the forgotten norms, endorsed what they prescribe and worked assiduously to revive them, such a person would be the one among the people to revive the Sunna which had been destroyed with the passage of time.

Now we will explain this subject in four sections. These are

1 The Necessity and Merit of Ordering Good and Forbidding Evil
2 The Basic Elements and Conditions of *Ḥisba*
3 Common Objectionable Practices
4 Ordering Princes and Sultans to do Good and Forbidding them from Evil.

**

The Necessity and Merit of Ordering Good and Forbidding Evil and Censure for Disregarding and Neglecting it

Aside from the general agreement of the community concerning them and what those of sound intellect inform us, these matters are demonstrated by the Qur'ānic verses and by the traditions.

As for the Qur'ānic verses, God said: "Let there be from among you a group of people calling for what is right, ordering good and forbidding evil. They are the ones who will prosper."[1] In this verse there is a statement of obligation, for the Almighty's words "Let there be ..." is an order and this obviously entails an obligation. This verse also contains a statement that prosperity is not granted unconditionally but is restricted to certain people: He said "They are the ones who will prosper". There is also a statement that it is a collective duty and not an individual one, that is, when a community ensures that someone undertakes it then not everyone has to do so. He did not say "You must all order what is good", but rather "Let there be from among you a group". Thus, whenever one person or a number of people undertake it, the others are not obliged to do so, and the prosperity is afforded to those who carry it out directly. If all the people refrain from performing it, then the responsibility to do so inevitably falls upon everyone who is able to do so.

God said: "They are not all the same. From the People of the Book there are some who are righteous. They recite the verses of God throughout the night and they prostrate themselves to Him. They believe in God and the Last Day. They order what is good and forbid what is evil and hasten to do good deeds. They are among the virtuous."[2] Here, God did not say they are virtuous simply because of their faith in Him and the Last Day, but also because they order good and forbid evil.

God said: "The believers, both men and women, protect each other. They order what is good and forbid what is evil and observe the prayers."[3] Here, God characterised believers as those who order good and forbid evil, and whoever does not do this is therefore dissociated from the believers described in this verse.

God said: "Curses were pronounced by David and Jesus the son of Mary on those people of Israel who abandoned their faith. This is because they disobeyed and continued in their excesses. They did not forbid each other from the evil which they committed. It was indeed evil that they did."[4] In this there is the greatest confirmation, since God stated that the people of Israel deserved to be cursed due to

[1] Qur'ān 3:104.
[2] Qur'ān 3:113-14.
[3] Qur'ān 9:71.
[4] Qur'ān 5:81-82.

the fact that they did not forbid evil. God said: "You are the best community which has arisen for mankind. You order what is good and forbid what is evil."[5] This verse is proof of the merit of ordering good and forbidding evil, since God made it clear that because they did this they were the best community.

God said: "When they forgot the warnings they had been given, We saved those who forbade evil, but We gave those who did wrong a terrible punishment because they were sinners."[6] Here, God makes it clear that they were saved because they forbade what was evil. The verse also proves the necessity of doing this.

As for the traditions, the Prophet said: "O people, God says that you must order good and forbid evil before you appeal to Him, otherwise you will receive no response."

The Prophet said: "Take care not to sit by the roadside." "We must do this," they replied, "it is where we gather to talk." He said: "If you must do this, do what is proper on the roads". "And what is it proper to do on the roads?" they asked. He said: "To avert one's eyes, to give no offence, to reply to a greeting, and to order good and forbid evil."

The Prophet said: "Whatever a man says is to his debit and not his credit, except for an order to do good or a forbidding to do evil or an invocation of God's name." He also said: "God does not punish the individual for the sins of his fellows unless they do what is objectionable and he is able to prevent this but does not."

Abū Amāma al-Bāhilī related that the Prophet said: "What would you do if your women were disobedient, your youth dissolute and you no longer strove in the way of God?" They asked: "Will this happen?" "Yes," he replied, "by the One in Whose hands is my soul. And worse is yet to come." They asked: "And what is worse than this?" He replied: "What would you do if you did not order what is good and forbid what is evil?" They asked: "Will this happen?" The Prophet replied: "Yes, by the One in Whose hands is my soul. And worse is yet to come." They asked: "And what

---

[5] Qur'ān 3:110.
[6] Qur'ān 7:165.

is worse than this?" He replied: "What would you do if you saw good as evil and evil as good?". They asked: "Will this happen?" "Yes" he replied, "By the One in Whose hands is my soul. And worse is yet to come". They asked: "And what is worse than this?" He replied: "What would you do if you ordered what is evil and forbade what is good?" They asked: "Will this happen?" "Yes," he replied, "by the One in Whose hands is my soul. And worse is yet to come. God says through me that He has sworn to bring a trial upon you in which the forbearing will become dismayed."

'Akrama related on the authority of Ibn 'Abbās that the Prophet said: "Do not be with a man who kills unjustly, for whoever is in his presence and does not prevent him is cursed. And do not be with a man who beats unjustly, for whoever is in his presence and does not prevent him is cursed." This tradition indicates that you should not enter into places where there is injustice and sinfulness, nor be present in situations in which there is evil if you cannot prevent it. For the Prophet has said that a curse will fall upon he who is present and that a man may not witness what is evil without having to excuse himself by saying that he is incapable of doing anything about it. For this reason, a group of our ancestors chose to isolate themselves because they were unable to prevent the evils they witnessed in the markets, during the religious festivals and in the mosques.

Regarding this, 'Umar b. 'Abd al-'Azīz said that people should not depart and abandon their homes and children except in bad times like these, when they see that evil has triumphed and that good has been vanquished, when they see that whoever speaks out is ignored, when they see dissensions from which they are not safe and that a punishment will befall the sinful from which they themselves will not escape. For they consider that associating with beasts of prey and eating whatever grows is preferable to associating with those people with all their comforts.

Ibn Mas'ūd related that the people in a village were acting sinfully, and among them were four men who were censuring what they were doing. One of these told them that they were doing such and such, and began to forbid them from it and to inform them of the shamefulness of their actions. But they started to argue with him and would not stop what they were doing. He cursed them, and they cursed him. He fought against them, but they got the better of him. So he withdrew from them, saying: "I have cursed them but they cursed me. I have fought against them but they have got the better of me." Then he departed. After this, the second man came and forbade them, but they did not obey him. So he cursed them, and they cursed him. Then he withdrew, saying: "By God, I have forbidden them, but they would not obey me, and if I had fought against them they would have got the better of me." Then he departed. After this, the third man came and forbade them but they would not obey him. So he withdrew, saying: "By God, I have forbidden them but they would not obey me. If I had cursed them they would have cursed me, and if I had fought against them they would have got the better of me." Then he departed. After this, the fourth man came and said: "By God, if I had forbidden them they would have resisted me, if I had cursed them they would have cursed me and if I had fought against them they would have got the better of me." Then he departed.

Regarding this, Ibn Mas'ūd said that the fourth man has the lowest standing of them all, and that among you there are few like him.

Abū 'Ubayda b. al-Jarrāḥ related that he asked: "O Prophet, who among the martyrs is more precious to God?" The Prophet replied: "The man who goes to a tyrannical ruler and orders him to do good and forbids him from evil and is killed for this. And if the ruler does not kill him, then no sin will be recorded against him no matter how long he might live."

From these proof texts it is evident that ordering good and forbidding evil is a duty, and that no capable person is absolved from this except when someone else performs it.

Let us now state the conditions and procedures of *ḥisba*.

**

The Basic Elements and Conditions of *Ḥisba*

Know that there are four basic elements of *ḥisba* - a term which comprehensively covers the ordering of good and the forbidding of evil. These are: (1) the *muḥtasib*; (2) the jurisdiction of *ḥisba*; (3) the one taken to account by the *muḥtasib*; and (4) the nature of *ḥisba*. These are the four basic elements and they each have their particular conditions.

1 The First Basic Element: The *Muḥtasib*

At this point, al-Ghazālī remarks that there are four conditions which have been laid down for the muḥtasib. These are (a) the muḥtasib must be a faithful Muslim; (b) the muḥtasib must not be a sinner; (c) the muḥtasib must be capable of acting; and (d) the muḥtasib must be commissioned by the ruler. al-Ghazālī does not always agree with these and in places offers arguments to the contrary.

(a) As for the first condition, that is, that the *muḥtasib* be a faithful Muslim, the reason for this stipulation is obvious. It is because faith is the basis of religion. How can someone be religious who rejects this fundamental principle of religion?

(b) As for the second condition, that is, moral probity, a number of people have considered this. They have said that a sinner cannot be a *muḥtasib*, and in this they are guided by the disapproval levelled against the man who orders what he himself does not do. God said: "Do you order people to be righteous and yet forget yourselves?"[7] and "It is loathsome to God that you say what you do not do."[8] There is also what was related about the Prophet, that he said: "While on *al-isrā'*[9] I came across some people whose lips were being cut off with scissors of fire. 'Who are you?' I asked. 'We used to order what was good but not do it ourselves,' they replied, 'and forbid what was evil, but do it.'" There is also what was related of God, that He revealed to Jesus that he should preach to himself, and only after this

[7] Qur'ān 2:44.
[8] Qur'ān 6:13.
[9] Muḥammad's night journey (*isrā'*) to Jerusalem, followed by his ascension to Paradise in one night. Under the guidance of Gabriel he is said to have talked with previous prophets and to have seen God.

should he preach to the people. If not, then he should be ashamed before God.

Or perhaps these people are guided by means of analogy with the maxim that guiding someone is dependent upon first guiding oneself, just as correcting someone is dependent upon first correcting oneself. For how can the unrighteous correct others?

All that these people have stated is a fantasy, for the truth is that a sinner may be a *muḥtasib*. The proof of this is seen when we ask: is it a condition of the *muḥtasib* that he should be utterly sinless? If this is a condition, then it is contrary to the consensus of opinion and renders the practice of *ḥisba* impossible. The Companions of the Prophet were not sinless, let alone the other people, and the prophets differed in the degree of their infallibility. The Qur'ān demonstrates the sins committed by Adam and by some prophets. For this reason, Sa'īd b. Jubayr said: "If the only person permitted to order good and forbid evil must be unimpeachable, then nobody will have the right to do it."

These people have claimed, however, that this condition does not relate to minor sins, so that someone who wears silk may prohibit adultery and the drinking of alcohol.

Thus, we ask them: may someone who drinks alcohol wage war against the unbelievers and act as a *muḥtasib* regarding them, prohibiting them from unbelief? If they answer no, they are going against the consensus of opinion, since among Muslim soldiers there are still both the pious and the profligate, the drinker of alcohol and those who oppress orphans, and they were never forbidden to wage war, neither in the period of the Prophet nor subsequently. If they answer yes, then we ask whether the drinker of alcohol may prohibit murder or not. If they answer no, we would ask what the difference is between this man and someone who wears silk since the latter is permitted to prohibit the drinking of alcohol, and murder is a much greater sin than this. There is no difference between drinking alcohol and wearing silk. But if they answer yes, and they make distinctions in that someone who commits an offence may not prohibit its like nor what is less serious, but may only prohibit what is more serious, then this is an arbitrary judgement. For since it is possible for the drinker of alcohol to prohibit adultery and murder, how can it be impossible for the adulterer to prohibit drinking alcohol? Indeed, how can it be impossible that someone should drink and yet prohibit his servants from drinking, saying that he is obliged to put a stop to it and forbid it? Because a man disobeys God in one matter must he then be forced to disobey Him in another? And if he is obliged to forbid, then how can this obligation be annulled because of what he himself does? It is absurd to say that he is obliged to forbid drinking alcohol as long as he does not drink, and that if he drinks then he should not do this.

We hold, however, that when a man knows that what he says regarding *ḥisba* will not be accepted because of the people's knowledge of his sinfulness, then he is not obliged to perform *ḥisba* by appealing to people's consciences. There is no use in him doing this as his sinfulness militates against his words being beneficial. When there is no use in his saying anything then he is not obliged to do so.

Some claim that a *dhimmī* may act as a *muḥtasib* over a Muslim if he sees him committing fornication because he is entitled to tell the Muslim not to fornicate. They say it is inconceivable that it is unlawful for him to do this; indeed it must be permissible or even obligatory.

Regarding this, we say that if an unbeliever actively prohibits a Muslim then he has gained control over him, and this is not permitted. God has not given the unbelievers mastery over the believers. As for him merely telling a Muslim not to fornicate, this is still unlawful, not because the unbeliever has forbidden a Muslim from fornication, but rather because it shows the audacity of judging a Muslim. In this there is humiliation for the one judged, and while the sinner deserves humiliation, this should not come from an unbeliever who deserves more to be humiliated than a Muslim.

(c) The third condition is that the *muḥtasib* should be capable of acting. It is obvious that anyone who is unable to remedy matters cannot undertake *ḥisba* except in his heart. Everyone who loves God hates sins and disapproves of them. Ibn

Mas'ūd said: "Fight the unbelievers with your hands, but if you are only able to look gravely in their faces, then do this."

(d) As for the fourth condition, that is, that the *muḥtasib* should be commissioned, the reason for this is obvious. For the one who is not commissioned is not obliged to do anything. What we mean is that this condition entails the necessity of performing the duties.[10] As for the possibility and permissibility of acting, this only necessitates that the *muḥtasib* be of sound intellect, even a discerning adolescent.

If the *muḥtasib* is not commissioned, however, he may still forbid evil. He may, for example, pour away alcoholic drinks and break musical instruments. When he does this, he thereby gains God's reward. No one may prevent him from this merely because he has not been commissioned. For these things are righteous deeds which bring one closer to God and he is entitled to do them, just like prayer, holding the office of prayer leader and other godly acts. His authority is not that of a sovereign power such that he must be commissioned. This is why we state that a slave and an ordinary person may undertake *ḥisba*.

In prohibiting by one's actions and in preventing what is objectionable there is indeed a kind of sovereign power and authority. But this is acquired merely through

---

[10] al-Māwardī states that there are nine differences between the Muslim who voluntarily undertakes the duties of *ḥisba* and the mandated *muḥtasib*:

"(1) The duty is incumbent on the *muḥtasib* due to his being mandated by the sovereign power, and his performance of this duty is considered sufficient to exempt others from it; (2) the *muḥtasib*'s undertaking his duty is one of the responsibilities of his office and he may not neglect it. The Muslim who voluntarily undertakes *ḥisba* does so as an act of supererogation which may be neglected in favour of something else; (3) the *muḥtasib* is authorised to ask for assistance in forbidding that which must be forbidden, whereas the volunteer is not authorised to do this; (4) the *muḥtasib* must respond to whoever requests his aid, whereas the volunteer need not; (5) the *muḥtasib* must seek out what is patently wrong so as to forbid it, and must search for any neglect of the good so as to order that it should be adhered to. But the volunteer does not have to seek out or search for such things; (6) in the pursuance of the duties to which he is appointed and commissioned, the *muḥtasib* may employ helpers thus making him more authoritative. But the volunteer may not deputise helpers for this purpose; (7) the *muḥtasib* may chastise for obvious wrongs which do not merit the punishments prescribed within Islamic law, but the volunteer may not chastise for any wrongdoing; (8) the *muḥtasib* may be remunerated from the public treasury for his performance of *ḥisba*, whereas the volunteer may not; (9) the *muḥtasib* may exercise his own independent judgement in that which concerns practice sanctioned by custom but not in that which concerns Islamic law. Customary practice involves such things as benches and extensions to buildings within the markets. He may approve or disapprove of such things according to his own reasoning, but the volunteer may not do this. These nine points show the differences between the one who holds the office of *ḥisba* and the

faith, like the authority to kill the polytheist, to remove his means of subsistence and to strip him of his weapons. A youth may do this when it is not dangerous, for preventing unbelief is like preventing sinfulness.

As for the *muḥtasib* being commissioned by the ruler or the governor, a number of people have laid down this condition and have not acknowledged that the ordinary citizen may act as *muḥtasib*. This stipulation is wrong since the verses and traditions we have quoted demonstrate that anyone who witnesses a forbidden practice is obliged to prevent it whenever and in whatever circumstances they come across it. To hold it as a strict condition that the *muḥtasib* be commissioned by the ruler is an arbitrary and groundless judgement.

The strange thing is that the Shi'ites have gone to extremes in this, and have stated that it is not permitted to order good until the infallible Imam appears, their Imam of Truth. These people are of too little standing to say anything. Indeed, the reply to them is to remark that if they went to the judiciary demanding their rights concerning blood revenge or their possessions, then they would prevail by an order to do good and gain their rights from those who treated them unjustly by forbidding what is evil. Demanding their rights is part of ordering good. But this is not the time to forbid injustice and demand one's rights because the Imam of Truth is still thought not to have appeared!

It is said that in ordering good there is a demonstration of sovereign power, legal authority and control over those who are judged, and for this reason the unbeliever may not act over the Muslim even though he is right. Thus, ordinary citizens must not act as *muḥtasib* unless they have the authorisation of the governor or the ruler.

To this, we say that as far as the unbeliever is concerned, it is indeed unlawful because of the sovereign power and authority entailed. The unbeliever is contemptible and thus has no right to have the power to pass judgement on a Muslim. As for the ordinary Muslim, he has a right to this power because of his religion and knowledge and the authority which results from this. Passing judgement

---

one who undertakes this voluntarily, even though the latter may order good and forbid evil" (*al-Aḥkam al-Sulṭāniyya* p. 207).

does not necessitate being commissioned to do so, just as the authority entailed in teaching and giving instruction does not. There is no disagreement regarding the fact that instructing as to what is unlawful and enjoining the ignorant person who in his ignorance does evil do not require any permission from the ruler even though these contain the force of directives and the one instructed has the ignominy of being called a fool. All that is required here is to be a pious Muslim, and the same applies to forbidding evil.

Here, al-Ghazālī discerns five methods of prevention open to the muḥtasib in the performance of his duties, and in what follows relates these to his premise that the muḥtasib need not be commissioned by the ruler.

Ḥisba has five stages:

The first is instruction.

The second is gentle exhortation.

The third is cursing and rebuke, and by cursing is not meant obscene language, but rather to say "You fool. You idiot. Have you no fear of God?" and such like.

The fourth is prevention by direct force, such as breaking musical instruments, pouring away alcohol, seizing silk clothes from those who wear them, and taking away clothes which have been stolen and returning them to their rightful owner.

The fifth is intimidation and the threat of a beating, and actually administering this so that the person stops what he is doing, such as the person who persists in calumny and slander. That is, if it is impossible to stop a man's tongue by other means, he may be persuaded to keep quiet with a beating. This might result in both sides seeking assistance and conscripting helpers, and may entail a fight.

It is clear that, aside from the last stage, the other stages do not require the ruler's permission. The last stage has some particular aspects which will be dealt with subsequently.

Regarding instruction and exhortation, how can these require the permission of the ruler? As for calling someone a fool and an idiot and saying that they have no fear of God and such like, this is true and it is necessary to speak the truth. Indeed, the best stage of *ḥisba* is a word of truth to a tyrannical ruler, as was stated in a tradition. Thus, if it is allowed to give judgement against a ruler and express disapproval, then how can his permission be required? This also applies to breaking musical instruments and pouring away alcohol, as these things are done in the knowledge that they are correct without having to resort to any personal judgement. They therefore do not require the permission of the ruler.

The practices of our ancestors regarding *ḥisba* over rulers were undertaken on the basis of the general agreement that specific authorisation to do so was unnecessary. If the ruler approved of whoever was ordering good, then this was fine, but if the ruler disapproved of him, this disapproval was an evil which had to be forbidden. So how can it be necessary to seek the ruler's permission to censure him?

Proof of this can be seen in the way our ancestors used to censure the rulers. For example, it is related that the caliph Marwān b. al-Ḥakam delivered a sermon before the prayer during one of the religious festivals. A man correctly told him that the sermon should come after the prayer, but Marwān ordered him to hold his tongue. Regarding this, Abū Sa'īd said that the man had done his duty, for the Prophet said: "Whoever among you comes across an evil, he should forbid it with his hand, and if he cannot do this then with his tongue, and if he cannot do this then with his heart. This is the least part of faith." From these general principles they understood that the rulers were subject to *ḥisba*, so how can their permission be required?

It is related that when the caliph al-Mahdī went to Mecca he stayed there for some time. When he started his circumambulations he pushed the people away from the Ka'ba, so 'Abd Allah b. Marzūq sprang forward, grabbed him by his robe and shook him. "What do you think you're doing?" 'Abd Allah said. "What gives you more right to the Ka'ba than those who have come from far away, so that when they get here you stop them reaching it? God has said '[... and the sacred mosque which We have made available to all men] whether they live there or come from the country.'[11] So what gives you more right?" al-Mahdī looked into the man's face and recognised him as one of his clients [*mawālī*]. "'Abd Allah b. Marzūq?" asked al-Mahdī. "Yes," he replied. al-Mahdī took him to Baghdad but did not want to punish him openly as the people would condemn him for it. So he put him in the stable to tend the animals and he was given an aggressive and ill-tempered horse to look after in the hope that it would injure him. But God calmed the horse down. Then they took him to a house and locked him in, al-Mahdī keeping the key. Three days later 'Abd Allah had escaped into the garden and was eating vegetables. al-Mahdī was informed of this. "Who let you out?" he asked. "The One who imprisoned me," replied 'Abd Allah. So al-Mahdī started to yell and shouted: "Aren't you afraid that I'll have you killed?" But 'Abd Allah looked him in the eyes and laughed, saying: "As if you had power over life and death!" He remained in prison until al-Mahdī died. Then they set him free and he returned to Mecca. He had vowed to himself that if God released him from their hands he would sacrifice a hundred camels, and he did not stop until he had done so.

It is related on the authority of Ḥibān b. 'Abd Allah, who said that the caliph Hārūn al-Rashīd was taking a walk in Dawīn with a man from the Banū Hāshim called Sulaymān b. Abī Ja'far. Hārūn said to him: "You have a slave girl who sings very well. Bring her to me." So she came and sang, but the caliph didn't enjoy her singing. "What's wrong with you?" he asked. "This isn't my lute," she replied. So Hārūn told a servant to go and bring her lute. As the servant was returning with the lute he came across an old man collecting date stones in the road. "Make way old man," said the servant. The old man raised his head and seeing the lute took it from the servant and smashed it on the ground. The servant grabbed him and took him to the chief of the quarter, saying: "Guard this man because the Commander of the Faithful wants to see him." The chief of the quarter replied: "There isn't a more venerable man in Baghdad, so how can he be wanted by the Commander of the Faithful?" "Just do as I say," the servant said. Then he entered into Hārūn's presence. "I came across an old man picking up date stones," he said, "and told him to make way. But he raised his head and seeing the lute broke it on the ground." At

[11] Qur'ān 22:25.

this, Hārūn fumed with rage. Sulaymān b. Abī Ja'far asked him: "Why are you so angry Commander of the Faithful? Send instructions to the chief of the quarter to have the man beheaded and thrown into the Tigris." "No," said Hārūn, "I will send for him and confront him first." So the messenger went and told the man that he had to go to the Commander of the Faithful. He asked him whether he would ride, but the old man refused, and thus walked until he stood before the gates of the palace. When Hārūn was informed that he had arrived, he asked his courtiers: "Can you see any forbidden thing in this room that we should remove before the old man enters? If so, should we move to another room?" "It's better that we move to another room in which there is nothing forbidden," they answered. So they went to another room in which there was nothing forbidden. Then the old man was ordered to appear, and he was brought in with a bag of date stones in his sleeve. "Take it out of your sleeve", the servant said, "and go in to see the Commander of the Faithful." "These are my dinner tonight," the old man said. "We will feed you," the servant replied. "I don't need your food." said the man. Hārūn asked the servant what the matter was and the servant informed him that the old man had some date stones in his sleeve. "I've ordered him to remove them", he said, "and then go in to the Commander of the Faithful." Hārūn told him to leave the man alone and let him keep the stones. So the old man went in, greeted them and sat down. Hārūn asked him: "Old man, what made you do what you did?" "And what is it that I've done?" he asked, and he made Hārūn embarrassed to say that he had broken the lute. When Hārūn went on at him, he said: "I have heard your father and your forefathers reciting this verse from the pulpit: 'God demands justice, the performance of good deeds and treating one's relatives well. And He forbids vile deeds, what is prohibited and injustice',[12] and I have seen what is prohibited so I have prevented it." He said "so I have prevented it", and nothing more. When the old man departed, the caliph gave one of his men a large sum of money saying: "Follow him and if you see him speaking of what went on between us, give him nothing. But if you find that he says nothing then give him the money." When the old man left the palace he found a date stone partially buried in the ground so he began to take it out and spoke to no one. The caliph's man said to him: "The Commander of the Faithful asks you to take this money." The man said: "Tell the Commander of the Faithful to return it to where he got it." It is related

[12] Qur'ān 16:90.

that when he had finished speaking he went back to the date stone and took it out of the ground, reciting:

> I see that the world brings cares the more of it you possess
> It demeans those who revere it, and it honours those who praise it less
> If you cannot do without a thing, take only this and leave the rest.

It is related that the caliph al-Ma'mūn heard that someone was acting as *muḥtasib* and going among the people ordering them to do good and forbidding them from evil, while not being commissioned by him to do so. So he ordered that the man be brought before him. When he appeared, the caliph said: "I have heard that you consider yourself qualified to order good and forbid evil without me having charged you to do so." Now, al-Ma'mūn had been sitting on a chair reading a document or a book, and he forgot about it and it fell on the floor under his foot where he was unaware of it. The *muḥtasib* said to him: "Lift your foot from the names of God, then say what you will." al-Ma'mūn didn't understand what the man meant and asked him three times to repeat what he had said, but still didn't understand. "Either you lift up your foot", the man said, "or give me permission to do it." Then al-Ma'mūn looked under his foot and saw the book. He picked it up, kissed it and was embarrassed. Then he resumed: "Why are you ordering good? God has given us, the members of the Prophet's family, the prerogative to do that. We are the ones about whom God said: 'They are the ones who, if We give them power on earth, will establish prayer, pay alms and order good and forbid evil.'"[13] The man said: "You have spoken the truth, Commander of the Faithful. You are as you have described yourself; you are a ruler and have authority, and I am one of your supporters in this. No one would deny this unless he is ignorant of the Book of God and the Sunna of the Prophet. God said: 'The believers, both men and women, protect each other. They order what is good.'[14] And the Prophet said: 'Muslims are to each other like parts of a building: they support each other.' You have been given power on earth, and this is the Book of God and the Sunna of His Prophet. If you adhere to them you would thank the one who helped you to revere them, and if you consider yourself above them and do not adhere to them then the One to Whom you belong and in

[13] Qur'ān 22:41.
[14] Qur'ān 9:71.

Whose hands lies your power or your debasement has decreed that whoever does good should not go unrecompensed. So now say what you will." al-Ma'mūn liked what the man said and was pleased with him. "People like you", he said, "may order good. So continue in what you were doing with my authorisation and according to my decision." And the man continued what he was doing.

Accounts like the above contain clear proof that permission to order good and forbid evil is not needed.

As for the fourth stage, there are some considerations in that forcefully taking property from someone's possession and returning it to its rightful owner, taking apart someone's silk clothes and breaking wine jars in someone's house could lead to humiliation and a lack of respect. This is prohibited and must be prevented, as also must remaining silent about something which is forbidden. Thus, two conflicting things are forbidden here, and which course of action to take depends on an independent decision guided by an assessment of the gravity of the evil and the extent to which someone's dignity will be infringed by assailing him. This is something which cannot be accurately determined.

As regards the pupil and the teacher, the situation is not so complex, since the one to whom respect is due is the teacher, the one dispensing wisdom regarding religion. There can be no respecting the scholar who does not act according to what he teaches; he must deal with the pupil on the basis of the knowledge which the pupil has learnt from him.

It is related that al-Ḥasan was asked how a son should act as *muḥtasib* over his father, and he replied that he should exhort him in a way that does not anger him, and if it does, he should remain silent.

2 The Second Basic Element of *Ḥisba*: The Jurisdiction of *Ḥisba*

Ḥisba relates to every objectionable practice, actually taking place, evident to the *muḥtasib* without his having to pry, and known to be objectionable without the need for independent judgement.[15] Thus, there are four conditions which we will discuss.

(a) The first condition is that the practice is an objectionable one.

By this, we mean that the practice is forbidden in Islamic law. We use the term 'objectionable' rather than 'sin' because an objectionable practice is more general than a sin. Thus, whoever sees a young boy or someone insane drinking alcohol, he must pour the alcohol away and stop it being drunk. Similarly, when he sees an insane man fornicating with an insane woman or an animal he must prevent him from this. This is not simply because of the abomination of the scene and because it takes place in front of people, for if the *muḥtasib* comes across these forbidden practices in a private place, he must still prevent them.

Ḥisba is not concerned with the major sins but rather with such as exposing one's genitals in the baths and being alone with or staring at women who are not members of one's family. All these are minor sins and must be forbidden.

(b) The second condition is that the objectionable practice is actually taking place. *Ḥisba* is therefore restricted in the case of someone who has drunk alcohol earlier but is not doing so now. It has no jurisdiction here as the objectionable practice is no longer in evidence. It is also restricted regarding something based on circumstantial evidence, such as when someone concludes from a man's behaviour that he is resolved to drink at night. In this case there can be no *ḥisba* except exhortation. If the man denies that he is resolved to drink, then he may not be exhorted since this is to distrust a Muslim who may perhaps be telling the truth. He also might not do what he has resolved to because something could prevent him.

[15] Arabic: *ijtihād*, that is, a discretionary opinion by a qualified legal expert regarding cases not already explicitly covered by the existing norms of Islamic law.

So let the *muḥtasib* pay attention to the point we have made, that objectionable practices which are being carried out at the moment are such as being alone with an unrelated woman, standing by the door of the women's baths and such like.

(c) The third condition is that the objectionable practice is evident to the *muḥtasib* without his having to pry. Thus, whoever commits a sin in his own home behind closed doors may not be spied on. God will deal with him. In this context is what was related about 'Umar, that he climbed onto a man's roof, went into the house and saw him doing something forbidden and thus censured him for it. "Commander of the Faithful," said the man, "if I have sinned against God in one respect, you have sinned against Him in three." "What are these?" asked 'Umar. The man replied: "God said 'Do not pry'[16] and you have pried. He said 'Go into houses through the doors'[17] and you have climbed up onto the roof. And He said 'Do not go into houses that are not yours until you have asked permission and greeted the people who live there',[18] and you have not greeted me." So 'Umar left him alone after asking him to repent.

You ask what being immediately apparent and being concealed amount to. Know that when a man closes the door of his house and is concealed within its walls, no one may enter to discover any sin without his permission. That is, except when someone outside the house can perceive what is going on inside, such as when the sounds of musical instruments are so loud that they pass through the walls of the house. Whoever hears this may enter the house and break the instruments. Similar is the situation where the voices of drunken people are raised in the familiar way such that they can be heard by people on the road. This is making the offence apparent and necessitates *ḥisba*.

Consider when, despite the intervention of the walls, a sound or a smell can be detected. If it is the smell of alcohol, then while it is likely that this is from prohibited alcohol it is not permissible to seek it out and pour it away even though

[16] Qur'ān 49:12.
[17] Qur'ān 2:189.
[18] Qur'ān 24:27.

the circumstances indicate that the people probably intend to drink it. *Ḥisba* is permitted only concerning what is immediately apparent.

A bottle of wine may be hidden in the sleeve or under the robe, as may musical instruments. If a dissolute person is seen carrying something under his robe, it is not permitted to ask him to reveal what he is concealing unless it is obvious, for his dissolute appearance does not prove that he has alcohol with him. The profligate also needs vinegar and such like. Thus, it is not permitted to draw conclusions from his concealing something even though he would not do so were it lawful. There are many reasons for concealment. If there is a smell, on the other hand, then this is cause for inspection and it is obvious that it comes under the *muḥtasib*'s jurisdiction, because this is a sign which arouses suspicion and suspicion is the same as knowledge in such cases. Also, a lute might be recognised from its shape when the robe concealing it is thin. The evidence of its shape is the same as that of a smell or a sound, and such evidence means that the thing is not concealed but rather revealed.

We have been instructed to conceal what God conceals and to censure anyone who reveals what they should not. Discovery can occur in a number of ways: sometimes through the sense of hearing, sometimes through the sense of smell, sometimes through sight and sometimes through the sense of touch. It cannot be restricted only to the sense of sight. Indeed, what is wanted is knowledge, and these other senses are also an aid to knowledge. Thus, it is permissible to break what someone has under their robe if the *muḥtasib* knows that it is alcohol, but he may not find out what it is by asking to be shown. This is prying and prying means to search for specific evidence. If clues come to light and knowledge is attained, then the appropriate measure is permitted. As for searching for evidence, this is absolutely forbidden.

(d) The fourth condition is that a practice is known to be objectionable without need of independent judgement. Whatever requires independent judgement does not come under the aegis of *ḥisba*. Thus, the follower of the Ḥanafī school of law may not censure the follower of the Shāfi'ī school of law for eating lizards and hyenas and not saying "In the name of God" before slaughtering; nor may the Shāfi'ī censure the Ḥanafī for drinking non-alcoholic wine, for inheriting from relatives on the maternal side, for possessing a house which he has acquired by what the Shāfi'ī considers to be unlawful means, and other such matters which require independent judgement.

3 The Third Basic Element of *Ḥisba*: The One Taken to Account by the *Muḥtasib*

It is a condition that the offender has the capacity to perform prohibited acts which merit censure. The minimum requirement is that he be a human being. It is not a condition that he be legally capable, since we have already stated that if a young boy drinks alcohol he must be prevented from this and be called to account by the *muḥtasib* even though he has not reached maturity. And it is not a condition that he be of sound mind, since we have already stated that if an insane man fornicates with an insane woman or an animal he must be prevented from this.

There are indeed some things which the insane person does which are not forbidden practices, such as neglecting the prayers, fasting and so on. But we do not want to consider the finer points here, for we could equally mention those concerning the one at home and the traveller, the sick and the healthy. Our intention is only to indicate the basic things which should be censured and not the details.

You might say that it is sufficient for the offender to be an animal and that we do not need to make the condition that he be a human being. For if an animal spoils a man's crops we would prevent it in the same way as we would prevent a madman from fornicating with a mad woman or an animal.

Know that there is no reason for calling this *ḥisba*, for *ḥisba* consists of preventing practices objectionable to God and is a safeguard against associating with these things. Preventing a madman from fornication and bestiality is to uphold God's rights over us, as is preventing a youth from drinking alcohol. A man should be stopped from destroying crops for two reasons: it is a wrong against God because it is a sin, and it is a wrong against the injured party.

4 The Fourth Basic Element of *Ḥisba*: The Nature of *Ḥisba*

Ḥisba has stages and rules of conduct. As for the stages, these are first knowledge, then instruction, then censure, exhortation and advice, then cursing and stern rebuke, then active prevention, then threatening with a beating, then actually giving a beating and drawing a weapon, then asking the assistance of helpers and getting people to assist in the fight.

(i) The First Stage: Knowledge

If by knowledge we mean seeking information that an objectionable practice is taking place, this is forbidden, as is the prying that we mentioned earlier. The *muḥtasib* must not eavesdrop by another person's house in order to hear the sound of a musical instrument, nor smell for alcohol, nor feel someone's robe for the shape of a musical instrument, nor ask the neighbours to find out what is happening in another house.

This is the case. But if without being prompted two men of good character give the *muḥtasib* information that such and such a person is drinking alcohol in his house or that he has alcohol in the house with the intention of drinking it, then at this point the *muḥtasib* may enter without asking permission. He may disregard the owner and enter so as to stop the objectionable practice by, for example, beating the man on the head to prevent him whenever this is necessary. This is as long as he has been informed by two men of good character.

There are considerations as to whether the *muḥtasib* is permitted to force his way into someone's house on the basis of an allegation. The basic principle, however, is that the *muḥtasib* should refrain from this, because it is the owner's right that no one enters his house without his permission, and the established right of a Muslim is not negated except on the testimony of two witnesses. This is a basic principle which must be upheld.

It is said that the inscription on King Luqmān's ring was "Keeping secret what I have seen is better than voicing my suspicions".

(ii) The Second Stage: Instruction

The man who engages in an objectionable practice does so out of ignorance, for if he knew that it was objectionable he would desist from it. This is like the simpleton from the countryside who prays but makes mistakes in bending the body and in the prostrations then learns that he is ignorant of the correct way to pray. But if he is content to neglect the fundamentals of prayer, then he should be instructed politely and gently. This is because instruction implies ignorance and folly, and accusing someone of ignorance is offensive. Men are seldom happy to be accused of ignorance of affairs, especially of Islamic law. For this reason, you will notice how a short-tempered man will be furious when he is informed of a mistake and of his ignorance, and how he will strive to deny the truth when it becomes known, afraid lest his ignorance is exposed. It is human nature to strive harder to conceal the deficiency of ignorance than to conceal one's genitals, because ignorance is a stain on one's self esteem, a black mark on one's character and the one who has it is reproached. The unsightliness of the genitals derives from one's image of the body, but the personality is more exalted than the body and thus a blemish on this is worse. The ignorant man is not to be blamed, however, because ignorance is something we are born with and something about which we have no choice. It is a blot which can be removed and changed only with the benefit of knowledge. While men are hurt when their ignorance is exposed, they are proud of their knowledge and are delighted when the excellence of their learning is revealed to someone else.

Since instruction discloses a deficiency and is insulting, its injury should be ameliorated with civility and gentleness. We should tell him that man is not born with knowledge, and that we too were once ignorant of the correct way to pray but those who know informed us. For perhaps there are no scholars in his village, or whatever scholar there is cannot fully explain and elucidate the prayers. The main requisite of prayer is to be composed while bending the body and prostrating.

In such a way, the *muḥtasib* should be civil and polite so that the man is instructed without offence. For to insult a Muslim is unlawful, just as ignoring his objectionable practice is unlawful. No rational person washes away blood with blood or urine, and whoever avoids the offence of doing nothing about an objectionable practice by unnecessarily insulting a Muslim, they have indeed washed away blood with urine. It is the same when you come across an error which is not concerned with religion: you must not dishonour a man because of this, for he will benefit from your knowledge; but he will become your enemy unless you are aware that he will avail himself of knowledge. Knowledge is much cherished.

(iii) The Third Stage: Censuring by Exhortation, Advice and Instilling Fear of God

This is used for someone who does a thing in full awareness that it is objectionable, and for someone who persists in doing something after he has learnt that it is objectionable. This includes, for example, the person who continues to drink alcohol, to act unjustly, to slander Muslims, and such like. He must be exhorted, fear of God must be instilled in him, he must be acquainted with the traditions which warn against these matters and told about the conduct of our forefathers and the god-fearing. This should be done tenderly and gently, not roughly or angrily. He should be dealt with compassionately and the sin he commits should be seen as a sin against his own soul. Indeed, Muslims are as one soul.

In this there is a great harm which the *muḥtasib* must guard against for it is pernicious. This is when one who has knowledge gives instruction and glorifies himself on account of his knowledge and belittles the others because of their ignorance. Perhaps by his instruction he intends to humiliate, to demonstrate the privileged position that knowledge provides and to degrade the man because of his ignorance. If this is the incentive, then it is a worse evil in himself than the evil to which he is objecting. Such a *muḥtasib* is like a man who saves someone from a fire but burns himself, and this is the height of folly. To act in such a way is highly contemptible, a terrible wickedness and is a temptation of the Devil which affects all men. That is, all except he whom God has made aware of his own imperfections, and whose eyes have been opened by God's divine guidance.

(iv) The Fourth Stage: Cursing and Stern Rebuke

This is resorted to when the *muḥtasib* is unable to prevent with gentleness and when the transgressor persists in what he is doing and ridicules the *muḥtasib*'s exhortations and advice. It is like Abraham's words: "Fie upon you and what you are worshipping to the neglect of God. Have you no sense?"[19]

By cursing we do not mean obscene language, using words related to fornication and its prelude, nor do we mean untruths. Rather, the *muḥtasib* should address the man in terms commensurate with what he has done but not in obscene language. He should say, for example, "You sinner. You idiot. You fool. Have you no fear of God?" or "You country simpleton", "You numbskull" and such like. For every sinner is an idiot and a fool, and if it were not for his stupidity he would not have disobeyed God. Indeed, whoever lacks intelligence is a fool, and the intelligent person is as the Prophet said: "The intelligent person is he who judges himself and aspires for what comes after death. The stupid person is he who follows his cravings and tells lies before God."

This stage has two rules of conduct. First, the *muḥtasib* should not resort to it except when necessary and when gentleness is of no avail. Second, the *muḥtasib* should only speak the truth and not go on at length, freeing his tongue to say what is not required. Rather, the *muḥtasib* should restrict himself to what is necessary. If he considers that his words of rebuke are not having the desired effect, then he must not say them, but should instead confine himself to showing anger, contempt and disdain because of the man's offence. If the *muḥtasib* considers that if he speaks he will be beaten, but that if he looks grave and shows disgust he will not be beaten, then he must do the latter. It is not enough for the *muḥtasib* to disapprove in his heart; rather, he must frown and show the man his disapproval.

(v) The Fifth Stage: Active Prevention

This includes such as breaking musical instruments, pouring away alcohol, taking silk from someone's head or body or preventing them from sitting on it, stopping someone retaining another person's property, evicting someone with a kick from an unlawfully possessed house, removing someone from the mosque if they are in a state of major ritual impurity, and so forth. Active prevention is, however, only for

---

[19] Qur'ān 21:67.

some offences, for as regards offences made by the tongue and in the heart, the *muḥtasib* cannot prevent these directly.

This stage has two rules of conduct. First, the *muḥtasib* should only actively prevent when he cannot leave it up to someone to take it upon themselves. Thus, if the *muḥtasib* is able to entrust it to someone to remove themselves from illegally possessed land or from a mosque, then he must not push or drag them away. And if he can trust someone to pour away alcohol, break musical instruments or remove silk stitching from a robe, then he does not have to do this himself. If the man does not take such things upon himself, then efforts must be made and they should be taken care of by someone who has no impediment to acting.

Second, the *muḥtasib* should limit his actions to what is necessary. Thus, he should not take hold of a man's beard or leg when evicting him if he can pull him by the hand. Similarly, the *muḥtasib* does not need to cause undue damage. He need not tear a silk robe but only remove the stitches, he need not burn musical instruments or the cross carried by a Christian but only stop their corrupting influence by breaking them. The objects should be broken so as to render them as difficult to repair as to make them anew from wood. In pouring away alcohol, the *muḥtasib* should guard against breaking the vessels if at all possible. But if he has no choice but to break them with a stone, then he may do so. The vessels have no importance if he must break them because of the alcohol. If a man prevents the *muḥtasib* from pouring the alcohol away or obstructs him, then he should beat him so that he can pour the alcohol away. In such a situation, a man will be concerned more to protect himself than he will his vessels.

If the alcohol is in long thin-necked bottles, and if the *muḥtasib* busies himself with pouring it away, this will give the offenders time to catch hold of him and stop him. This is a good reason for the *muḥtasib* breaking the vessels. He must not waste his energies and thwart his intentions simply because of the vessels. But when it is easy to pour away the alcohol without breaking anything, then the *muḥtasib* is answerable for any damages.

(vi) The Sixth Stage: To Threaten and Intimidate

This is such as when the *muḥtasib* says “Stop that or I’ll break your head!” or “I'll cut your head off!” or “I'll have you punished!” and so forth. If possible, this must take precedence over an actual beating.

The general rule in this stage is that the *muḥtasib* should not threaten anyone with what he is not permitted to implement, such as when he says “I’ll confiscate your house!” or “I’ll beat your children!” or “I’ll curse your wife!” and so on. That is, if he says these things intending to do them, this is forbidden, and if he says them without intending to do them, he is a liar. If the *muḥtasib* threatens to beat and humiliate the man, then he may resolve to do this to an extent commensurate with the circumstances. He may threaten more than he intends to carry out if he considers that this will restrain and prevent the man. This is not an unlawful lie. Indeed, it is normal to exaggerate in such things. It is the kind of exaggeration employed when a man reconciles two people or makes peace between two wives, and he is permitted to employ this when necessary. This is similar to what the *muḥtasib* intends, for he endeavours to improve a person. Regarding this intention, some people have pointed out that it is not disgraceful to threaten what one will not do, since failing to keep a threat is magnanimous, but it is shameful to make a promise that you will not keep. We do not agree with this, for what has earlier been said should not be gone back on, whether it be a promise or a threat. This can be seen as rightfully due to the servants of God. To do otherwise is, however, not unlawful.

(vii) The Seventh Stage: Beating and Drawing Weapons

This includes striking with the hand, kicking with the foot and such like. These things are permitted to ordinary citizens on condition that they are necessary and that they are resorted to only insofar as they are needed to achieve the aim. When the objectionable practice has been prevented then the *muḥtasib* must stop.

The judge might make someone against whom there is an proven legal claim honour this by imprisoning him. If the one imprisoned still refuses to comply, while the judge is aware of his ability to discharge the claim and of his obstinacy, he may force him to honour it by beating him, gradually increasing these beatings as is necessary. Likewise, the *muḥtasib* should consider how severe the beating ought to be. Thus, if the only way of preventing an objectionable practice is by drawing a weapon and wounding, then the *muḥtasib* may do this as long as it does not cause civil strife. Similarly, if a licentious man takes hold of a woman, for example, or is playing a musical instrument, and between him and the *muḥtasib* is a river or some other obstruction, then the *muḥtasib* make take his bow and say "Leave her alone, or I'll shoot you." If the man does not let her go, the *muḥtasib* may shoot him. He must not, however, intend to kill the man, but should aim at his legs, thighs and such like, and should assess how severe he needs to be. The *muḥtasib* may also unsheathe his sword and say "Stop that evil or I'll strike you."

All these things are ways to prevent objectionable practices, and this must be done by all means possible.

(viii) The Eighth Stage: The Use of Helpers

This is when the *muḥtasib* is not able to act alone but requires helpers who withdraw their weapons. Perhaps the offender will also acquire helpers, and this will then lead to the two sides coming face to face and fighting. There is some disagreement as to whether this necessitates the permission of the ruler.

Some people say that ordinary members of the community may not do this on their own initiative because it may lead to civil strife, disorder and the destruction of the town. Others say that permission is not necessary. This latter opinion is more logical, since if the ordinary citizen is permitted to order good, then the first stage of *ḥisba* inevitably leads to the second, and the second to the third and so on, and this might inevitably result in conflict which gives rise to people assisting each other. So the *muḥtasib* should not take the possible consequences of *ḥisba* into consideration; and its highest stage is enlisting men to fight in obedience to God and preventing sins against Him. We permit prominent citizens to come together and fight and suppress whichever group of unbelievers they choose. In the same way, suppressing the depraved is also permissible. Since it is admissible to kill the unbeliever, it is similarly admissible to kill a sinner who tries to defend his moral depravity. When a

Muslim is killed fighting the unbelievers he becomes a martyr, and when the *muḥtasib* is unjustly killed in acting correctly he becomes a martyr.

In general, however, it is rare in *ḥisba* for the situation to reach such a state. Nevertheless, its occurrence does not militate against the logic of the various stages of *ḥisba*. Indeed, it is said that whoever is able to prevent an objectionable practice may do so with his hand and his weapon, alone or with assistants. The situation is thus permissible, as we have stated.

These are the stages of *ḥisba*. Now we will turn to its rules of conduct, God willing.

The *Muhtasib*'s Rules of Conduct

We have mentioned some particulars concerning the rules of conduct which apply when dealing with the different stages of *ḥisba*. Now we will refer to them in general and to their origins. Thus, we say that all the *muḥtasib*'s rules of conduct originate in three qualities which the *muḥtasib* should possess: knowledge, piety and a good character.

As for knowledge, this is needed so that the *muḥtasib* is aware of the jurisdiction of *ḥisba*, its boundaries and its courses of action and thus is able to proceed according to Islamic law.

As for piety, this is needed to prevent the *muḥtasib* from acting contrary to what he knows. For not everyone who has knowledge acts according to it. On the other hand, perhaps the *muḥtasib* is aware that he is over-zealous in his application of *ḥisba* and is going beyond the legally permissible limits, but he is prompted to do this for a particular purpose and so that his words and exhortations are acted upon. Nevertheless, if the sinner acts as *muḥtasib*, he may be ridiculed and treated with disdain.

As for a good character, this enables the *muḥtasib* to be courteous and gentle and is the main requirement. Knowledge and piety are insufficient, for when someone gets in a rage these are not enough to control him if they are not combined with a good character. Certainly, piety cannot be achieved without a good character alongside the ability to suppress cravings and anger. A good character also enables the *muḥtasib* to endure the hardships of acting in the religion of God. If he does not possess this, then when his honour, possessions or person are attacked in any way he will forget *ḥisba*, disregard the religion of God and think only about himself. Indeed, such a person might originally undertake *ḥisba* only looking for fame and prestige.

With these three qualities *ḥisba* becomes favourable to God and by means of them objectionable practices are removed. But if they are lacking, then this will not be the case. Indeed, *ḥisba* will perhaps itself become objectionable.

Some of these qualities are referred to in the Prophet's words: "No one should order good and forbid evil unless they are gentle in what they order and gentle in what they forbid, mild-tempered in what they order and mild-tempered in what they forbid, knowledgeable in what they order and knowledgeable in what they forbid." This demonstrates that it is not a condition that the *muḥtasib* be simply knowledgeable in what he orders and forbids, but should also be mild-tempered.

Ḥasan al-Baṣrī said: "If you are one of those who orders good, then be one of those who abide by it. If not, you are doomed." It was also said

> Do not reproach a man when you do the same.
> Whoever does this is also to blame.

We do not mean by this that ordering good becomes prohibited because the *muḥtasib* is seen to be sinful, but rather that its influence on people's hearts will cease. It is related that Anas b. Mālik said: "O Prophet, we say that we will not order good unless we abide by it, and we will not forbid evil unless we avoid it". The Prophet replied: "No, order good even if you do not abide by it, and forbid evil even if you do not avoid it."

One of our forebears gave advice to his son. He said: "If someone wants to order good he must prepare himself to be forbearing and to rely on the reward from God.

Whoever relies on the reward from God will not be harmed." Thus, one of the rules of conduct of *ḥisba* is to prepare oneself to be forbearing. For this reason, God linked forbearance to the ordering of good. God quoted what Luqmān said: "My son, institute the prayers, order good, forbid evil and be forbearing in the hardships which afflict you."[20]

Another rule is not to let personal allegiances interfere with the work, so that the *muḥtasib* is not afraid to act because of them, and to stop needing people's approval, so that the *muḥtasib* will not be a prey to flattery. Indeed, it is related that a venerable old man had a cat and that every day he used to get some offal from the butcher next door for it. Then he saw the butcher do something objectionable. So he first went into the house and got rid of the cat, then he acted as a *muḥtasib* over the butcher. "I won't give you anything for your cat after this," the butcher said. The man replied: "I only acted as a *muḥtasib* over you after I had got rid the cat and was no longer in need of you." And it is as the man said, for whoever does not stop needing people cannot perform *ḥisba*, and whoever desires that people will think kindly of them and praise them will not find *ḥisba* easy.

Ka'b al-Aḥbār asked Abū Muslim al-Khawalānī: "How much do your people love you?" "Very much," he replied. Ka'b said: "The Torah says that when a man orders good and forbids evil he is no longer liked by his people." Abū Muslim said: "The Torah has spoken the truth, and I am wrong."

A demonstration of the necessity of gentleness is al-Ma'mūn's reply to someone who rudely admonished him. He said: "Be courteous, for God has sent people better than you to people worse than me", and he ordered him to be so. God said: "Speak to him mildly for perhaps he will remember and fear God."[21]

In being gentle, let the *muḥtasib* follow the example of the prophets. Abū Amāma related that a young man approached the Prophet and said: "O Prophet, will you give me permission to commit fornication?" The people yelled at him to go away, but the Prophet told them to bring the youth forward. They did this, and when the young

---

[20] Qur'ān 31:17.
[21] Qur'ān 22:44.

man sat before him, the Prophet said: "Do you want it for your mother?" "No, God forbid!" replied the youth. The Prophet said: "Likewise, the people do not want it for their mothers. Do you want it for your daughter?" "No, God forbid!" the youth replied. The Prophet said: "Likewise, the people do not want it for their daughters. Do you want it for your sister?" Ibn 'Awf added that the Prophet went on to mention maternal and paternal aunts, and that for every one the youth replied "No, God forbid!" and the Prophet said "Likewise, the people do not want it." Both narrators of this tradition related that the Prophet put his hand on the youth's breast and said: "O God, purify his heart, pardon his sin and deliver him from evil. For there is nothing more hateful to God than this", that is, fornication.

Ḥammād b. Salma said that Ṣila b. Āshīm once came across a man who had let his loincloth fall to the ground. Ḥammād's companions wanted to seize him roughly. "Leave it to me," he told them. Then he said to the man: "Friend, I need you to do something for me." "What do you need, sir?" he asked. "I want you to put your loincloth back on," Ṣila replied. The man said: "Gladly, and out of respect to you," and put it back on. Ṣila said to his companions: "If you had grabbed him he would have said no, would have had no respect and would have cursed you."

Muḥammad b. Zakariyā al-Ghalābī said that one night he saw 'Abd Allah b. Muḥammad b. 'Ā'isha when he had left the mosque after the evening prayer and was making his way home. In the road there was a young man from the Quraysh who was drunk and had seized a woman and was pulling her. She called for help and the people gathered and beat the youth. Ibn 'Ā'isha looked at him and recognised him. "Leave the dear man alone," he told the people. Then he said to the young man: "Come here friend." At this, the young man became ashamed, went up to him and Ibn 'Ā'isha embraced him. Then he said: "Come with me," and the young man went with him until they arrived at the house and Ibn 'Ā'isha invited him in. Ibn 'Ā'isha said to one of his servants: "Let him spend the night near you, and when he sobers up tell him what has happened. But don't let him go until you have brought him to me." When the young man sobered up the servant told him what had happened and the young man became ashamed, started to cry and made to leave. "I've been ordered to take you to Ibn 'Ā'isha," the servant said, and took him there. "Aren't you ashamed of yourself?" said Ibn 'Ā'isha, "Don't you feel the stain on your honour? What would your children say? Be god-fearing and stop what you are doing." The young man bowed his head and cried. Then he raised his head and said: "I have made a vow to God about which He will question me on the Day of Judgement. I will not drink wine again and will stop everything I have been doing. I am repentant." "Come here," Ibn 'Ā'isha said, and he kissed the young man's head, "You have done the right thing, my son." After that, the young man always accompanied Ibn 'Ā'isha and wrote down the traditions he knew. All this was due to the blessing of Ibn 'Ā'isha's gentleness. Ibn 'Ā'isha said: "The people are ordering good and forbidding evil, but their good is evil. So you must be gentle in all your orders and you will be obeyed."

Fatḥ b. Shakhraf said: "A man had seized a woman and was molesting her. He was a strong man and had a knife in his hand with which he wounded everyone who came near. While the people were standing back and the woman was crying out as he held her, Bashr b. al-Ḥārith came by. He approached the man and rubbed his shoulder against the man's shoulder. At this, the man fell to the ground and Bashr went on his way. The people went up to the man, who was sweating profusely, while the woman went about her business. They asked him what had happened and he replied: 'I don't know. But a venerable old man rubbed against me and said 'God is watching you and what you do' and when he said this my legs became weak and I was terrified of him. I don't know who he was.' The people told him that the man was Bashr b. al-Ḥārith. 'O God,' he said, 'what have I done?' That same day he was stricken with fever and died seven days later."

In such a way did the faithful apply *ḥisba*. We have now concluded our examination of the stages of *ḥisba* and its rules of conduct. God gives success by His generosity. Praise be to God for all His blessings.

**

Common Objectionable Practices

We will indicate these in general terms so that they will serve as examples of their like. There is no intention to enumerate them all or to be inclusive.

1 Objectionable Practices in the Mosques

Know that objectionable practices are divided into those which are 'reprehensible' and those which are 'prohibited'. So, when we say that such a thing is a reprehensible objectionable practice, this means that its prevention is desirable, that is, neglecting to prevent it is not punished, but its prevention is rewarded by God, and doing nothing about it is reprehensible. It is not unlawful except when the perpetrator is aware that it is reprehensible. Thus, it must be brought to his attention because reprehensible practices are regulated by Islamic law and whoever does not know of them must be informed. And when we say that such a thing is a prohibited objectionable practice or is absolutely forbidden, this means that it is forbidden, and doing nothing about it when able to do so is similarly forbidden.

One thing often witnessed in the mosques is impairment of the prayer by a lack of composure in the bending of the body and in the prostrations. This is an objectionable practice which invalidates the prayer, according to the tradition. It must therefore be prohibited by all except the Ḥanafīs who believe that it does not invalidate the prayer and thus that there is nothing to be gained by censuring it. Whoever observes an error in the way someone performs the prayer and yet does nothing about it, he is an accomplice. This is what the tradition said regarding both the slanderer and the listener being accessories to the sin, stating that the listener is an accomplice of the one who speaks. Other things which invalidate the prayer are a stain on a man's clothing which he has failed to notice and not facing in the correct direction because of darkness or blindness. All these things are concerns of *ḥisba*.

Among other things often witnessed in the mosques is reciting the Qur'ān in a tuneful manner. This must be forbidden and the correct method must be taught. If the man who often recites the Qur'ān in this way is able to learn then he should not recite until he has studied. But if this is difficult for him, if his tongue will not obey him and most of his recitation is tuneful, then he must leave it and endeavour to study the first chapter of the Qur'ān and to recite this correctly. If most of what he recites is correct but he is unable to do this consistently, then there is no objection to him reciting, but he must lower his voice so that no one else can hear. Some would forbid him reciting even silently, but if he is doing his very best and if he has a liking for recitation and is intent on doing it, then I see no objection to this. But God knows best.

Among other matters is for the muezzins to perform the call to prayer all at the same time, to draw out the words, not to face the correct direction, or to perform the call to prayer singly but not wait until the call of another has ceased such that it is difficult for those present to hear the call due to the clashing of voices. All these things are reprehensible objectionable practices which must be explained to the perpetrators. If the muezzin knows what his doing but still persists then he should be prevented and become subject to *ḥisba*.

Another reprehensible practice is successively to repeat the call to prayer in one mosque after daybreak. There is nothing to be gained from this whether it be done in one mosque or many, as no one will still be asleep in the mosque, nor will the sound coming from the mosque awaken people in other mosques. All these are reprehensible practices which are opposed to the normative behaviour of the Companions of the Prophet and our forebears.

Another reprehensible practice is for the man who delivers the Friday sermon to wear black clothing made mostly of silk, or to hold a golden sword. In this case he is a sinner and must be rebuked. As for simply wearing black, this is not reprehensible but is undesirable. The clothes most beloved of God are white. Whoever maintains that black clothes are reprehensible and a heresy means by this that they were not well known in the early period. If they do not want them to be forbidden then they should not call them a heresy and reprehensible, but rather simply say that they should not be worn in preference to white clothes.

Another reprehensible practice is for the story-tellers and the preachers to include innovations in what they have to say. If the story-teller lies in his narrations then he is a sinner and must be rebuked. Similarly, the heretical preacher must be restrained. It is not permitted to attend his sessions except with the intention of refuting him, whether by all the people if they are able or by some of those present around him. If they are unable to do anything about it then they should not listen to his innovations. God said to His prophet: "Turn away from them until they speak of other things."[22] Whenever the preacher's words tend to lessen the people's fear of God and encourage them to commit sins, and they become increasingly foolhardy because of what he says and certain of God's forgiveness and mercy, this is an objectionable practice and he must be prevented from doing it as it is a great corruption.

A partition should be erected between the men and the women which will prevent them seeing each other. This is also a situation in which immorality is likely to occur, as is confirmed by experience. If there is any fear of the women subjecting the men to temptation, they should be prevented from entering the mosques to pray and from attending the gatherings in which God's name is repeated. 'Ā'isha, the favourite wife of the Prophet, prevented the women from doing these things. When she was told that the Prophet had not stopped them attending the congregations, she said: "If the Prophet had known what the women would cause after his death, he would have stopped them."

As for women passing through the mosque while veiled, this should not be prevented. The principle is, however, that the mosque is not a thoroughfare.

Another reprehensible practice is for people to gather on Fridays to sell utensils, foodstuffs and talismans, and, for example, to present petitions, to recite the Qur'ān, read poetry and such like. For some of these things are unlawful since they are fraudulent and untrue. There are, for instance, doctors who are deceitful, magicians, tricksters and many purveyors of charms who manage to sell their wares to children and people from the countryside. Such things are unlawful both in the mosque and

[22] Qur'ān 6:68.

outside it and must be prevented. Indeed, every sale is unlawful in which there is deceit, fraud and concealing defects from the buyer.

There are some things which are allowed outside the mosque, such as sewing and selling utensils, foodstuffs and books. These things are similarly not unlawful within the mosque except when they cause obstructions, that is, when they leave little room for those praying and disturb the prayers. If they cause no harm, then they are not unlawful. In principle, however, they should not be done. They are only permissible on condition that they take place infrequently, for if the mosque was always to be treated as a shop this would be unlawful and would have to be stopped. In general, among the things which are permissible are those which are considered so only on condition that they do not take place very often, since if they happened more frequently they would become minor sins; just as with crimes there are those considered minor so long as that they are not repeated. Although these things might rarely take place, if they were given free rein there would be a fear that they would become more frequent and would have to be prohibited. This prohibition is the prerogative of the governor or those responsible for the interests of the mosque on behalf of the governor because it does not require independent judgement. The ordinary citizen must not prohibit what is in itself permissible out of concern that it might increase.

Other reprehensible practices include drunken youths and the insane entering the mosque. There is nothing wrong with young people entering the mosque as long as they do not always play games. It is not in itself unlawful for them to play games in the mosque, but it is when they regularly use it as a playground. This must be prevented and is another example of the permissibility of something when it is done infrequently and its impermissibility when it is done often.

As for the insane, there is likewise nothing against them entering the mosque unless it is feared that they will dirty it, curse and use foul language or do objectionable things such as revealing their genitals and so on. But if the insane person is quiet and calm and has learnt to control himself, then he must not be removed from the mosque. It is the same for a drunkard. If it is feared that he will vomit or be verbally offensive then he must be removed from the mosque. This is also the case if he is irrational, which is always to be feared. If a man is not intoxicated but has been drinking and this can be smelled on him, this is a very reprehensible objectionable practice. How could it not be so, since the Prophet even prevented anyone who had eaten garlic or onion from entering the mosques? This latter, however, is merely reprehensible; concerning alcohol it is worse.

It is said that a drunken man should be beaten and forcibly expelled from the mosque. We disagree with this. Whenever he is rational he may stay in the mosque but be prevailed upon and ordered to stop drinking. As regards giving him a beating to stop him, this is not up to the ordinary people, but rather to the governor and then only upon the man's confession or the testimony of two witnesses. This is not the case when the man merely smells of alcohol. Certainly, when a man is staggering in such a way that he is clearly drunk, then whether he is in the mosque or outside it he may be beaten to stop him showing the effects of his intoxication. To reveal the effects of something repugnant is itself repugnant, and sins must be renounced. After an offence, it and its effects should be concealed, and it is not then permitted to pry to discover it. There might be a smell without a man having drunk, caused by sitting in a place where there is alcohol or by putting it to his lips without swallowing when there was no intention to drink.

2 Objectionable Practices in the Markets

Among the common objectionable practices in the markets is deceit in re-selling commodities for a profit and in concealing defects. For example, whoever falsely claims that he bought a certain item for, say, ten dinars and that he is making a profit on it of so much, is a sinner. Whoever is aware of this falsehood must inform the buyer, for if he keeps quiet for the sake of the seller he becomes an accessory to the deception and commits a sin by his silence. Similarly, when someone knows that there is a defect he must inform the buyer of it, otherwise he consents to a fellow Muslim wasting his money, and this is unlawful. Also, disparities in the values of the cubit, weights and measures must be rectified by anyone who becomes aware of them or the matter must be referred to the governor for him to rectify them.

Other objectionable practices include selling musical instruments and models of animals made for children during the religious festivals. These latter must be broken and, like musical instruments, their sale must be prevented. There is also the selling of vessels made of gold and silver, silk clothes and caps of silk and gold, by which I mean those clothes suitable only for men or which are customarily worn only by men. All these are 'prohibited' objectionable things. There is also the person who habitually sells used clothes that have been bleached claiming that they are new. This is unlawful and must be prevented. Similarly, there is the deceitful mending of ripped clothes and anything else that aims at deception. Also included is every kind of contract of sale whose object is to deceive.

It would take a long time to enumerate all these matters, so let the *muḥtasib* draw analogies from the things we have mentioned when dealing with those we have not.

3 Objectionable Practices on the Public Highways

Among the common objectionable practices on the public highways is the erecting of columns, placing benches adjacent to private buildings, planting trees, making windows and extensions, dumping wood and leaving loads of grain and foodstuffs. All these things are forbidden if they lead to obstructions on the roads and inconvenience to the passers-by. On the other hand, if they do not cause any harm because the road is sufficiently wide, then they should not be prevented. Indeed, it is permitted to unload firewood and foodstuffs in the road in the amounts which will be taken to the houses, for everyone needs to do this and it is not possible to put a stop to it. Likewise, tying up riding animals in the roads when this causes an obstruction and dirties the passers-by is an objectionable practice which must be prevented except insofar as it is required for mounting and dismounting. This is because roads are for the use of all and not for one single person. As regards animals, roads are usually most needed for transporting fodder.

Another thing is driving animals which are carrying thorn bushes when these rip the people's clothes. This is an objectionable practice if it is possible to tighten and gather the loads together so that they do not do this, or when it is possible to take the loads on a wider road. If this is not possible, then it must not be prevented as the people of the town need such things. Indeed, nothing should be left on the roads for longer than it takes to transport it. Similarly, burdening animals with loads heavier than they can bear is an objectionable practice and the owners must be prevented from doing this.

There are also butchers who slaughter outside their shops and soil the roads with blood. This is an objectionable practice which must be prohibited, as butchers should slaughter in their shops. If not, they obstruct the roads and do harm to the people because of their spreading filth around and offending people. There is also throwing rubbish in the roads and scattering melon skin, or spilling water where it might cause someone to slip and fall. All these things are objectionable practices. Similar is letting water escape onto narrow roads from drain pipes coming out of walls, since this soils people's clothes or makes the roads impassable. But it should not be forbidden on wide roads if people can walk around it. As regards leaving rainwater, mud or ice on the roads without clearing it away, this is an objectionable practice. But no single person is responsible for this except as regards ice which one person will have thrown on the road and water which collects in the road from a certain drain pipe. In these latter cases, the person responsible must clear it away. As for brushing away rainwater, this is everyone's duty and the governor should charge the people to do it; ordinary citizens may only exhort that it is done.

Similarly, if a man keeps a voracious dog at the door to his house which harms people, he must be prohibited from this even when the only damage the dog does is to foul the road. But if he can stop this from happening, then he may keep the dog as it is. If the road is obstructed by the dog lying down, this must be stopped. Indeed, an owner must not allow his dog to sleep in the road or sprawl out and thus cause an obstruction. The dog must be kept under control.

4 Objectionable Practices in the Baths

Among these are the pictures which are on the door of the bath or inside and which must be removed by anyone entering if they are able to do so. But if they are out of reach then no one may enter the bath except when absolutely necessary and must go elsewhere, for witnessing an objectionable practice is not permitted. It is sufficient to deface them and thus render them unrecognisable. Apart from pictures of animals, drawings of trees and other objects are not prohibited.

Other things include exposing one's genitals and looking at those of other people. In general, there is also the masseur exposing someone's thighs and below the navel to remove dirt. There is also putting one's hand under a man's loincloth, for to touch another person's genitals is unlawful, as is looking at them.

Another thing is lying face down in front of the masseur for him to massage the thighs and backside. This is, however, merely reprehensible if done over a covering, and is not prohibited if there is no fear that it will arouse carnal appetites. Similarly, exposing one's genitals to a cupper who is a *dhimmī* is an indecency, for a woman may not even reveal her body in the baths to a *dhimmī* woman so how can it be permissible for her to expose her genitals to men?

There is also putting one's dirty hands or pots and pans in water when there is little of it, and washing dirty loincloths and cups in the water trough when it is only partially filled, for this taints the water. The school of Mālik do not agree with this so it is not permissible to rebuke a Mālikī concerning it, but it is permissible to rebuke a Ḥanafī and a Shāfi'ī. If there is a Mālikī and a Shāfi'ī in the bath together the Shāfi'ī may only censure the Mālikī in this regard by courteous request. That is, he should say something like "We must wash our hands first, so let's put them in the water. But you do not have to harm and sully me." This is because in areas where independent judgement is necessary *ḥisba* may not be forcibly applied.

Also included is for there to be any slippery flagstones at the entrances to the rooms within the bath and beside the water channels on which the unwary might slip. This is objectionable, must not be allowed and the bath attendant should be rebuked for it, for it will lead to someone falling and perhaps breaking or dislocating a limb. Leaving lotus leaves used for washing and slippery soap on the floor are also objectionable practices. When someone leaves such a thing in a place where it is difficult to see it and thus avoid it, and then someone slips on it and breaks one of his limbs, then the responsibility is shared between the one who left it and the bath attendant as it is the latter's responsibility to keep the bath clean. The main principle, however, is that on the first day it is the responsibility of the one who left it, and on the second day that of the bath attendant.

5 Objectionable Practices in Hospitality

Among these is laying down silk on the ground for the men to sit on, for this is unlawful. Likewise, there is burning incense in a silver or gold censer or drinking alcohol or using rose water from silver containers or those whose rims are made of silver. There is also setting up a screen which has pictures on it and listening to musical instruments and singers.

Similar is women gathering on roof terraces so as to look at the men below whenever there are youths present. This might cause a disturbance. All these things are prohibited objectionable practices which must be stopped. Whoever is unable to stop them must leave since they are not permitted to witness objectionable practices. As for designs on cushions and carpets, this is not forbidden. This also applies to designs on trays and bowls, but not to containers which are formed into shapes of things. The tops of censers are sometimes made to look like birds, but this is unlawful and they should be broken.

There are disagreements regarding kohl containers made of silver. Aḥmad b. Ḥanbal once left a gathering because of one.

Whenever the food is unlawful, the place illegally acquired or the floor coverings unlawful, then these are among the most objectionable things. If there is only one person drinking alcohol, then it is not permissible to stay, as it is not allowed to attend gatherings where people drink even if you yourself do not. It is impermissible to sit with a sinner while he is committing his offence. Similarly, a man wearing silk or a gold ring is a sinner and it is not allowed to sit with him unless absolutely necessary.

There are differences of opinion regarding a child who is not legally of age wearing silk clothes. The truth of the matter is that it is an objectionable practice and the clothes must be taken from him. The Prophet told people: "These two things [silk and gold] are unlawful for the men of my community." In a like manner, a man must not allow a child to drink alcohol, not because he is charged to do this but because he wants to help him, for when the child reaches legal age it will be difficult for him to give it up. Similarly, a child will always want to adorn himself with silk if he gets used to it. These are seeds of corruption planted in his breast from which will grow a tree of firmly established appetites and which the child will not easily uproot once he has reached maturity.

Certainly, it is permissible for women to adorn themselves with gold and silk in moderation. But I can see no licence to pierce a young girl's ears so she can be made to wear golden earrings, as this is a painful injury and elsewhere such injury is a case for punishment. Injury like this is not allowed except for a very important reason, such as blood-letting, cupping and circumcision. Although piercing the ears is customary it is unlawful and must be prevented.

Among other objectionable practices is to show hospitality to someone who speaks of heresies. It is permissible for someone to be present as long as he is able to refute him and determines to do so. But if this is not possible, then one is not allowed to be present. If the offender does not talk of his innovations, then it is permissible to be present as long as one shows aversion for him and shuns him. It is not permissible to sit with someone who likes to tell amusing stories and various anecdotes and who makes people laugh with his obscenities and lies. If you are present, you must rebuke him. But if someone jokes without being obscene or lying, then this is permissible as long as it does not happen too frequently. It is not permissible when it becomes a regular occurrence and habitual. When a lie is clearly such, and is not intended to deceive people, then this is not an objectionable practice. For example, it is not improper for someone to say "I've looked for you a hundred times today" or "I've told you a thousand times" and such like, where it is obvious that they do not mean this literally.

Other objectionable practices are to spend lavishly on food and on one's dwelling. Indeed, there are two objectionable practices concerning possessions: one is to squander and the other is to be immoderate. For to squander money is to waste one's wealth to no avail and is like burning or ripping clothes, destroying a building for no purpose, or throwing money into the sea. Included here is spending money on a hired female mourner, a singer and all kinds of immoralities, for according to Islamic law it is unlawful to avail oneself of these things and they leave no benefit. Squandering might lead to a desire to spend money on a hired female mourner, a singer and other objectionable things. It could lead to spending money on things which in themselves are permissible, but with immoderation.

Immoderation varies as do the circumstances. So we hold that if a man has only one hundred dinars, for example, and he has children and other dependants who have no means of subsistence apart from him, then he spends it all on a banquet, he is a squanderer and must be prevented. God said: "[Do not tie your hand like the niggardly,] nor stretch it out as far as it will go so that you become blameworthy and destitute."[23] This was revealed concerning a man in Medina who had abused his wealth, left nothing for his dependants and was asked to pay maintenance but could afford nothing. God said: "Do not squander your wealth like a spendthrift. Spendthrifts are brothers of the devils."[24] God also said: "Those who neither squander nor are niggardly when they spend [are blessed]."[25] Whoever squanders must be rebuked and the judge must declare him legally incompetent. If the man has no dependants and is genuinely able to place himself in God's hands, then he may disburse all his wealth in charitable gifts. But whoever has dependants or is incapable of relying on God's charity may not donate all his wealth as alms. If a man spends all his money on painting the walls of his house or on decorating the building, this is likewise unlawful squandering. If, however, the one who does this is very wealthy then this is not unlawful because to decorate one's house is a legitimate aim. The mosques continue to be decorated and have their doors and ceilings painted even though this is nothing but a mere cosmetic. It is the same for houses. The idea of adorning oneself with fine clothes and eating lavish food is the same: these things are in themselves permissible and whether it is squandering or not depends on the particular circumstances of the man involved and how wealthy he is.

---

[23] Qur'ān 17:29.
[24] Qur'ān 17:26-27.
[25] Qur'ān 25:67.

There are too many objectionable practices similar to these for us to list them all, so judge the remaining ones according to those we have referred to. The sessions of the judges, the government offices of the sultans, the schools of legal scholars, the hospices of the Sufis and the hostels in the market place - there is not a place in which there are no reprehensible or prohibited objectionable practices. To study all the objectionable practices requires an understanding of the particulars of Islamic law, its sources and branches. So let us be content with what we have mentioned.

6 Objectionable Practices in General

Know that in these times whenever someone remains in their house, wherever it may be, they are committing an objectionable practice in that they are not guiding and instructing the people or urging them to do good. For even in the town most people are ignorant of the rulings of Islamic law concerning the conditions for prayer, so how must it be for the villagers and the nomads among whom are Arabs, Kurds, Turks and other ethnic groups?

In every mosque and part of a town there should be someone versed in Islamic law who instructs people in their religion. The same applies to every village. Every legal expert who has completed his individual duty and is applying himself to the collective duty should go out to the Arabs, Kurds and others who live in the rural areas near his town and instruct them in their religion and the obligations of Islamic law. He should take along his own provisions and not eat their food for most of this is acquired illegally. If one man undertakes this, then the others do not have to. If not, then everyone is responsible for it until it is done.

As for the learned man, he is at fault if he does not go out to others; and as for the ignorant man, he is at fault if he stops learning. Every blind man who is aware of the conditions for prayer should teach others, otherwise he is an accessory to any sin committed. It is clear that man is not born with a understanding of Islamic law but needs to be taught by the people of knowledge, and anyone who has learnt something is a person of knowledge in that subject.

Indeed, it is worse for legal scholars to sin in this way since they are more capable of avoiding it and it is their calling to teach the people. If skilled people neglect their professions then our way of life would cease, for they have taken upon themselves something essential for people's welfare. The situation of the legal scholar and his profession is as was transmitted on the authority of the Prophet: that the scholars are the heirs of the prophets.

A man may not remain at home and not go to the mosque because he considers that the people do not pray correctly. On the contrary, if he is aware of this he must go to instruct and to forbid. Similarly, if anyone knows for certain that something objectionable is being committed in the market, either continually or at that particular time, and which they are able to prevent, then they may not ignore this by staying at home. Rather, they must attend to it. If someone is not able to prevent every objectionable practice and does not want to witness them, but can prevent some things, then he must attend to these. This is because if he goes out with the intention of stopping those things which he is able to stop, it will not harm him to see those which he cannot. It is only forbidden to witness an objectionable practice when there is no legitimate reason for being present.

It is the responsibility of every Muslim to begin with himself, improve himself through devotion to the religious duties and by renouncing what is unlawful. Then he should instruct the members of his household in this. Once this is achieved, he should turn his attention to his neighbours, then to the people of the quarter, then to the people of the town, then to the people in the countryside surrounding the town, then to the Kurdish, Arab and other nomads, and in this way to the ends of the earth. When a man who lives nearby attends to these matters then the one who lives further away does not have to. If the man who lives nearby does not do this then every able man must undertake it whether he lives near or far. A man's responsibility does not cease as long as there remains on the face of the earth someone ignorant of a single religious duty and he or another person is able to deal with this and inform them of the duty. This is the chief concern of all who attach importance to their religion. It distracts them from giving their time to esoteric sidelines and becoming absorbed in the intricacies of sciences which are non-obligatory collective duties. Nothing takes precedence over this concern except an obligatory individual duty, or a collective duty when this is of more significance.

**

Ordering Princes and Sultans to do Good and Forbidding them from Evil

We have mentioned the stages of *ḥisba*, which include instruction, exhortation, sharp rebuke, active prevention and inducement by beating and punishment. Of these, the only ones permissible with sultans are the stages of instruction and exhortation. As for active prevention, ordinary citizens may not do this with the sultans as this causes public disorder, brings about disaster and results in more problems than it solves. Concerning a sharp rebuke, such as saying "You sinner. You who have no fear of God", if this leads to dissension affecting other people then it is not permissible. But if the *muḥtasib* only need fear for himself, then it is permissible, indeed it is his duty to give it. It was normal for our forefathers to expose themselves to danger and affliction by forbidding with no regard for their lives, and to open themselves to all kinds of torture in the knowledge that this was martyrdom. The Prophet said: "The best of the martyrs is Ḥamza b. 'Abd al-Muṭṭalib, and after him the man who goes to a ruler and in the name of God orders him to do good and forbids him from evil and is then killed for this." The Prophet also said: "The best thing in fighting for God is a word of truth to a tyrannical ruler."

When those who were rigorous in their religion learnt that the best word is one of truth to a tyrannical sultan, and that if the man who gives it is killed he becomes a martyr, as mentioned by the traditions, they began to do this reconciling themselves to death, suffering all manner of torture, enduring this for the sake of God and earning God's reward for their sacrifices.

The method of exhorting the sultans, ordering them to do good and forbidding them from evil is transmitted from our learned forebears. We will now confine ourselves to relating some stories which show how to exhort the sultans and how to forbid them.

In one account, ‘Abd Allah b. ‘Amr said: “While the Prophet was in the open square around the Ka‘ba, ‘Uqba b. Abī Mu‘ayyaṭ came up and seized him by the shoulder, twisting his robe around his neck and strangling him. Then Abū Bakr came along, took hold of ‘Uqba’s shoulder and pushed him away from the Prophet. “Would you kill someone because he says ‘my Lord is one God’?” asked Abū Bakr. “And he has brought you clear statements from your Lord.”

It is related that the caliph Mu‘āwiya imprisoned al-‘Aṭā’ b. Abī Rabāḥ and that Abū Muslim al-Khawalānī stood up and said: “Mu‘āwiya, this man is not a trouble to you, nor to your father or your mother.” At this, Mu‘āwiya flew into a rage and descended from the pulpit saying to the people: “Remain where you are.” He stayed away for one hour, then he returned having washed himself. “Abū Muslim made me angry with his remarks,” Mu‘āwiya said, “but I have heard the Prophet say ‘Anger comes from the Devil and the Devil was created from fire. Fire is put out by water, so if one of you becomes angry go and wash yourself.’ So I went and washed myself. Abū Muslim told the truth: the man is not a trouble to me nor to my father, so I am releasing your ‘Aṭā’.”

It is related that al-Aṣma‘ī said: “‘Aṭā’ b. Abī Rabāḥ went into the presence of the caliph ‘Abd al-Malik b. Marwān who was sitting on his couch surrounded by eminent men from every tribe. This was in Mecca when ‘Abd al-Malik performed the pilgrimage during his caliphate. When the caliph saw him he sat him down next to him on the couch and said: ‘Abū Muḥammad, what is it you want?’ ‘Aṭā’ replied: ‘O Commander of the Faithful, fear God with regard to what He has made unlawful and what His Prophet has made unlawful. And fear Him with regard to the children of those who did the hijra with the Prophet from Mecca to Medina, and those of the people who gave the Prophet sanctuary after his arrival there, for you are sitting with them now. And fear God with regard to the people at the frontier posts for they are as a citadel for the Muslims. And look after the Muslims, for you bear sole responsibility for them. And fear God with regard to those who are at your door lest you should forget them. And do not close your door to them.’ ‘Abd al-Malik replied:

‘I will certainly do as you ask.’ Then ‘Aṭā’ got up to leave, but the caliph stopped him, saying: ‘Abū Muḥammad, you have told me about what other people need and I have said that I will attend to it. But what about you?’ ‘Aṭā’ replied: ‘I have no need of anything in this world,’ then departed. ‘Abd al-Malik said: ‘Both he and his father are indeed noble men.’”

It is related that Ḥaṭīṭ the oil-dealer was taken to the governor al-Ḥajjāj. When he appeared before him, al-Ḥajjāj said: “Are you Ḥaṭīṭ?” “Yes,” Ḥaṭīṭ replied. “Ask me what you will, for I have vowed to God that I will have three qualities: to tell the truth when questioned, to endure when I am afflicted, and to give thanks when I am forgiven.” al-Ḥajjāj asked: “So what have you to say about me?” Ḥaṭīṭ replied: “You are one of God’s enemies on earth, you violate what is inviolable and you kill on mere suspicion.” “And what have you to say about the Commander of the Faithful ‘Abd al-Malik b. Marwān?” asked al-Ḥajjāj. Ḥaṭīṭ answered: “I say that he is more sinful than you and that you are just one of his crimes.” al-Ḥajjāj ordered: “Torture him.” The torture led to them splitting canes, tying them to his naked body, then pulling them out piece by piece until they rubbed his flesh away. But they did not hear him say a word. al-Ḥajjāj was told that he was at his last breath. “Take him and throw him in the market place,” said al-Ḥajjāj. Ja‘far said: “So myself and one of Ḥaṭīṭ’s friends went to see him, and we asked him: ‘Ḥaṭīṭ, is there anything you want?’ ‘A drink of water,’ he replied. So we gave him a drink of water. Then he died. He was eighteen years old. God have mercy on his soul.”

On the authority of ‘Abd Allah b. Mihrān who said that when al-Rashīd made the pilgrimage he passed by Kufa and stayed there for a few days. Then he resumed his journey and the people came out from the area of al-Kunāsa to see him, among whom was the madman Bahlūl. The children were insulting and inflaming Bahlūl. Then they saw Hārūn’s camel litters approaching, so they stopped what they were doing. When Hārūn arrived Bahlūl called at the top of his voice: “O Commander of the Faithful!” and Hārūn opened the curtain which was concealing him. “What is it, Bahlūl?” the caliph asked. “O Commander of the Faithful,” said Bahlūl, “Ayman b. Nā’il told us on the authority of Qudāma b. ‘Abd Allah al-‘Āmirī who said that he saw the Prophet leaving Arafat on a red camel and he did not beat or drive it or urge it on in any way. O Commander of the Faithful, to show humility when you travel is better for you than arrogance and haughtiness." At this, Hārūn wept until his tears fell to the ground. Then he said: "Bahlūl, tell me more, may God have mercy on you." "Very well," said Bahlūl, "if God gives a man money and handsomeness and he donates the money and ignores his handsomeness, his name will be written in God's most excellent register alongside the names of the righteous." "You have spoken well," said Hārūn, and he gave him a reward. Bahlūl said: "Give it back to the person you took it from. I have no need of it." "Bahlūl," Hārūn said, "if you have a debt then let me settle it." Bahlūl replied: "O Commander of the Faithful, there are many scholars in Kufa and they have all agreed that one may not settle a debt by incurring another." "Bahlūl," said Hārūn, "then let me give you something for your maintenance or lodging." Bahlūl raised his face to the sky and said: "O Commander of the Faithful, we are both children of God and it is impossible that He should remember you and yet forget me." At this, Hārūn drew the curtain and went on his way.

Aḥmad b. Ibrāhīm al-Maqrā said that Abū al-Ḥusayn al-Nūrī was not a very inquisitive man, did not ask about what did not concern him and did not seek what he did not need. If he saw any objectionable practice he would prevent it even though there might be harm in this for him. One day, he went down to a drinking place near the river, known as the drinking place of the coal merchants, to perform his prayers. There, he saw a boat loaded with thirty containers on which was written in tar 'Benevolence'. He read it and disapproved of it because he did not know of anything in either commerce or sales called 'benevolence'. "What's in those containers?" he asked the boatman. "And what's it got to do with you?" the boatman replied. "Mind your own business." Now, when al-Nūrī heard the boatman say this his curiosity was further aroused. "I want you to tell me what's in those containers," he said. The boatman replied: "What's it got to do with you? You're nothing but a busybody. This is wine for the caliph al-Mu'taḍid who wants to supply his court with it." "It's wine?" asked al-Nūrī. "Yes," answered the boatman. So al-Nūrī said: "I want you to pass me that oar." At this, the boatman became exasperated and told his assistant to give the oar to al-Nūrī so he could see what he would do with it. When al-Nūrī got hold of the oar he climbed into the boat and didn't stop until he had broken all the containers apart from one. The boatman called for help and the bridge-keeper arrived, at that time Ibn Bashr Aflah, who grabbed hold of al-Nūrī and took him to al-Mu'taḍid. Now, al-Mu'taḍid always used the sword before words, and no one doubted that he would have al-Nūrī executed.

Abū al-Ḥusayn said that he went into al-Mu'taḍid's presence and found him sitting on an iron throne and turning a staff around in his hand. "When he saw me he asked me who I was. 'A *muḥtasib*,' I replied. 'And who commissioned you with *ḥisba*?' he asked. 'The same One who entrusted you with rulership entrusted me with *ḥisba*, O Commander of the Faithful,' I answered. al-Mu'taḍid looked down at the floor for what seemed like an hour, then he raised his head to me and asked: 'What made you do what you did?' 'It was my concern for you,' I replied. 'I have lent you a helping hand to avert what is reprehensible from you, but did not complete my task.' al-Mu'taḍid lowered his head thinking about what I had said. Then he looked up at me and said: 'How was it that one container was spared out of all the others?' 'There is a reason for that,' I replied, 'and with your permission, Commander of the Faithful, I will tell you what it is.' 'Tell me,' said al-Mu'taḍid. 'O Commander of the Faithful', I said, 'I attacked the containers because it was my duty to God to do so, and my heart was overwhelmed with the exaltedness of what I had to do. I feared no one and in this state fell upon the containers until I came to the last one. Then I became aware of my pride in what I had been bold enough to do to someone like you, so I stopped myself. If I had continued in the state I was in at first, and the whole world was full of such containers, I would have broken them without a care.' al-Mu'taḍid said: 'Go on your way, I am giving you a free hand to prevent whatever objectionable practice you want to prevent.' 'O Commander of the Faithful,' I said, 'it is odious to me to prevent these things because I used to act on behalf of God, but now I act on my own behalf.' 'Then what do you want?' asked al-Mu'taḍid. 'O Commander of the Faithful,' I replied, 'just let me go.'"

al-Mu'taḍid did this and Abū al-Ḥusayn went to Basra. He spent most of his days there afraid that someone would ask him what had happened with al-Mu'taḍid. He stayed in Basra until the caliph died, then returned to Baghdad.

The above shows the conduct and practices of the learned in ordering good and forbidding evil, and their lack of concern for the sultans' power. They put their trust in the grace of God to protect them, and were content that God would bless them with martyrdom. When they were sincere to God in their intention to make their words affect hardened hearts, God softened those hearts and removed their hardness. As for today, greed has tied the tongues of the learned and they have fallen silent. When they do speak their own behaviour does not support what they say, so they are unsuccessful. If they were sincere and accepted the responsibilities of knowledge, they would be successful. The corruption of the citizens is due to the corruption of the rulers, the corruption of the rulers is due to the corruption of the scholars, and the corruption of the scholars is due to love of wealth and fame. Whoever is possessed by a desire for the world is incapable of applying *ḥisba* to the common people, so how can they apply it to rulers and the powerful? We ask God for help in every situation.

The treatise on ordering good and forbidding evil is completed in praise of God, with His assistance and the blessings of the success He grants.

APPENDIX II

The Diploma of Investiture

The diplomas drafted upon the appointment of the *muḥtasib* illustrate not only the style of such texts but also mention some of the duties considered to be under the *muḥtasib*'s aegis.

The earliest extant diplomas date from the Buwayhid period (932-1055). The following example, which is the earliest known, is taken from *Rasā'il al-Ṣāḥib b. 'Abbād* (Cairo, 1947, pp. 39-41). al-Ṣāḥib b. 'Abbād (938-95) was the wazīr of Mu'ayyid al-Dawla (r. 945-67).

This is a diploma from Mu'ayyid al-Dawla Abī Manṣūr b. Rukn al-Dawla Abī 'Alī, the patron (*mawlā*) of the Commander of the Faithful, for such and such a person.

According to what we have been informed and what we have learnt of your attested knowledge, your great discretion, your status among the leading *faqīh*s and your skill and ability, we have seen fit to employ you for that which the Imams have sanctioned and which is necessary for the community. This is *ḥisba*, which works for the welfare of the people and which combines the bitterness of truth with the sweetness of compassion. Thus, taking care of the citizens and seeking their advantage, we have commissioned you to perform the duties of *ḥisba* in Rayy. For *ḥisba* comprises ordering what is good and suppressing what is objectionable, exhorting to what is commendable and renouncing what is repugnant. God is our guide and our support, our helper and the One who directs us on the correct path, the Best Disposer of Affairs upon Whom we rely.

So attend to that which we have bestowed upon you, and always act in fear of God. *Ḥisba* is the way and the resource, the support which will aid you, the path which will deliver you from error and the protection from deficiency. Whoever adheres to its terms and dons its protective armour will be sure-footed and will be secure in this world and the next. But whoever does not fulfil its obligations and ignores its stipulations will stumble and will be burdened with his sins. The worthiest man to follow its guiding light and to raise its banner is the man of perception and knowledge, discernment and deliberation. Those of God's servants who fear Him are those with knowledge.

Implement with honesty the responsibilities imposed upon you so that others emulate your example and imitate you in your intentions and aims. For whoever improves his soul will have his call for good deeds answered and his words will act as an example in desisting from what is objectionable. Act severely against the immoral so as to educate them and to remedy their sins, to improve them, to correct those who go astray and prevent them from doing evil. For when such people do not meet firm opposition nor have fear of strong rebuke, they abandon themselves to their carnal appetites and persist in their evil ways. Be gentle with those who are known for their discretion and honesty so that the good people will join them. This is the straightest path and the correct method. God guides whom He wants on the straight path.

Pay attention to the weights and measures, the scales and balances, as business transactions are dependent on these and buying and selling rely on them. In the Qur'ān God has shown particular concern for the wickedness of giving short measure and the sin of underweighing. He said: "Woe unto those that deal fraudulently; those who when they receive by measure exact it in full, but when they have to give by measure or weigh, give less than is due. Do they not think that they will be called to account on the Last Day?"[1]

Deter the citizens from transgressing by forbidding what is prohibited and condemnable. In this, make no distinction between the wealthy and the prosperous and the needy and the poor, for they are all servants of God and His laws apply to them equally. Indeed, the rich - except for those whom God preserves - are more prone to commit what is objectionable and more able to satisfy their appetites by extravagance. When God is generous you must be righteous.

[1] Qur'ān 83:2-3.

When the women enter the markets and the shops, go onto the roads and come into contact with the men, you must make them cover their breasts and veil their faces. This is the best way to avoid the glances and stares of the licentious, and is more seemly for the modest and virtuous servant of God. For this reason God ordered that one should avert one's eyes; just as He ordered that a woman's chastity be protected: "Tell the Muslims that they must avert their eyes and protect their chastity. This is more befitting them."

Keep an eye on the merchandise on sale and ensure that it is not adulterated, for there are great sins and heinous crimes connected with this. Contracts of sale may be corrupted and business transactions impaired, to the detriment of the Muslims and to the people of the protected religions. You must praise highly whoever is always correct in the handling of his merchandise and will have nothing to do with what is defective, so that he will be a model for others and an example to those in his position. God does not desist from punishing those who do wrong.

Do not allow the wares and instruments, goods and appliances of the merchants to obstruct the streets for the passers-by. No one may obstruct the roads which Muslims use or block the roads with what might impede them. All merchants must have a set place for buying and selling which they must not move beyond nor extend. To harm a Muslim is unlawful, and to hinder his passage is a sin. God does not reward the artifices of those who deceive.

Ensure that the people of the protected religions wear the *ghiyār* and the *zunnār*[2] and that they are distinguished from the Muslims whom God has invested with power, whom He has exalted and singled out even in their outward appearance and clothing, and guarded from submissiveness and abasement, even though the unbelievers dislike this.

You are permitted to detain whoever ought to be detained, and to chastise whoever allows himself to be led astray, so that good prevails and corruption is rooted out, so that evil is reduced and impropriety is prevented. This should be done after a

[2] See Chapter 39 notes 3 and 4 for an explanation of these terms.

caution, a warning and a rebuke. For if words suffice then this is the easiest procedure and the best means of instruction. But if more than words are required then God's law must be applied, and that which arouses God's displeasure should not be countenanced. Indeed, God has no love for wickedness.

This is what we have commissioned you with and what God has commissioned you with. We have done our best to remind you of these matters, even though you are aware of them. We have informed you of all we know, even though you may already have full knowledge. So ask God, the Nourisher, for guidance, for He will guide your work and will lead you as long as you live. We do nothing but with His permission. We depend on Him for all we intend. He is the Best Supporter and the Surest Ally.

**

The remaining diplomas presented here were composed during the Fatimid (906-1160) and Ayyubid (1171-1250) periods and are preserved by al-Qalqashandī in his *Ṣubḥ al-A'shā* (Cairo, 1919).

The first was written during Fatimid times and although the writer is not mentioned it would have been composed on behalf of the caliph. It states (11:210-12):

Praise be to God the Renewer of good deeds, the Force behind the protectors of our state of al-Qāhira in these radiant times ...

This man is the most worthy and we have generously summoned him in order to elevate his rank, to fill his full moon with brilliance, to exalt him and to notify the righteous protectors of the honour bestowed upon him. God does not fail to recompense he who does good deeds, and our munificence does not disappoint he who has proved his obedience in these celebrated times of ours. He is the one whose previous service still brings him close to God, averts him from the paths to the abyss, reminds him of God and increases his good works. To this he has added the ordering of good, giving succour to the troubled, the forbidding of evil, doing pious deeds in the way of truth which he has endowed with all that God's creatures praise and extol. He has avoided worldly renown, made endeavour which pleases God and pleases us in its adhering to our distinguished way of life, insisted on the truth to the point where he was spoken of and was elevated, treated the people gently except concerning heresies which violate the sanctity of Islam or concerning deception which while not affecting the elite nevertheless harms the general public.

He is the one who dedicated himself to our service - which exalted him among us - and gave obedience to us. This demanded his drawing close to us and our summoning him, and promoted the interests of the citizens over which we made him responsible. He was worthy of our praise for his efforts in all his deeds. Thus it is our sublime decision to appoint him to the position of *muḥtasib*. Let him proceed in this post, diligent in all that avails the people. His position is beneficial for them.

Let him prohibit those who in affluence begin to meddle in that to which they have no right, or who oppress the poor by monopolising the wealth which God has made available to them.

Let him defend the weak by enforcing the divine statutes and preventing their contravention, telling the people to be just in their dealings on the basis of those transactions which are prohibited and those which are allowed, and showing them with fairness the guiding light of correct scales (for perhaps they will listen), and chastising those of them whom he finds giving short measure: "Those who when they receive by measure exact it in full, but when they have to give by measure or weigh give less than is due."

Let him order the people of the markets to perform the ordinary prayers and the Friday prayers, and discipline anyone who does not attend to this, thus causing those who persist in their negligence to amend their ways.

Let him compel those of good character to adopt that respectability which befits their status, corresponds to their rank, ensures that their profits are honourably gained and preserves them from suspicion whether they are present or absent.

Let him not enable the salespeople to cheat weak and ignorant citizens, nor give them the opportunity to increase their prices unjustly or to give the people short measure.

Let him urge all of them to be correct in their transactions, to make contracts which are permitted by the sublime Islamic law, and let him deter them from imperfect contracts and from ruses which deceive by adulterating commodities which are selling badly. He is the most experienced regarding sales which the sublime Islamic law has deemed immoral, and the most knowledgeable regarding tradespeople who do not correct their measures and scales when these give small amounts and underweigh.

So let him attend to these things whenever they are necessary, and by this means anticipate God's reward in the Hereafter for his pious deeds and be a *muḥtasib*. Let his words concerning these matters be cheerful, let his control in all this be wide-reaching and let him defend the instructions upon which he relies. Let him direct his representatives to do the same, explain every obscure circumstance to them by his own example, in every command show piety to Almighty God and pursue the favour of God alone. The noble text above is authorisation to this effect.

**

The following diploma is similarly from the Fatimid period and concerns the re-appointment of a *muḥtasib* over Fusṭāṭ in Egypt. (11:212-14)

Praise be to God, the Orderer of Good and the Forbidder of Evil, the Testament of Justice by Whom the word of faith is strengthened and rendered victorious, the One overflowing with boundless generosity and limitless grace.

Whereas Almighty God has established our authority based solely on justice and beneficence, and confirmed our noble commands so as to raise the light of goodness supported by God, and our laws celebrated for their rightfulness and whose merits are recorded on the pages of the age; And whereas He has inspired us with adherence to the sublime Islamic law which has nurtured the hearts of our subjects in peace and happiness, we have sought to elect to the ranks of religion and virtue he whose family is still exalted and who is characterised by all manner of commendable and praiseworthy acts.

He is the one who has inherited eminence from his virtuous forbears, received happiness from a family whose branches are pious and who was thus surrounded with magnificent and blossoming gardens, a family whose hearts were gladdened with the excellence of his conduct and his behaviour, holding within himself a religiosity which revealed the signs of his goodness. He was assigned to the religious ranks and excelled in his good conduct towards others, was exemplary in following the road of integrity and relied upon analogy and comparison concerning that in which he was deficient. The measures and scales were beneficiaries of what he pronounced with justice. All the honest people who do good deeds appealed to him, while those who transgress and lie feared him. The blessed office of *ḥisba* in divinely protected Miṣr was acquainted with his judgements and rulings, knew by experience his fairness and praised both his refutations and confirmations. Then he voluntarily withdrew from it against its will, but it has returned to him speaking to his deep sense of honour which knows no peer.

Thus, the exalted and noble order has been recorded to entrust him with the post of *muḥtasib*. Let him announce the benevolence of God in the performance of his duties and raise the light of his office by administering its sublime ordinances. Let him examine the weights and measures which are the speaking voice of truth, unfurl the banner of justice which has often streamed in our times, so that the evildoer's heart begins to tremble. Let him thoroughly examine the eating houses and the drinking places, and restrain the heretics whether they hide by night or declare themselves openly. Praise be to Almighty God that he possesses that fine intelligence which guards him against prolixity in his instructions and assists him in overcoming all obstacles in the rendering of judgements and the settling of disputes.

And how could this not be case, while he is well acquainted with what transpires and has a heart which does not obstruct what is correct when it is seen? Let Almighty God raise him up as a symbol of justice, clothe him with good fortune in our exalted times as a sign of His rewards. The noble document above is authorisation to this effect.

**

The following diploma has no indication as to date (11:114-15).

He has been given authority in this position and entrusted personally to supervise the interests of those who surrender to the will of God in so far as this concerns *ḥisba.* So let him look into both the trivial and the important, the great and the small, that which involves quantities and that which does not, that concerning which goodness is ordered and evil is forbidden, what is bought and what is sold, that which brings one close to Heaven and far from Hell even though between them there is only the span of the outstretched arms or the length of an arm. Let him look into all the ways of earning a living, both during the day and at night, and that whose amount cannot been known except when the tongue of the scales speaks or the mouth of the measure talks. Let him act as a balance for every trade and as a gauge when measures are before him, so it is known who has done wrong and who has acted justly. Let him inspect most of these things and warn against adulteration, for most diseases come from food and drink. Let him be acquainted with the prices and gather information in every market without forewarning the people there. Let him put reliable men in charge of the tradespeople who will represent him in his supervision and in whom he can place his trust whether he is present or not. He will instruct them to inform him of all that is difficult to understand and to consult him when needed, for the opinion of such as he is to be preferred.

Regarding the mint and the coins which are dispersed from it, there may be counterfeit among these which only come to light after some time. So let him apply himself to this with his breast which knows no anguish and let him submit to a test that which does not succeed in confusing him insofar as he is able.

As for broken pieces of gold, fragments of silver, and those things whose solder has been either wholly or partially melted by fire, let him assign inspectors over these matters and put in charge of such gold he who will control this as the heat of the sun controls the colour of the chameleon. And let him employ responsible men over the perfumers and street pedlars to prevent them from selling curious medicaments, except those traders concerning whom he has no misgivings and who are well-known. Medicine should only be given to a sick person after a prescription has been written by a skilled physician.

As for street pedlars, astrologers and all those groups of people of Sasanian origin, those who take money from people by ruses and trick them with the tongue, and any evil person of this type who is in reality a devil and not a man at all, you should absolutely forbid them and break them like glass until they are beyond repair, and shower warnings upon them. Otherwise, what is the benefit of having punishment? You should put an end to all these wicked affairs, and prevent the weak people from emulating these disgraceful things.

And whoever you discover has cheated a Muslim, has falsely acquired a dirham, has overcharged a customer or departed from customary practice, proclaim his name in the town and apply the whip to his back until he can endure no more. Apart from the *faqīh*s of the schools, the learned women and others who are alarmed by the ravaging wolf in a herd of gazelles and calves, whoever has the audacity to do these things and their like and is unheeding, fire your arrows at them, make their feet stumble with your fearlessness, and do not overlook any of them except he whose honesty you know well and who you think it best to defend.

As for your deputies, do not be satisfied with any except he who is perspicacious. You will be awarded a remuneration for their employment if, when you are asked, you indicate those you have deputised.

Devotion to God is the most wonderful path. In all we have mentioned, or most of it, you must act according to the legal school of Mālik.[3]

**

[3] Mālik b. Anas (d. 795), who compiled one of the very earliest compendiums of Islamic law and after whom a school of law is named.

The final diploma is from the Ayyubid period (10:460-62).

He is the one whose qualities have been praised, whose methods are correct, who is safe from error in that with which he is entrusted, whose relations with the people are based on absolute justice, whose proper actions have opened roads and passes through obscurity and who has embraced honesty as a constant companion in his dealings. He is the one who has attained a merit from which no obstacle impedes him, who has been rightly extolled by the voice of experience, who is worthy to be spoken of by everyone in the best of terms, to be supported in the realisation of his desires and the attainment of his hopes, the fire of whose intentions should be kindled in order to see the brilliance of his deeds. He is the one who deserves to be helped towards success in the windings of his path and the tortuousness of his road, and who should persevere in his jurisdiction so that he will receive the sign of beneficence. Praise will be not because of him but because of what he has performed, and he will drink and fully quench his burning thirst from the well of success. He will be distinguished with the marks of productivity by which he is characterised, and in his curing of the shortcomings of others he will cure his own.

As, O shaykh, you possess all the above qualities, answer fully and with great credit to this description, are so enriched with your own abilities as to need no appeal to a distinguished lineage, are entitled to be considered as a person of discretion because you are such, contain so much goodness that it cannot be briefly described, are so far above base qualities that you do not deem permissible or lawful that which is not, are extolled for services all of which have made you as pure gold, have a domain in which your deeds testify to your pre-eminence and excellence, use your integrity which has strengthened your avoidance of any suspicion and which has aroused powerful sentiments among the people - our protector, the caliph of the age, has directed that you be employed over *ḥisba* in such and such a place.

So attend to its duties as someone who strives for piety, and consider nothing but *ḥisba* as the watering place of the thirsty. God does not think proper what He has forbidden. Never order or forbid anything unless God has done so. Only consider proper what *ḥisba* reveals, in the knowledge that it is God who considers it so.

Proceed in it as he who spares no effort, as he who is steadfast in what benefits the people rather than what benefits himself, who by improving the nature of people demonstrates the purity of his own nature, who repays the excellence of God's benefactions to him with the excellence of his own deeds, who takes it upon himself to exercise his virtues in prohibiting what it has been ordered to prohibit and to prevent.

In your applications of *ḥisba* follow the school of endeavour and the straightest road. Be as diligent in it as someone clinging to the strong rope and firm cord of piety. Prevent a man being alone with an eligible woman. Examine the affairs of the eating houses and the drinking places and correct everyone who deviates from the obligatory customary practices concerning these. Test the accuracy of the weights and measures for they are the instruments which people use in their commercial dealings, and strive to remain blameless of any misdeed by keeping them clean and unsoiled. Caution against making an animal carry more than it can bear and chastise whoever intends to do this.

Instruct that the mosques and places of worship be cleaned so that they shine with the cleanliness of their passageways just as their dark areas are illuminated with lamps. This reveals their glory and beauty and instils a desire to protect their splendour from tarnish and debasement. Do not allow anyone to be in the mosques except for prayer or remembrance of God, and prevent disputes and the formulation of abominable ideas. As for those who turn them into markets for merchants, with this insolence they have become depraved, for the mosques are domains of the soul and the scales for judging what the people do outwardly and what they possess within. It is more befitting that only those who pray should be in the mosques at night and not those who sit in conversation; has God permitted any but His name to be exalted in them?

Prohibit anything which blocks or hinders free passage on the roads, and prevent and rebuke any offender concerning this. Compel the Christians, the Jews and other non-Muslims to wear the *ghiyār* and the *zunnār* for this demonstrates the glory of Islam and the baseness of non-adherence, shows non-Muslims that they should prepare for the passage to Hell, and distinguishes between the believers and the unbelievers.

Chastise anyone who gives short weight or measure and who is dishonest in his trading, and reprimand and intimidate anyone who repeats his offence.

By the will of God, be aware of all these things and act accordingly.

Bibliography I

This lists the articles and monographs used in the present translation. It does not include those works which provide information specifically concerned with *ḥisba* and the *muḥtasib*. A bibliography of these follows.

Abū'l-Fidā', 'Imād al-Dīn Ismā'īl. *al-Mukhtaṣar fī Akhbār al-Bashar*. Beirut, 1968.

al-'Aynī, Badr al-Dīn. *al-Sayf al-Muhannad*. Cairo, 1966.

al-Azraqī, Aḥmad b. Muḥammad. *Akhbār Makka*. Beirut, 1965.

al-Balādhurī, Aḥmad b. Yaḥyā. *Ansāb al-Ashrāf*. Jerusalem, 1936.

Brockelmann, C. *Geschichte der Arabischen Litteratur*. Leiden, 1937.

al-Bustānī, Buṭrus. *Muḥīṭ al-Muḥīṭ*. Beirut, 1983.

Gibb, H. A. R. "The Fiscal Rescripts of Umar II". *Arabica* 2 (1955) 3-16.

Goitein, S. D. *A Mediterranean Society*. Berkeley, 1971.

Ḥājjī Khalīfa, Kātib Celebī. *Kashf al-Ẓunūn 'an Asāmī al-Kutub wa'l-Funūn*. Cairo, 1892.

Ibn 'Abd al-Barr al-Qurṭūbī. *al-Isti'āb fī Ma'rifat al-Aṣḥāb*. Cairo, n.d.

Ibn Ḥazm, 'Alī b. Muḥammad. *Jamharat Ansāb al-'Arab*. Cairo, 1962.

Ibn al-Jawzī, Abū'l-Faraj 'Abd al-Raḥmān. *al-Muntaẓam fī Tarīkh al-Mulūk wa'l-Umam*. Hyderabad, 1358 AH.

Ibn Khaldūn, Abū Zayd 'Abd al-Raḥmān. *Muqaddimah*. Translated by F. Rosenthal. Princeton, 1958.

--------. *Kitāb al-'Ibar*. Cairo, 1971.

Ibn Khallikān, Shams al-Dīn. *Ibn Khallikan's Biographical Dictionary*. Translated by B. M. De Slane. London, 1843.

Ibn Manẓūr, Muḥammad b. Mukarram. *Lisān al-'Arab*. Lebanon, n.d.

Ibn Miskạwayh, Aḥmad b. Muḥammad. *Tajārib al-Umam*. Cairo, 1914.

Ibn Muyassar, Muḥammad b. 'Alī. *Akhbār Miṣr*. Cairo, 1981.

Ibn al-Nadīm, Abū'l-Faraj Muḥammad. *The Fihrist of Ibn Nadim*. Translated and edited by B. Dodge. Columbia, 1970.

Ibn al-Qifṭī, 'Alī b. Yūsuf. *Tarīkh al-Ḥukamā'*. Leipzig, 1903.

Ibn Sa'd, Muḥammad al-Zuhrī. *Kitāb al-Ṭabaqāt al-Kabīr*. Leiden, 1908.

Ibn Sallām, Abū 'Ubayd al-Qāsim. *Kitāb al-Amwāl*. Cairo, 1976.

Ibn Taghrībirdī, Jamāl al-Dīn. *al-Nujūm al-Zāhira fī Mulūk Miṣr wa'l-Qāhira*. Cairo, n.d.

Ibn Ẓāfir, Jamāl al-Din 'Alī. *Akhbār al-Duwal al-Munqaṭi'a*. Cairo, 1972.

al-Iṣfahānī, Abū'l-Faraj. *Kitāb al-Aghānī*. Beirut, n.d.

Kaḥḥāla, 'Umar Riḍā. *Mu'jam al-Mu'allifīn*. Damascus, 1957.

al-Khaṭīb al-Baghdādī. *Tarīkh Baghdād*. Cairo, 1931.

al-Kindī, Ya'qūb b. Isḥāq. *Kitāb al-Wulāt wa Kitāb al-Quḍāt*. Beirut, 1908.

--------. *The Medical Formulary of al-Kindī*. Translated by M. Levey. New York, 1966.

Lane, E. W. *The Manners and Customs of theModern Egyptians*. London, 1860.

--------. *Arabic-English Lexicon*. Cambridge, 1984.

Maimonides, Moses. *Glossary of Drug Names*. Translated and edited by F. Rosner. Philadelphia, 1979.

al-Maqrīzī, Taqī al-Dīn. *Itti'āẓ al-Ḥunafā'*. Cairo, 1967.

--------. *al-Mawā'iẓ wa'l-I'tibār fī Dhikr al-Khiṭaṭ wa'l-Āthār*. Beirut, 1947-48.

al-Mas'ūdī, 'Alī b. Ḥusayn. *Murūj al-Dhahab*. Paris, 1873.

al-Musabbiḥī, 'Izz al-Mulk Muḥammad b. Aḥmad. *Akhbār Miṣr*. Paris, 1978.

Muslim, Abū'l-'Abbās Aḥmad b. 'Umar. *Ṣaḥīḥ Muslim*. Lahore, 1976.

al-Ṣāḥib Ismā'īl b. 'Abbād. *Rasā'il al-Ṣāḥib b. 'Abbād*. Cairo, 1947.

al-Shayzarī, 'Abd al-Raḥmān b. Naṣr. *al-Nahj al-Maslūk fī Siyāsat al-Mulūk*. Cairo, 1326 AH.

al-Subkī, Tāj al-Dīn. *Mu'īd al-Ni'am wa Mubīd al-Niqam*. Cairo, 1948.

al-Ṭabarī, Muḥammad b. Jarīr. *Tarīkh al-Rusul wa'l-Mulūk*. Leiden, 1879-1901.

al-Tanūkhī, Ḥasan b. Abū Qāsim. *Nishwār al-Muḥāḍara*. Beirut, 1971.

Tritton, A. S. *The Caliphs and their Non-Muslim Subjects*. London, 1930.

al-Wakī', Muḥammad b. Khalaf. *Akhbār al-Quḍāh*. Cairo, 1947.

Wiedermann, E. "al-Karasṭūn". *Encyclopaedia of Islam*. First edition, Leiden, 1927, vol. 2 pp. 757-60.

Wüstenfeld, F. *Geschichte der Arabischen Aertze und Naturforscher*. Göttingen, 1840.

Bibliography II

The following lists the articles and monographs which either deal wholly with *ḥisba* and the *muḥtasib* or contain important relevant information. It is not entirely comprehensive, but includes the majority of works in European languages.

Articles

Abribat, J. "Notes sur la hisba (police)". *Revue Tunisienne* (1911) 20-31.

Amedroz, H. F. "The Hisba Jurisdiction in the Ahkam Sultaniyya of Mawardi". *Journal of the Royal Asiatic Society* (1916) 77-101, 287-314.

Arié, R. "Traduction annotée et commentée des traités de hisba d'Ibn 'Abd al-Ra'ûf et de 'Umar al-Garsîfî". *Hesperis-Tamuda* 1 (1960) 199-214, 349-86.

Behrnauer, W. "Mémoires sur les institutions de police chez les Arabes, les Persans et les Turcs". *Journal asiatique* No.16, 5 serie (1860) 347-92; No.17, 5 serie (1861) 5-76.

Bhatia, M. L. "The Functioning of the *Muḥtasib* under Aurangzeb". *Islamic Culture* 57 (1983) 263-76.

Boukani, S. "Le mohtassib et la protection du consommateur". *Revue Franco-Maghrébine de Droit* 2 (1994) 105-9.

Buckley, R. P. "The Muḥtasib". *Arabica* 39 (1992) 59-117.

Cahen, C. and Talbi, M. "Hisba". *Encyclopaedia of Islam*. New edition, Leiden, 1971, vol. 3 pp. 485-89.

Chalmeta Gendron, P. "La hisba en Ifrîqiya et al-Andalus: étude comparative". Cahiers de Tunisie 18 nos. 69-70 (1970) 87-105.

--------. "El 'kitab fi adab al-hisba' (Libro del buen gobierno del zoco) de al-Saqatî". *al-Andalus* 33 (1968) 143-95, 367-434 .

Chemoufi, A. "Une traité de Hisba (Tuhfat an-nâzir wa gunyat ad-dêlair fî hifz aš-ša'â'ir wa tagyîr al-manâkir) de Muḥammad al-'Uqbânî al-Tilimsânî (juriste mort à Tlemcen en 871/1467). Edition critique". *Bulletin d'études orientales* 19 (1965-66) 133-334.

Floor, W. "Das Amt des Mutasib im Iran - zur Kontrolle der 'offentlichen Moral' in der iranischen Geschichte". *Mardom Nameh* (1980) 122-39.

Foster, B. R. "Agoranomos and Muhtasib". *Journal of the Economic and Social History of the Orient* 13 (1970) 128-44.

Garcia Gomez, E. "Unas 'Ordenanzas del zoco' del siglio IX: traduccion del mas antiquo antecedente de los tratados andaluces de Hisba, por un autor andaluz". *al-Andalus* 22 (1957) 253-316.

García Sánchez, E. "Les traités de *ḥisba* andalous: en example de matière médicale et botanique populairs". *Arabica* 44I (1997) 76-93.

García Sanjuán, A. "La organisatión de los oficios en Al-Andalus a través de los manuales dc *ḥisba*". *Historia Instituciones Documnetos* 24 (1997) 201-33.

Glick, T. F. "Muhtasib and Mustasaf: A Case Study of Institutional Diffusion". *Viator* 2 (1971) 59-81.

Goudefroy-Demombynes, M. "Sur quelques ouvrages de hisba". *Journal asiatique* 230 (1938) 449-57.

Hamarneh, S. "Origin and Function of the Hisba System in Islam and its Impact on the Health Professions". *Archiv für Geschichte der Medizin* (Sudhoffs) 48 (1964) 157-73.

al-Husaini, I. M. "Hisba in Islam". *Islamic Quarterly* 10 (1966) 69-83.

Imamuddin, S. M. "al-Hisbah in Muslim Spain". *Islamic Culture* 36 (1962) 159-66.

Izzi Dien, M. "Hisba and the Legal Ethics of Islam". *Culture: Unity and Diversity: Proceedings of the Annual Conference of the British Society for Middle Eastern Studies. 1994, the University of Manchester*. (Durham, 1994) 284-91.

Kabir, M. "Administration of Justice during the Buwayhid Period (A.D. 946-1055)". *Islamic Culture* 34 (1960) 14-21.

Klingmüller, E. "Agoranomos und Muhtasib. Zum Funktionswandel eines Amtes in islamischer Zeit". *Festschrift E. Seidl* (Cologne 1976) 88-98.

Latham, J. D. "Observations on the Text and Translation of al-Jarsifi's Treatise on 'Hisba'". *Journal of Semitic Studies* 5 (1960) 124-43.

Lévi-Provençal, E. (ed.). "Risala fi al-Qada wa al-Hisba of Ibn 'Abdun of Seville". *Journal asiatique* (1934).

Lévi-Provençal, E. and Colin, G. S. (eds.). "The Kitab fi Adab al-Hisba of al-Saqati of Malaga". *Journal asiatique* (1931).

Levy, R. "Muḥtasib". *Encyclopaedia of Islam*. First edition, Leiden, 1936, vol. 3 pp. 702-3.

Mantran, R. "Règlements fiscaux ottomans. La police des marchés de Stamboul au debut du XVIème siècle". *Cahiers de Tunisie* 4 (1956) 213-41.

--------. "Un document sur l'ihtisab de Stamboul à la fin du XVIIe siècle". *Mélanges Louis Massignon* 3 (1957) 127-49.

--------. "Le *bitirme*, taxe de l'ihtisab d'Istanbul". *Mémorial Ömer Lútfi Barkan* (1980) 141-48.

Marcais, G. "Considerations sur les villes musulmanes et notamment sur le role du mohtasib". *Recueils de la Société Jean Bodin* 6 (1954) 249-62.

Pellat, C. "Un 'traité' de hisba signé: Saladin". *Studi in onore di Francesco Gabrieli nel suo ottantesimo compleanno* (1984) 593-98.

Serjeant, R. B. "A Zaidi Manual of Hisbah of the 3rd Century (H*)*". *Rivista degli studi orientali* 28 (1953) 1-34; also in Serjeant, R. B. *Studies in Arabic History and Civilisation* (London, 1981) VII 1-34.

Shoshan, B. "Fatimid Grain Policy and the Role of the Muḥtasib". *International Journal of Middle Eastern Studies* 13 (1981) 181-89.

Talbi, M. "Quelques données sur la vie sociale en Occident musulman d'après une traité de hisba du XVe siècle". *Arabica* 1 (1954) 294-306.

Wickens, G. M. "al-Jarsîfî on the Hisba". *Islamic Quarterly* 3 (1956-7) 176-87.

Wilson, B. R. "Glimpses of Muslim Urban Women in Classical Islam". (Ḥisba manuals from North Africa and Spain) *Annals of Scholarship* 2ii (1981) 95-106.

Monographs

Chalmeta Gendron, P. *El Senor del Zoco en Espana*. Madrid, 1973.

Ibn Bassām, Muḥammad b. Aḥmad. *Nihāyat al-Rutba fī Ṭalab al-Ḥisba*. Baghdad, 1968.

Ibn Taymiyya, Taqī al-Dīn Aḥmad. *al-Ḥisba fī'l-Islām*. Cairo, 1318 AH. Translated by M. Holland as *Public Duties in Islam: The Institution of the Hisba*. Leicester, 1982.

Ibn al-Ukhuwwa, Muḥammad b. Muḥammad. *Ma'ālim al-Qurba fī Aḥkām al-Ḥisba*. Cambridge, 1937.

Ibn 'Umar, Yaḥyā. *al-Naẓar wa'l-Aḥkām fī Jāmi' Aḥwāl al-Sūq*. Tunis, 1975.

Izzi Dien, M. *The Theory and Practice of Market Law in Medieval Islam*. Warminster, 1997.

al-Ghazālī, Abū Ḥāmid Muḥammad. *Iḥyā' 'Ulūm al-Dīn*. Cairo, 1915.

al-Māwardī, 'Alī b. Muḥammad. *al-Aḥkām al-Sulṭāniyya*. Cairo, 1983.

al-Qalqashandī, Abū'l-'Abbās. *Ṣubḥ al-A'shā fī Ṣinā'at al-Inshā'*. Cairo, 1913.

al-Shayzarī, 'Abd al-Raḥmān b. Naṣr. *Nihāyat al-Rutba fī Ṭalab al-Ḥisba*. Cairo, 1946.

Tyan, E. *Histoire de l'organisation judiciare en Islam*. Lyon, 1943.

INDEX

The index refers only to the introductory sections, to al-Shayzarī's *Nihāya* and accompanying footnotes. Items are not listed where these are clearly the subjects of a particular chapter.

Aaron, 33
Abbasids, 5, 7, 17
'Abd Allah b. 'Uṭba, 4, 28 n. 1
'Abd Allah b. al-Zubayr, 4
ablutions, ritual, 106
abortion, 115
Abū 'Abd Allah the Shi'ite, 30 n. 9
Abū Bakr (caliph), 124 n. 1
Abū Hurayra, 81
Abū al-Qāsim al-Juhnī, 31 n. 10
Abū al-Qāsim al-Ṣaymarī, 131, 132
Abū Sa'īd al-Iṣṭakhrī, 85 n. 1
Abū Sa'īd al-Khadarī, 41, 82
al-Abzarī, 126 n. 1
acacia, 116
al-'Āḍad (caliph), 28 n. 1
adulterer, 125
agoranomos, 6
Aḥadī dirhams, 94
ahl al-dhimma, *see dhimmī*s
Aḥmad b. al-Ṭayyib al-Sarakhsī, 7, 30 n. 9
akshūt, 73
The Alchemy of Cooking, 58
The Alchemy of Perfume, 69
alcohol, 122, 125, 126
Aleppo, 13, 41, 42, 110
Alexandria, 10
'Alī b. 'Abbās al-Majūsī, 76 n. 3
'Alī b. Abī Ṭālib (caliph), 6, 125
alkali, 134
almonds, 63
  ground, 68
  oil of, 68
aloe, medicament from, 109
aloes-wood, 71, 74
ambergris, 71, 72, 74
'āmil al-sūq, 2, 4, 5, 6, 7, 8, 16, 28 n. 1
amulets, 115
Anas b. Mālik, 29
animals, 38, 135
  illnesses of, 101
anfaq oil, 75
apostates, 121
apricot stones, 68
  oil of, 75
'arīf, 23, 35 n. 22, 36-37, 52, 57, 60, 62, 63, 74, 85, 92, 118 (*see also* assistants; deputies; helpers; servants)
aristolochia, 70
ash, alkaline, 98
  of cane, 79
  of ground plants, 53, 58
'Āṣim al-Aḥwal, 7, 17, 28 n. 1
assistants, 34, 35 (*see also 'arīf*; deputies; helpers; servants)
aswāq, 102 n. 1
Atabek Tughtakīn (sultan), 12, 31
atheists, 121
Avicenna, *see* Ibn Sīnā

Baalbek, syrup from, 79
backgammon, 119
Baghdad, 7, 41, 93, 104 n. 1, 131
al-Baghdādī, 104 n. 1
Bahā' al-Dawla (amir), 104 n. 1
bahaṭa, 58
bakeries, 46
bakers, 18, 35 n. 22, 36, 37 n. 5, 49, 124 n. 1
balm of Gilead tree, 68
bamboo concrete, 66
Banū Munqidh (tribe), 41
Bāqī al-Khādim al-Aswad, 8, 37 n. 5
barbaṭ, 126
barbers, 106
bark, of frankincense, 67
  of oak, 70
  of olive tree, 74
  of pine 67
basandūd, 63
baths, 122, 134
Bāṭiniyya, 128
bazaar criers, 83
beans, 47, 109
  flour of, 46, 67

beansprouts, 62
beards, 127
beef, 60, 72 (*see also* cows, meat of)
beeswax, 71
Behrnauer, Walter, 14
ben tree oil, 74, 75, 116
Bible, 122
bikr, 125
bitumen, 79
blankets, 89
bleachers, 87
blood, 54
  dragon's, 68, 70-71, 73, 109
  gazelle's, 71
  young goat's, 71
blood money, 115
bones, 66
  of cows and camels, 60
  of the cuttlefish, 71, 72
  of the human body, 117
booth, of the *muḥtasib*, 62
borax, 48
boys, as servants, 49
brains, 58
bran, 50
brazilwood, 73
bread, unleavened, 48
breadcrumbs, 63
bribery, 35, 53
brick, powered baked, 68
brocade, 87
Brockelmann, Carl, 12, 13
brokers, 83
burials, *see* funeral
Buwayhids, 15, 18, 31 n. 10

camels, 52
  meat of, 58, 60, 62
camphor, 72, 74
candles, 67
capers, 79
caravans, 38
caraway seeds, 79
carob beans, 79
cassia tree, pods of, 68
caster-oil plant, 72
ceremonies of investiture, 8
charcoal, 118
chard, 50, 108
chalk, red, 116
cheese, 78, 79
chick-peas, 134
  flour of, 46, 47, 67
chicken breasts, 72
Chinese rhubarb, 65
Christians, 121, 122
cinnabar, 97
cinnamon, 60, 71
civet, 74
clarified butter, 91
clay, 54
  red, 68, 118
cloth, 87
  merchants, 6, 36, 84
  beaters, 87
cloves, 71
coinage, 94
collusion, 81
Companions (of the Prophet), 40 n. 2, 120
cooks, 36
copper, coinage, 98
  containers, 54
  red, 50
coriander, 45
cornstarch, 58, 63, 64, 73
corpses, washing of, 130
costus, 66
covenant of protection, 121
cows, meat of, 58, 60, 62 (*see also* beef)
Cretan bindweed, 66
Crusaders, 31 n. 10, 32 n. 11
crust, 47, 48
cubit, 83, 93
cucumbers, 134
cumin, 79
  white, 48
  black, 48
cuttlefish, bone of, 71, 72

Damascus, 41, 42, 43, 124 n. 1
dānaq, 41
Daniel (prophet), 30 n. 9
al-Danyālī, 30 n. 9
Dār al-Ḍarb, *see* mint
Dār al-ʿIyār, 44 n. 3
darnel, 46, 47
dates, 78
  stones of, 72

juice, 77
Dāwūd b. Ya'qūb al-Kutāmī, 102 n. 1
Dawwās b. Ya'qūb, 124 n. 1
De Medici Tentatione, 116 n. 2
deputies, 44 n. 3 (*see also 'arīf*; assistants; helpers; servants)
dharīra, 72
*dhimmī*s, 16, 102, 131
dice, 119
dinar, 94, 98, 122
diplomas of investiture, 9, 15
dirham (coin), 82, 83
dirham (weight), 44, 70, 71, 73, 74, 98
dirra, 34, 124, 126
al-Dīwān al-Sulṭāniyya, 44 n. 3
donkey-drivers, 135
dough, 47, 49, 50
kneader of, 47
dragon's blood, 68, 70-71, 73, 109
drains, 38
Dumat al-Jandal, 2
dung, 38
dust, 46, 48, 85
dyers, 87

eagle water, 48, 49
earthenware, sellers of, 134
effeminate men, 127
eggs, 53, 59
for gambling, 119
Egypt, 10, 90
Egyptian opium, 65
elecampane roots, 66
elephantiasis, 106
emblic myrobalan, 70
embroiderers, 87
euphorbia resin, 66
eye salves, 116

Fakhr al-Dawla (amir), 31 n. 10
fals, 95 n. 5
fānīd, 76
faqīh, 7, 28
Fatimids, 2, 8, 11, 18, 21, 23, 28 n. 1, 32 n. 11, 35 n. 22, 37 n. 5, 40 n. 1, 44 n. 3, 122 n. 5
felt, 93
fenugreek, 73
figs, 134
fig tree, sap of, 45
"Fiscal Rescript" of 'Umar, 40 n. 2
firewood, 38
carriers of, 135
fish, 49, 62
flax, from Giza, 90
from Nablus, 90
fleawort, 45
flour, 50, 57, 58, 63, 64, 85
barley, 46, 47
bean, 46, 67
chick pea, 46, 47, 67
rice, 47, 58, 63
lentil, 63
wheat, 79
fly-whisks, 47, 62, 63, 79
fox whiskers, 93
frankincense, 66, 75
bark of, 67
frying pans, 50
funeral, ceremonies, 127
processions, 127
Fusṭāṭ, 10, 19

Gabriel, 29
Galen, 112, 116, 117
gall bladder, of an ox, 66, 98
gambling, 119
garlic, 134
gazelle, blood of, 71
intestines of, 71
gazelle's ankle, 63
Geniza, records of, 11 n. 36, 37 n. 5
ghāliyya, 73, 74
Ghāmid, the woman from, 125
gharī, 67
al-Ghazālī, 1, 13
Ghazna, 32
ghirāra, 42
ghiyār, 121
Giza, flax from, 90
glass, ground, 73
glue, 87, 88
goats, blood of, 71
heads of, 56
meat of, 52, 53, 58
tails of, 53
tallow of, 67
gold, 31, 43, 84, 94
governors, 133

grain, 37 n. 6
barley, 45
merchants, 6, 18, 38 n. 6
wheat, 45
granaries, 38 n. 6
grapes, 74, 78
pulp of, 63
graves, 127
graveyards, 127
Greece, physicians of, 114
greengrocers, 134
gum, 65, 66, 116
gypsum, 45, 72
roasted, 85

ḥabaq, 99
ḥabba, 41, 43, 45
ḥadd (pl. *ḥudūd*), 22
al-Ḥajar, 2
Ḥājjī Khalīfa, 12
al-Ḥākim b. Amr Allah (caliph), 10, 22, 28 n. 1, 122 n. 5, 126 n. 1
Ḥākim b. Umayya, 3
Hama, 41, 42
Ḥamīd al-Mufliḥ, 8
al-Ḥārith b. al-Ḥakam, 4
Hārūn al-Rashīd (caliph), 94 n. 5
hawkers, 74
heads, cooked, 55, 62 (*see also* sheep, heads of; goats, heads of)
heart, 62
helpers, 23, 34, 35 n. 22 (*see also* *'arīf*; assistants; deputies; servants)
haematite, 47, 98
henna, 79, 92
heretics, 121
Hippocratic oath, 115
al-Ḥīra, 2
ḥisba, performed by caliphs, 6
treatises, 1, 5, 15, 18, 21, 22
Ḥisba al-Kabīr, 30 n. 9
Ḥisba al-Ṣaghīr, 30 n. 9
hiyājī nāṭif, 63
hoarding, 37-38 (*see also* monopolising)
Homs, 41
honey, 50, 54, 59, 63, 68, 79
hoof, shoeing of, 100
horn, ground, 67
horned poppy, 67, 116
horse, stomach of, 71
humours, 113
Ḥunayn b. Isḥāq, 112 n. 4, 116
hunters of sparrows, 53
al-Ḥusayn b. 'Alī, 131 n. 19
al-Ḥusayn b. al-Qāsim, 30 n. 9
ḥuwwār, 37 n. 5

al-iblīq, 74
Ibn Bassām, 14
Ibn al-Ḥajjāj, 30 n. 9, 120
Ibn Hammām al-Salūlī, 29
Ibn Qutayba al-Dīnawarī, 130
Ibn Sīnā, 76 n. 4
Ibn al-Tuwayr, 20
Ibn al-Ukhuwwa, 13, 14
Ibrāhīm b. 'Abd Allah, 30 n. 9
Ibrāhīm b. Batha, 34 n. 21
idol worshippers, 121
Iḥyā' 'Ulūm al-Dīn, 1
Imām, 121, 125, 128, 130
incense, 106
increment, 97 (*see also* interest; profit; usury)
Indian pepperwort, 70
indigo, 116, 118
inheritances, *see mawārīth*
ink, 71, 92
interest, 81 (*see also* increment; profit; usury)
intestines, of gazelle, 71
Islamic law, *see* law, Islamic
Iyās b. Mu'āwiya, 4, 28 n. 1
'Izz al-Dawla Bakhtiyār (amir), 30 n. 9

Jābir b. Manṣūr al-Jawdarī, 8, 9
jawārshanāt, 76
Jazīrat al-Rawḍa, 10 n. 33, 20
jewels, 97
Jews, 121
jizya, 121, 122, 123
jubba, 89
judges, 2, 10, 11, 22, 28 n. 1, 131
chief of, 131
court of, 132
jūdhāb, 59
juice, barberry, 77
date, 77
of lycium, 66

sugar cane, 63, 76, 78, 79
jujube, 77

kaddān, 79
Kāmil al-Ṣinā'a al-Ṭayyiba, 76 n. 3
Kata Genos, 117
kayl, 42
khabīṣa, 64
khalūq, 73
kharāj, 11
khil'a, 9
khushkar, 37 n. 5
kidney, 55, 67
al-Kindī, Ya'qūb, 30 n. 9, 58
kishk, 63
kishkanānij, 64
Kitāb al-Anwā', 130
Kitāb al-Aqrabadhīn al-Kabīr, 76 n. 2
Kitāb al-Iḥtisāb, 16, 36 n. 3
kneading troughs, 47
kohl, 67
Kufa, 4, 7
Kunnāsh, 117

labaniyya, 58
lac, 68
ladanum, 74
Lakhmids, 2
lamb, 54 (*see also* mutton; sheep, meat of)
latex, 67
lavender, 106
law, Islamic, 2, 22, 32, 40, 85, 94, 114, 123, 128, 130, 131, 135
lead, 54, 72, 93
pellets, 71
white, 76
leather, 44, 106
lemon juice, 54
lentils, 107
flour of, 63
lepers, 106
lettuce, 134
wild, 65
Levy, Rubin, 14
lily, oil of, 68
lime, 118, 134
liver, 54, 58, 62, 71
lizard, droppings of, 71
lotus tree, leaves of, 105
Ma'ālim al-Qurba fī Aḥkām al-Ḥisba, 14
Ma'arra, 41, 42
al-Madā'in, 7
musk from, 75
madder, 92
madīra, 58
Magians, 121
al-Mahdī (caliph), 7
Mahdī b. 'Abd al-Raḥmān, 4
Maḥmūd of Ghazna (sultan), 32
Mā'iz b. Mālik, 125
makkūk, 42
Mamluks, 10
al-Ma'mūn (caliph), 31 n. 10, 33
manna, 41
al-Manṣūr (caliph), 7
al-Maqrīzī, 20
maranj, 97, 98
marandajūn, 92
marble, 67, 68, 72, 74
trimmers of, 72
marjoram, 67
markets, (*see also aswāq*)
flax, 127
horse, 102 n. 1
slave, 7, 102 n. 1
women's, 3
yarn, 127
marsh mallow, 79, 105
marzubān, 42
mashāsh, 63
masseurs, 106
mastic, 48, 60, 68
al-Māwardī, 1, 13, 16, 20, 95 n. 5
mawārīth, 7, 11
measures, 45, 134
Mecca, 2, 3, 52
Medina, 2, 3, 4, 7, 52
melilot seeds, 67
melons, 134
skin of, 78
menstruation, 108, 112, 113, 131, 132
milk, 76, 78
millers, 37 n. 5
minaret, 128, 129
minced meat, 54
mint (coinage), 95 n. 5
Miṣr, 10, 19
mithqāl (coin), 96

mi'zafa, 126
mizmār, 126
monopolising, 37 (*see also* hoarding)
moon, mansions of, 129-30
Moses, 33
mosques, 119, 128
  of Aḥmad b. Ṭūlūn, 9
  of 'Amr b. al-'Āṣ, 9, 9 n.27
  attendants of, 128
  of Friday prayer, 128, 131
moss, water 78
Mu'ādh b. Jabal, 41
muezzins, 128, 129, 130
Muḥammad (prophet), 2, 3, 52 (*see also* prophet Muḥammad)
Muḥammad b. 'Abd Allah, 30 n. 9
Muḥammad b. Ya'qūt, 32 n. 11
Mu'izz al-Dawla (amir), 31 n. 10
mukul tree, 66
mukūs, 35 n. 22
mukūs al-ḥisba, 35 n. 22
al-Muqtadir (caliph), 32 n. 11
Muṣ'ab b. Zubayr, 4
musical instruments, 126
musk, 70, 71, 73, 74
  bags, 70, 109
  from al-Madā'in, 75
  pastilles, 109
  from Sughd, 70, 75
al-Mustaẓhir billah (caliph), 131
mustard, 73
al-Mu'taḍid (caliph), 7, 30 n. 9, 40 n. 1
mutton, 45, 60 (*see also* lamb; sheep, meat of)
al-Muwaffaq (caliph), 104 n. 1
myrobalan, black, 68
  burnt stones of, 117
  emblic, 70
  Kabuli, 68
  yellow, 68
myrrh, 67, 109
myrtle, 75

Nabateans, 121 n. 2
Nablus, flax from, 90
nafaqa, 85 n. 1
Nāfi' b. 'Abd al-Raḥmān, 7
nard, down of, 66
nāṭif, hiyājī, 63
  poppy seed, 63
  yellow, 63
natron, 134
nāẓir aswāq, 102 n. 1
nāẓir al-sikka, 94 n. 5
neckbands, 122
nūbiyya, 64
nutmeg, 71

oak, apples, 92
  bark, 70
oil, 50, 54, 57, 58, 60, 61, 62, 78, 79, 91
  almond, 68
  anfāq, 75
  apricot stone, 75
  balm of Gilead tree, 68
  ben tree, 74
  cotton seed, 75
  dregs of, 45, 58, 66
  lily, 68
  saffron, 98
  sesame, 50, 57, 78
olive tree, bark of, 74
omelettes, 59
onions, 62, 134
opium, Egyptian, 65
opopanax, 68
ornamental stitchers, 87
ovens, 70 (*see also tannūr*)
oxymel, 77

palm, fibres of, 93, 106
paper, 93
papyrus, 74
Paul of Aegina, 117
pepper, 73, 117
pepperwort, Indian, 70
perfumers, 36
pharmacopeia, 76
pickles, 78, 79
pickling brine, 79
pigs, 122
  hair of, 93
pine, 75
  bark of, 67
  resin of, 70
pistachio nuts, 74
pitch, 79
plums, 66

poll-tax, *see jizya*
polypody, 67
pomegranite skins, 79, 106
poppy, horned, 65, 116
seeds, 63
ports, 8, 11, 19, 102 n. 1 (*see also aswāq*)
pot-sherds, 50
prayers, 129
preachers, 127
prices, setting of, 37
princes, 133
profit, 84, 94, 98 (*see also* increment; interest; usury)
prophet Muḥammad, 6, 28, 30, 31, 32, 33, 35, 37, 38, 53, 81, 82, 107, 113, 119, 125, 127, 128, 132, 133 (*see also* Muḥammad)
pulses, sellers of, 134

qabā', 89
qaddaḥ, 38 n. 6
qāḍī, *see* judge
qāḍī al-quḍāt, *see* judges, chief of
al-Qāhira, 10, 19
Qairouan, dirhams from, 94
qafīz, 42
*qalansuwa*s, 87
Qānūn, 76
qarāṭīs, 96
Qashan, dinars from, 95
Qāṭājānus, 117
qaṭṭāra, 63
qīrāṭ, 41, 42, 48
quicklime, 48
Qur'ān, 1, 2, 29, 41, 119
quotations from, 6, 40 n. 1, 125, 131, 132, 133
reciters, 7, 130, 131
Qūṣ, 19

rabbit fur, 109
radishes, 134
rāmik, 70
raṭl, 44, 53, 57, 60, 64 n. 10, 68, 78
Rawāfiḍ, 120, 131
rawand al-dawābb, 65
register, of the *muḥtasib*, 47, 54, 65, 102, 103
representatives (legal), 133
resin, 66, 67
black, 71
euphorbia, 66
of mukul tree, 66
of pine, 70
of the savin juniper, 66
white, 72
rhubarb, Chinese, 65
rice, 59, 72
Rome, ancient, 36
rose water, 71, 77
rosin, 66, 67

ṣā', 60
ṣābūniyya, 64
Sabur, dinars from, 95
Sābūr b. Sahl, 76 n. 2
ṣadaqāt, 16 n. 45
sādhanj, 97
safflower, 78
saffron, 52, 65, 68, 71, 72, 73, 116
hairy, 72, 73
oil, 98
ṣāḥib al-sūq, 5
al-Sā'ib b. Yazīd, 3-4, 121 n. 2
Sa'īd b. Mīna, 4
Sa'īd b. Sa'īd al-'Āṣ, 3
sal ammoniac, 72
Ṣalāḥ al-Dīn, 12, 44 n. 3
salt, 48, 53, 54, 56, 57, 134
Samrā bint Nuhayk, 3
sanbūsak, 62
sand, 67, 79, 87, 98
sandalwood, 74
sandarac, 71, 72
al-Sarakhsī, *see* Aḥmad b. al-Ṭayyib
sarcocol, 70
Ṣarī' al-Dilā', 120
sausages, 59
savin juniper, resin of, 66
sawāḥil, 19, 20 (*see also* ports)
scales, 78 80
scalpels, use of, 100, 110
scammony, 67
seal, of the *muḥtasib*, 60 (*see also* stamp),
seasoning, 62
semolina, 50, 58
servants, 34, 35 (*see also 'arīf*; assistants; deputies; helpers)

sesame, oil of, 50, 57, 78
seeds, 48, 63, 68, 74
shādūrān, 70, 71, 74, 77
al-Shāfi'ī, 131
school of law of, 106
sharī'a, see law, Islamic
Shayzar, 12, 41, 42
sheep, 52
meat of, 52, 53, 58 (*see also* lamb; mutton)
tails of, 53
al-Shifā bint 'Abd Allah, 3
ships, owners of, 20
shoemakers, 106
shop bench, 36
Shu'ayb, 29
shurṭa, 8, 11, 31, 32 n. 11
shurṭa al-suflā, 8 n. 22
shurṭa al-'ulyā, 8 n. 22
sieves, 47, 72
silk, 31, 87, 92, 109
silver, 43, 48, 94, 97, 98
slaves, 108 (*see also* women, as slaves)
market of, 102 n. 1
snake's eye, 79
soap, 105
sodomy, 125
solder, 97
Spain, 5
sparrows, hunters of, 53
spices, 62, 79
spikenard, 71
stamp, of the *muḥtasib*, 34 n. 21 (*see also* seal)
starch, 88, 91, 116
steelyards, 43
Byzantine, 44
Coptic, 44
storax, 109
straw, 38
Successors, 40 n. 2
sugar, 59
cane, 63, 76, 77, 78, 79
ground, 73
Sughd, musk from, 70, 75
sukk, 74
Sulaymān b. 'Azza, 38 n. 6
sulphur, 98
sumach, 56, 79
sunbul, 42
Sunna, 28, 52
sūq al-raqīq, *see* markets, slave
swimming instructors, 34 n. 21
Syria, 40, 41, 65, 67
syrup, 63
from Baalbek, 79

al-Ṭā'i (caliph), 31 n. 10
Tāj al-Dīn al-Subkī, 95 n. 5
*Ṭālibī*s, 120, 131
tallow, goat's, 67
tamarind, 66
tanning, 106
tannūr, 47, 54, 64 (*see also* ovens)
tar, molten, 73
taro, 58, 60, 66
ṭaylasān, 122 n. 5
ta'zīr, 2, 22, 33, 34, 75, 125
The Ten Treatises of the Eye, 116
Tendunyas, 19
tharīda, 56
thread, 87, 93
thyme, 134
Tiberias, 13
Tigris, 34 n. 21
Torah, 122
town crier, 127
treasury, 23
head of, 10
The Trial of the Physician, 116
trinkets, 97
trotters, of sheep and goats, 56
ṭunbūr, 126
turbans, 8, 9
turdīn, 59
turmeric, 73, 79, 116, 118
ṭurṭūr, 34, 124, 126
Tyre, dinars from, 94

'Ukāẓ, 2
'Umar b. 'Abd al-'Azīz (caliph), 40 n. 2
'Umar b. Hubayra, 4
'Umar b. al-Khaṭṭāb (caliph), 3, 4, 6, 7, 52, 81, 121, 122, 125
Umayyads, 4, 5
'ushr, 121 n. 2
usury, 94, 95 (*see also* increment; interest; profit)

‘Uthmān (caliph), 4

veins, 100, 108, 109, 110-13
vegetables, 134
verdigris, 50, 67
vetch, 47
vinegar, 68, 72, 73, 76, 77, 78
violet water, 77
vitriol, 92, 97, 109
green, 67, 68
“volunteer” *muḥtasib*, 31 n. 10

waqiyya, 41, 44, 60
Walīd b. ‘Abd al-Malik (caliph), 4
walnuts, ground, 68
washermen, 134
Wāsiṭ, 4
water, bags, 134, 135
carriers, 134
containers, 38, 47
moss, 78
waterskins, 134
waterspouts, 38
wax, 43, 67, 71, 74
weavers, 84
weighing pans, 57
weights, standard, 44
iron, 44
stone, 44
wood, 44
wheat, 46, 60, 79
whip, 125
whipping, 125
white lead, 76
wine, 73
women, 39, 89, 90, 115, 127
slaves, 102, 120
slippers of, 93
Wüstenfeld, F., 13

Yaḥyā b. ‘Umar, 5
Yaḥyā b. Zakariyā, 7, 30 n. 9
Ya‘qūb b. Yūsuf b. Killis, 11
al-Ya‘qūbī, 104 n. 1
yarn, 85
Yazīd II (caliph), 4

al-Zahrāwī, 117
Zaydī manual, *see Kitāb al-Iḥtisāb*
zulābiyya, 63
zunnār, 122